OUT FROM UNDERDEVELOPMENT

Out from Underdevelopment

Prospects for the Third World

James H. Mittelman
Professor of Political Science and
Dean of the Faculty of the Social Sciences
Queens College, City University of New York

St. Martin's Press   New York

First published in the United States of America in 1988

ISBN 0-312-01189-1 (cl.)
    0-312-01189-X (pkb.)

Library of Congress Cataloging-in-Publication Data

Mittelman, James H.
Out from underdevelopment : prospects for the Third World/James
H. Mittelman.
p.   cm.
Bibliography: p.
Includes index.
ISBN 0-312-01188-1 : $35.00.   ISBN 0-312-01189-X (pkb.) : $12.95
1. Developing countries—Economic policy.   2. Developing
countries—Economic conditions.   I. Title.
HC59.7.M5337 1988
338.9′009172′4—dc19   87-22927
                                                          CIP

For my family

Contents

Preface

As a petulant 20-year-old embarking on graduate school, I quickly lost patience wading through the standard fare of university education in the US. My courses suffered from a kind of single-mindedness that seemed to stifle creativity. The staff were so orthodox in their own work and with their students that there was little feeling of pleasure in learning. Scholarly activity was presented as a 'discipline'.

Frustrated with staid, unimaginative courses, I confronted the dean, a strait-laced drill-sergeant who politely listened to my reasons as to why I should be allowed to use my fellowship for travel abroad. The sergeant caught me by surprise when he uttered, 'All right, sir. Where do you aim to study overseas?' Improvising, I said, 'Africa', a continent I knew nothing about. Cocking an eyebrow, he inquired, 'Where in Africa?' At a loss for an answer I glanced fretfully at my watch, dutifully noting that I was late for my class. 'Could we meet again to discuss the details of my proposal?' I queried.

I immediately telephoned a friend far more experienced in world affairs than I and explained my dilemma. 'The sergeant asked me where I want to study in Africa. What should I say? Do they have universities there?' My friend, an Oxford-educated diplomat with an advanced degree in African studies, replied, 'Of course, there are excellent universities in Africa. I recommend Makerere in Uganda and Ibadan in Nigeria. Since Nigeria may soon erupt in civil war, I would choose Makerere.' This advice prompted me to thumb through my world atlas. Aha, I learnt that Uganda is a landlocked country in East Africa, the source of the Nile.

When the dean and I resumed our conversation, I stated my choice, Makerere. He reacted in a word: 'What?' I explained, 'Makerere is in Uganda. It's an outstanding university, you know.' Three days later his secretary called to say that he had approved my request.

Months slipped by without so much as an acknowledgement, let alone an acceptance or rejection from Makerere. One of my professors, an esteemed philosopher, consoled me and urged me not to go. 'Good God, man,' he exclaimed, 'do you intend to study #&*@

barbarism?' Finally, I placed my first overseas telephone call. The operator asked for the name of the city, not the country. I told her to try the capital city. Unrelentingly, she demanded the name of the capital. Back to my reliable atlas: 'Either Kampala or Entebbe,' I shouted. 'I can't tell from the map. The binding in the middle of the page runs right through Uganda.' Nonetheless, the call went through in a minute. 'Oh yes, my dear chap. We have received your application. Of course you are accepted. Can you come right out?'

PROVINCIALISM

When I stepped off the plane in Uganda, I gazed at Lake Victoria, royal blue under the tropical sun, encircled by a verdant quilt of banana trees and a patchwork of ruddy clay roads. To an unseasoned traveller, the 26-mile journey from Entebbe, the old colonial headquarters, to Kampala, the capital since the accession to independence in 1962, seemed otherworldly. My eyes were riveted on the lush plant life: brilliant purple bougainvillaea shrubs, fiery red flame trees, and sturdy witch-like baobab trees. The perfume of flowers was everywhere. Dotting the expanse were men clad in *kanzu*, long white gowns, topped by Western-style sports jackets. Trailing behind some of the men were their wives frocked in *basuti*, high-shouldered, multicoloured dresses inspired by fashion during the Edwardian period of colonial rule, with babies resting on their backs.

At the university, I was shown to my room in Mitchell Hall, a dormitory named after a colonial governor. When the bell rang, I joined the crowd assembling in the dining hall. No one said a word to me. My first impression was that I was the only white student present. Although the language of instruction at Makerere is English, the African students conversed in their own tongues. I could not ask for the food because such staples as *matoke*, boiled green bananas, were unknown to me. After lunch I made my way to the town centre. I came upon the Clock Tower where, I was told, nearly every day the country's leading politicians and intellectuals would hold a public debate over burning social issues.

In the university community, I met an American professor from my home town. We became close friends and at the end of the academic year, he asked if I would give an exam to his first-year class while he was up-country lecturing at a high school. Gladly, I said. Now in those days Uganda had quite a reputation for its rollicking night club life. Not a person of great willpower, I accepted an invitation to accom-

pany friends to 'the Susana' on the eve of the exam. And what a time
we had! Consuming our fair share of beer and *waragi* (a potent
gin-like drink brewed locally), we mingled with the other patrons – a
convivial crowd ranging from local notables, including government
ministers, to the common man and woman – and danced until the first
flickers of morning light summoned us away from the festivities.
Mindful of my responsibilities at the university, I dashed back to
campus at 7.00 a.m., one full hour before I was to appear in the
classroom.

In the British educational system, I found out, exams are taken
very seriously. There is no periodic evaluation, as is the North
American custom. Rather, since undergraduates are often tested only
twice – at the end of their first and third years in a three-year degree
programme – the results of a single exam can determine one's future
life chances. The gravity of the occasion was impressed upon me by
the appearance of solemn students bedecked in red gowns, a remnant
of the Oxford–Cambridge tradition, for the three-hour exam. After I
distributed the question sheets and the booklets, not a peep could be
heard in the large, austere lecture hall. Within minutes, I was asleep,
my head cushioned by my arms on the table in front of me.

Next thing, someone was tugging at my shoulder, barking in a
starchy accent: 'Young man, young man, are you invigilating here?'
Rubbing my eyes in wonder, I whispered, 'Pardon me'. A dowdy
woman glared at me and repeated, 'Are you invigilating here?' Again
I said, 'Pardon me'. The same sequence followed. Evidently a one-
track mind, she persisted: 'I want to know if you are invigilating here'.
With more than 100 African students listening to this breakdown in
communication between a Yank and a Brit, I became embarrassed.
What could she possibly mean?

Thoroughly confused, I decided that this whole business about
invigilating sounded terribly crude. I stood up, to my full five feet five
and five-eighths inches, and counterblasted: 'I assure you, ma'am, I
would not do anything like that in public and surely not in front of
students!' Instantaneously an uproar of laughter filled the room. My
inquisitor stormed out, slamming the door behind her. What had I
done?

UNDERSTANDING OTHER PEOPLE'S WAYS

During my first year in Uganda, the loneliest and most important
period in my life, I discovered that social realities are not what they

appear to be. On that initial occasion in the dining hall, I totally misread the behaviour of other students. That they focused their attention on me without initiating conversation had nothing to do with the colour of my skin. Later, many times over, I saw Makerere students relate to new Ugandan students in exactly the same way they had received me. Makerereites are observant, and I had been ethnocentric: more than to most places, foreigners (myself included) come to Africa with specific notions about it. Having been raised in a *de facto* segregated city, I mistakenly projected racial preconceptions formed in the US on a different social reality. To be sure, there is considerable racial prejudice in Uganda, but its causes and manifestations are unlike the pattern in the US.

In contrast to the way in which my bigoted professor of political philosophy characterized Africa, I came upon a vibrant intellectual culture in Uganda, unhappily interrupted by Idi Amin's reign of terror. Much like Athenian democracy during the Age of Pericles, the Ugandan polis in the 1960s made strides towards melding knowledge and an active pursuit of the good life. The populace readily welcomed accomplished intellectuals who engaged in open political debate, a favourite pastime of Ugandans in the early years after independence. Compare the tradition in the US where, despite near universal literacy, intellectuals are suspect in politics. The rule of thumb for the intelligentsia who enter American politics is either to come clean and bear the stigma of being an egghead, as did presidential candidate Adlai Stevenson, or to play down your PhD and credentials as a former professor, as has George McGovern, who also sought the presidency.

My experience administering an exam at Makerere taught me that understanding societies which encompass a myriad of cultures is a complex affair. Not only was I immersed in an African culture, but I also learnt to decipher a host of distinctive local societies as well as an overlay of Asian and European customs. In Kampala I encountered a medley of Bantu and Nilotic ethnic groups; refugee communities from nearby states, some of which arrived in the country as long ago as the late nineteenth century; many religious denominations, including a sect of Ugandan Jews established at the beginning of the twentieth century; a diverse lot of Indians and Pakistanis whose forebears built the railway from Lake Victoria to the Indian Ocean; and Europeans, who ruled for but a brief interlude in the history of East Africa. Thus one must unravel a cultural tapestry in order truly to understand the workings of institutions in post-colonial Uganda, as I discovered in the educational system.

When I told my tale about the testy woman rabidly yanking my shoulder, bemused English friends explained that invigilation means keeping watch over students at an examination. Asked what it is called in the US, I said that we normally use the term proctoring, a construction which my friends, rightly or wrongly, insisted is a distortion of the English language.

DELVING DEEPER THAN POPULAR BELIEF

Intrigued by such cultural differences and intellectually drawn into African history, there was no turning back. I was hooked on debates over development and simmering social issues in multi-ethnic societies as well as on new-found cuisine and the delights of language learning. Following my second tour in Uganda, when I taught at the university, an unforgettable period punctuated by Amin's rise to power, I faced a crossroads: should I establish a home base where I could make sense of my experience, or should I join an international band of gypsies straying from one far-off berth to another? Among these gypsies are my fascinating and talented cohorts from Makerere, whom I still repeatedly encounter in the novels and short stories of V. S. Naipaul and Paul Theroux.

My wandering took me to liberated zones amid anti-colonial wars in southern Africa, republics lorded over by tight-fisted dictators in Latin America, and the states which have inherited the mantle of great civilizations in Asia. Reminiscent of the personal journey described by the philosopher René Descartes in the seventeenth century, as a young man I had resolved to seek knowledge beyond the world of books. I found great profit in becoming acquainted with other people's customs. But something was missing. I realized that the observation of experience did not satisfy me. So too for Descartes who, frustrated with the indeterminacy of book learning, had given up his studies in search of experiential knowledge only to detect just as much difference of opinion among the general populace as among men of letters. As described in his *Discourse on Method*, nine years passed before Descartes decided to stop his peripatetic ways and 'to lay the groundwork of a philosophy more certain than popular belief'.

Similarly, in my youth, I made up my mind to draw on two sources, experiential knowledge and the great books, in order to understand the promise and predicaments of the Third World. At that time, I set my sights on two problems: the historical puzzle of how people get embroiled in underdevelopment, and the practical question of how whole societies can escape it. As a scholar and as a practitioner working for international development agencies, these two questions have engaged me ever since.

I believe that it is crucial for all concerned people to re-examine the traditional lore about the Third World. Insofar as the Western public is concerned about this segment of the globe – which includes three-quarters of humankind – attention is centred on the wrong issues and neglects major questions. The media typically transmit a random accumulation of facts without regard for the tenets behind practical policies. In bombarding us with information, reporters largely cover the activities of politicians, thus allowing government to set the bounds of what the public thinks about. In my view it is wrong to accept these inhibiting parameters of inquiry.

My concern in this book is to raise different questions about Third World development for an informed but non-specialist audience open to critical reflection. This project first took shape in my mind as an undergraduate course on 'The Political Economy of the Third World'. In searching for readings to assign, I discovered that the basic issues about the causes of, and solutions to, underdevelopment had not yet been presented in any satisfactory fashion. Neophytes seek an account that demystifies the issues, while many experts write about what their fellow experts say about the topic, which presumes that the audience has a prior familiarity with the literature. Rather than attempting to negotiate the demands of these two constituencies, this book deals with the issues *per se*, not how individual authors explain the issues. Above all, I try to assign and derive personal meaning from structural, or impersonal, processes.

Unhappily, the abstract ideas in scholarly works are tough going. Academic inquiry needs to be brought to life. In this volume, the discussion of heavy-duty concepts will be kept to a bare minimum (to be found in Part II). Without considering them, a treatment of concrete issues would be a mere exercise in storytelling. A country-by-country narrative – the Marco Polo approach of marching from one land to another – would perhaps be entertaining. However, its deceptive simplicity would render a disservice to readers.

Running through this book is a reappraisal of conventional and radical thinking. Versions of both ways of thinking are defective, yet some central themes seem to withstand critical scrutiny. Observers of the Third World must think about long-term prospects, and re-examine capitalism's fortunes and misfortunes over the last century.

Then we can discern the basic motor forces behind global capitalism and fathom why peoples succeed or fail in the quest to achieve societal goals. Equipped with this knowledge, we are prepared to answer the practical question which ranks with the menace of nuclear war as the major social issue of our time: what works in the Third World?

My core argument is that underdevelopment is not inevitable. It is caused by identifiable processes. Underdevelopment may be best understood in terms of the interplay of capital accumulation, the state and class forces. The relationship among these factors defines the strategy of development adopted in a given historical context. The three typical strategies of development are joining global capitalism, withdrawing from the world system, and balancing the ties of dependency. Each option offers its own promises and risks. Moreover, each strategy must be seen in a realistic, non-romantic and highly problematic manner.

J.H.M.

Acknowledgements

In my efforts to combine first-hand experience and researched analysis, I have had considerable help from others. Robert Ostertag (an undergraduate at the City College of the City University of New York) and Glenn Adler (a postgraduate student at Columbia University) gathered and wrote up basic research information for Chapters 5 and 6, respectively. They are excellent colleagues whose substantive contributions were invaluable. Mustapha Pasha, Marlene Guzman and Stanlie James – students at the Graduate School of International Studies, University of Denver – provided enormous assistance with editing, updating materials and verifying information.

Several scholars gave me unusually thorough and thoughtful criticisms on the entire manuscript. Although I may not have answered all their questions or followed all their suggestions, I am indebted to Mark Anikpo, Robert W. Cox, Kenneth Grundy, Mustapha Pasha, Joel Samoff, George Shepherd, Jr and Linda Yarr. As the revisions progressed, I was guided by George Houser, Haider Ali Khan, John McCamant, Christopher Nwodo, Richard Sandbrook, Timothy Shaw, Peter Van Ness and Christine White. Their ideas and queries on individual chapters have deepened my understanding.

The case-studies in Part III of this book are based on official documents, secondary sources and visits to Brazil in 1970, the People's Republic of China in 1986 and Mozambique in 1971, 1975, 1978 and 1981. For arranging travel and access to information, I am grateful to the China Centre for the International Exchange of Personnel in Banking and Finance and the African Studies Centre at Eduardo Mondlane University, Mozambique, whose director, the late Aquino de Bragança, was a purveyor of consistent encouragement and a fountain of knowledge.

My appreciation also goes to Sherle Schwenninger of the World Policy Institute. A grant from the Transnational Academic Program of the World Policy Institute supported the preparation of this manuscript. My thanks to the staff at the Graduate School of International Studies, University of Denver – Arline Fink, Diane

Reed, Asma Barlas and Diane de Rose Libero – for lightening my administrative load and typing and retyping many drafts. Finally, Queens College of the City University of New York – especially Helen Cairns, Sandra Carbone and Florence Friedman – assisted in the completion of this book.

To my wife, Linda, and our children, Alexandra, Jordan and Alicia, for being towers of strength and sources of inspiration, I am most grateful of all.

JAMES H. MITTELMAN

List of Abbreviations

ANC	African National Congress
AID	Agency for International Development
CIA	Central Intelligence Agency
CCP	Chinese Communist Party
COMECON (also known as CMEA)	Council for Mutual Economic Assistance
ECLA	Economic Commission for Latin America
FNLA Frente de Nacional de Libertação de Angola	National Front for the Liberation of Angola
FRELIMO Frente de Libertação de Moçambique	Mozambique Liberation Front
GNP	Gross National Product
IMF	International Monetary Fund
ITT	International Telephone and Telegraph Company
MAT	Mutual Aid Team
MNR (also known as RENAMO) Movimento Nacional da Resistência de Moçambique	Mozambique National Resistance Movement
NACLA	North American Congress on Latin America
NIC	Newly Industrializing Country
NIEO	New International Economic Order
NSSM	National Security Study Memorandum

OPEC	Organization of Petroleum Exporting Countries
PRI Partido Revolucionario Institucional	Institutional Revolutionary Party
SADCC	Southern African Development Coordination Conference
UAE	United Arab Emirates

UNITA
União Nacional para
  a Independência a Total
  de Angola
	National Union for the Total Independence of Angola

A Note on Style

For the sake of brevity and clarity of style, I prefer not to encumber the text with footnotes. My sources and key references for each chapter are indicated in the Notes and References section at the end of the book (pp. 187–96). This section includes both selective bibliography used in the preparation of this work and suggestions for further reading. Although my publisher has introduced British conventions of style, we have agreed to use billion in the US sense of thousand million (rather than million million, as is the practice in the UK).

J.H.M.

Part I
Introduction

1 Public Platitudes and Unfounded Attitudes

From listening to commentators on television and reading the news-papers, you may have the impression that many, if not most, non-oil-exporting Third World countries are in the position of a castrated man in a harem: impotent and unable to do anything about their incapacity. Nowadays the media frequently refer to such countries as Bangladesh and Haiti as 'basket cases'. Some of these have been assigned to the 'Fourth World'. I used to think that this meant the bottom of the barrel: then *Time* magazine even suggested that we must distinguish a 'Fifth World'.

Is this gloomy view warranted? Or are the past successes of the oil cartel, new-found industrialization and the growth of manufacturing portents that the Third World may escape the doldrums?

Any assessment of the prospects for development must, of course, turn on the questions asked. A crucial task, then, is to determine what are the essential features of development and underdevelopment. This is a complicated business which this book seeks to unscramble. After exploring competing arguments over what ails the Third World, I will show that aspects of one interpretation – political economy – offer a master key to explaining historical trends and current realities both in Third World countries and in the world at large. Of overriding practical importance is to eliminate underdevelopment by devising alternative strategies of development. The panorama is huge, but obfuscations can be avoided if we pinpoint questions targeted at the heart of the controversies over development and underdevelopment.

AMERICAN RITES

The difficulty in getting a grip on fundamentally different ways of thinking about history and politics was apparent in a 1979 interview with President Fidel Castro. Speaking on national television in the

US, ABC News Correspondent Barabara Walters posed several penetrating questions which the Cuban leader answered with much grace and aplomb. Castro, however, was dismayed when the line of questioning dwelt on his personal life. It is instructive to quote the interview at length:

Walters: You are a man of great mystery to us. First of all, why the mystery? You come from nowhere, you seem to disappear, we hear you have no one home, you are a man of secrecy and mystery.

Castro: So then we could say we are facing the theory of mystery. So I ask myself, I'm the first to ask myself, where is the mystery? Because, well, there are certain things that we had to do since the beginning of the Revolution. That is, if a trip is made why should we tell the CIA and the terrorists that we are going to make a trip?

Walters: Do you have a house where you live? No one seems to know where it is.

Castro: Yes, of course and I even have a bed where I sleep.

Walters: Are you married?

Castro: What marriage do you mean, what do you call marriage?

Walters: What do I call marriage?

Castro: Marriage in the bourgeois type? No.

Walters: Wait, wait, many of your people, your brother is married in a bourgeois way. You were married once in the bourgeois way, you have a son.

Castro: Yes, I married once.

Walters: And are you divorced? Many people in this country are married. You considered them all bourgeois people?

Castro: No, no. Well, there are many interpretations about all this. That is, there are marriages with a different feeling also. There is no longer the girl that became educated to marry a millionaire. There are differences. But I am going to make a question.

Walters: Why not an answer?

Castro, somewhat puzzled by this emphasis, continued to respond politely, albeit with uncharacteristic reserve. Still, Walters inquired about romance and his family:

Walters (voice over): We advanced the oft-voiced opinion that his closest companion was Celia Sanchez, first secretary of the Communist Party, and one of the women who served with him in the mountains. He wouldn't affirm or deny this. We then asked about his sister.

Walters: You have a sister, Juanita, who lives in the United States.

Castro: Yes . . . ?

Walters: She has been very critical of you, she has even written to President Carter about you . . .

Castro: Yes . . .

Walters: I have two questions . . .

Castro: Don't you think it is monstrous that a sister says something like that about a brother?

Walters: Yes, I wonder why.

Castro: Well, I can tell you the following: we are children of course from the same father and the same mother, we have the same blood but we have different ideas. I am a socialist, I am a Communist, although her, in her passion, even gets to the extent of stating that I am not a Communist. She has different political ideas, she is an enemy of socialism, she is an enemy of communism. Actually an error is made, a mistake is made in trying to identify Castro as the symbol of all the evil things in the world. But, anyways, that is not the fundamental question. I am a citizen of this country, a country with nine-and-a-half million inhabitants. I would say the following very much according to my convictions: I have nine-and-a-half million brothers. I have a different vision of the world. My family is very large, my family is not only Cuba. My family is the Angolans, the liberation movements in Africa, my family is made up by all progressive and revolutionary peoples of the world. But a sister who attacks me because we are revolutionaries, that does not eliminate my honor, that does not even hurt me.

Walters: I have one final personal question. Will you ever shave off that beard?

Castro: As an exchange for what? The ceasing of the blockade? (Laughs)

Barbara Walters would have none of this blend of reticence and frivolity. She persisted in probing the Cuban's private life on the ground that the public is interested in a 'man of secrecy and mystery', whereupon Castro retorted: 'What is the importance of my being married or not and who cares whether I'm married or not? These are totally my problems. They do not belong to the international public opinion, they belong to me.' Punching home the point, he added: 'I can tell you the following: I'm a man that is totally free and that owns my own life. The rest is detail, untranscendental details that have nothing to do with the Revolution nor politics.' Undaunted by this appeal to talk further about affairs of state, the interlocutor said: 'Aha, but also, . . . you know the expression [marriage].' Then, Castro stoutly asserted that they should discuss love and marriage on another occasion and not in front of a large public audience.

This impasse epitomizes the gulf between the way of thinking of a stellar television interviewer and a structural perspective of international affairs. In the US, from an early age and in our schooling, we are trained to think in terms of discrete events and individual personalities. Customarily in high school history courses, many of us were required to regurgitate long lists of dates and battles in the American Revolution and the Civil War. When it came to the test, I could never recall the bulk of them and received a grade showing as much despite (or because of) my light-minded attempts at memorization the night before. The traditional lore was and still is a tale of superexcellent deeds by peerless superheroes. Clearly the 'great man' explanation of history is the basis of the general American view that, through the accomplishments of individuals and hard work, the US earned its material abundance.

Unlike the libertarian view, a structural perspective, more pronounced in European education and in some quarters in the Third World, emphasizes underlying social forces and impersonal processes such as trends in population growth and movement, changes in patterns of consumption, and the relative mobility or immobility of labour. A structural perspective is grounded in theory – a dirty word to many practically minded North Americans – and takes a long-range view of history.

In foreign affairs, large numbers of US citizens believe that Castro and other Third World leaders are hostile to the US because they want what we have attained on the basis of our own initiative and resources. There is the feeling that the demands for a new international deal thinly disguise a desire to take away the unparalleled achievements of the people of the US, whose only crimes are to allow political liberty to flourish and to start up mighty engines of economic growth.

What has rankled Senator Daniel Patrick Moynihan, a former US ambassador to the UN, for instance, is the attempt by small-time dictators in the Third World to claim what rightfully belongs to the US. For cudgelling his pro-Third World critics, Moynihan gained a tremendous national following. 'There are those in the country,' he argued, 'whose pleasure, or profit, it is to believe that our assailants are motivated by what is wrong about us. *They* are wrong. We are assailed because of what is *right* about us. We are assailed because we are a democracy.' Moreover:

> We repudiate the charge that we have exploited or plundered other countries, or that our own prosperity has ever rested on any such relation. We are prosperous because we are – or were – an energetic and productive people who have lived under a system that has encouraged the development of our productive capacities and energies. We also consider that we have been reasonably helpful and generous in our dealings with other countries.

That statement I take to be a fair summary of a cross section of US public opinion concerning the Third World.

The ordinary citizen in other countries may be no more open-minded than Americans, but the US is so powerful that its values affect virtually all nations. To a huge majority in the Third World and Europe, American perceptions of international relations are provincial in the extreme. This much was acknowledged by Adlai Stevenson who, as US ambassador to the UN, reportedly quipped that the technology Americans need most is a hearing aid. The inability to grasp other people's beliefs reflects misconceptions sown in our minds.

MISGUIDED ATTITUDES

Global processes are often seen as chaotic, complex and remote from daily life. Most people recognize that in comparison with national and local governments, international institutions are lacking in power and the ability to exact compliance. The branches of a national government enact and effect the rule of law, whereas the UN Security

Council and General Assembly pass lofty and unenforceable resolutions; the Secretary General has neither a mandate nor a standing army to make these pious pronouncements binding, and the International Court of Justice has a docket ordinarily uncluttered by cases.

The differences between the national realm and the international sphere are fairly palpable. What is less evident, though, is the effort of government officials to foster the image of world disorder. Zbigniew Brzezinski, US national security adviser under President Jimmy Carter, described the challenge of formulating a sound foreign policy thus: 'My overwhelming observation is that history is neither the product of design nor of conspiracy but is rather the reflection of continuing chaos.' Rejecting the charge that the Carter administration failed to pursue a consistent foreign policy, Brzezinski insisted on the importance of the inherent 'complexity' of the modern world. 'The question I find meaningful,' he underlined, 'is not whether it is possible to pursue a consistent policy, but whether it is possible to pursue a *complex* policy.' What Brzezinski overlooked is a keystone of a democratic polity: the principle that matters of public policy are comprehensible and open to the influence of the ordinary citizen. Never mind, he seemed to imply: comprehension of international relations, intricate as it is, is beyond the ken, as well as the reach, of the common people.

The image of global affairs as chaos and confusion is accurate, but only as far as it goes. It omits structural processes – regularities and patterns – in the world system. What must be taken into account is hierarchy and the global division of labour. The pecking order ranges from the upper echelon in the most powerful nations and their local accomplices in the Third World, to the teeming mass of downtrodden in a multitude of countries whose life chances are seemingly nil.

Ingrained images of the Third World have been forged by the media. While striving to present a balanced treatment of foreign affairs – to be sure, a difficult task – the media in the US have come under fire from various quarters. Former Soviet Foreign Minister Andrei Gromyko, usually a dour, melancholy sort, was asked his opinion of an article about him in the *New York Times*. 'About half is true and half is false,' he answered. 'Since The Times is a balanced newspaper, that is to be expected.'

By now it is commonplace to note that the media and films have traditionally fostered racist images of Third World peoples: Tarzan was the strongest man and Jane had the most voluptuous breasts in the African jungle. Whites portrayed superior beings, while blacks played subordinate roles. The impression of *exoticism* lingers because it is a simple and convenient technique for imposing intellectual order on an unknown Africa and a veiled Orient. *Islamic fundamentalism* is a label to tag diverse phenomena; religion is surely the idiom but not the basis of political protest in the Middle East. Similarly, *tribalism* is a term that conjures up images of primitive behaviour and an incapacity to manage the affairs of state.

Why should Nigeria's Ibo, Yoruba and Hausa-Fulani be stigmatized as tribes while the numerically smaller Basque, Flemish and Welsh are dignified as nations or ethnic groups? Furthermore, in explaining the outcome of an American election, say, a mayoral race in Boston, one of the first questions routinely asked is: who got the Irish, Jewish and black vote? Taking a cue from *The Federalist Papers*, American schools teach that myriad loyalties are the basis of countervailing sources of power which offset the relentless passions of humankind. Publius, a composite of the three authors of *The Federalist* (John Jay, Alexander Hamilton and James Madison), warned that mortal feuds between factions spread like contagion and infect a body politic. But a proper balancing of interests could stem this paroxysm, argued Publius. Two centuries later, the image of a promised balance is rather tarnished as a result of the realities of racial strife. Even so, it is still widely believed that multiple forms of identification are a sign of health in a pluralist democracy, yet Americans often regard such ties as a pathology elsewhere in the world.

In today's Third World, tribal loyalty – ethnicity is a preferred term – is as much a product of colonialism as it is an aspect of indigenous cultures. It was the divide-and-rule tactics employed by the European powers which gave Third World peoples the incentive to identify along ethnic lines. In the early colonial period in south-western Uganda, for example, British administrators found rural dwellers – Americans would call them rugged individualists – who farmed the irregular ranks of steep slopes. They belonged to clans and shared religious practices but did not truly coalesce until the British, or their local agents (drawn from the Baganda, the heartland ethnic group), offered tangible rewards – bore holes for water, modern medicine and mission schools – for establishing the type of political structures favoured by the colonizers. These structures were in fact a means of installing political control.

It would be a grave error to deny that ethnicity is a major *form* of conflict in contemporary Africa. When a Langi, one of former President Milton Obote's kin, gunned down a Kakwa, a compatriot from

Idi Amin's home area, the motive may well have been tribal animos-
ity. But it is tautological to reckon that Tribe A fights Tribe B because
of tribalism. Properly understood, tribalism is an ideology moored in
the history and social structure of a people.

Tribalism is not the lens through which crises in the Third World
ought to be viewed. The American media's harping on tribalism
during the Congo crises of 1960 and 1964 misled the public, and this
slant is still the order of the day. The Western press continues to ask
us to swallow a naive and prejudicial notion of tribal confusion. In a
peevish magazine article whose title – 'Misunderstanding Africa' –
does ironic justice to its content, correspondent Xan Smiley encapsulates this unfortunate tendency: 'tribalism is incorrigibly stronger
than a spurious nationalism based on recently drawn colonial boundaries, and remains by far the most important power in politics
throughout the continent'. The antidote to tribal impulses, says
Smiley, has been adopted by a 'brave band of sub-Saharan countries –
Senegal, Gambia, Zimbabwe, Nigeria, Botswana, Mauritius – that
have allowed their people a measure of pluralist choice'. In effect, his
prescription for the 1980s is none other than the Western model, the
same old institutions and procedures which failed to take root in
Africa during that continent's first stage of decolonization: the transfer of political power which ushered in a climate of disillusionment
in the 1960s and 1970s.

This is one of the central themes in *Petals of Blood* by Ngugi Wa
Thiong'o. Ngugi, Kenya's foremost novelist, chaired the literature department at the University of Nairobi until the government stripped
him of his position and placed him in detention. For a time the
authorities had tolerated his biting novels about post-colonial Kenya.
They were written in English, which many Kenyans do not read, and
sold at around $5 per copy, a steep price by local standards. But his
plays, composed in Kikuyu, a local language, and enacted by
villagers, provoked the ire of the government.

In *Petals of Blood*, the protagonists are soured, their lives in total
disarray, because of the authorities' betrayal of the struggle for
Kenya's independence. As Wanja, an enchanting and reflective
woman turned prostitute, puts it:

They [the big men] want to encourage the formation of various
tribal organisations. Each tribal union would have its oaths binding
its members, on point of death, to an absolute loyalty to the group.
Then the leaders from all the unions would form a National Front

. . . It would be the duty of each union to eliminate disloyal elements under the pretext that such elements were betraying the tribe and its culture and its wealth to other tribes.

But what has caused this to happen? Her companion asks what is the basis of leadership? In a word, Wanja responds: 'Property'. The wielders of power fan the flames of tribalism in order to deflect attention from the *underlying causes* of conflict, thereby maintaining their own position on top of the heap.

Ngugi's compelling novel reflects an acute appreciation of the underpinnings of social conflict in the Third World. Clearly such an appreciation does not provide operational answers to the problems stalking underdeveloped countries, but it does lead one to pose fruitful questions and to avoid certain traps.

One such trap is the widespread belief that it is a gap that sets apart the Third World from the advanced countries. Certain countries, the argument runs, have fallen behind in their historical development. They are said to be caught in a vicious circle: poverty begets more poverty. A mounting population eats up economic growth.

The influential 1980 Report of the Independent Commission on International Development Issues, chaired by Willy Brandt, takes as a cornerstone of its study the premise that the gap separating rich and poor countries is so serious that human beings are divided into different universes. To paraphrase the report: the advanced countries, bracketing the West and Eastern Europe, have one-quarter of the world's population and four-fifths of its income, whereas the Third World, including China, holds three-quarters of the globe's population and one-fifth of its income. In the advanced countries life expectancy on average is over 70 years, more than 20 years greater than in most Third World countries. There one in four children die before the age of 5; one in five people suffer from hunger and malnutrition; and 50 per cent of the people have no opportunity to become literate.

Numerous documents compiled by international organizations provide statistical indicators to show the severity of the gap. According to the World Bank, 1980 income per person in the industrial countries was approximately five times that of the developing countries as a whole, 12 times that of the low-income oil importers. The bank indicates that 750 million people now live in absolute poverty in the Third World and that that number could increase to 850 million by the year 2000.

Beneath the aggregate statistics, however, lay another story. It would be a mistake to allow global data to jumble the wide variation among countries. So, turning to national figures assembled by the World Bank, let us look at two indicators of the gap between countries: average income and average energy consumption. In 1981, per capita income in Bangladesh was $140; India, $260; Tanzania, $280; and China, $300. The corresponding amount for Sweden was $14 870; West Germany, $13 450; the US, $12 820; and France, $12 190. In 1980, energy per capita consumption in Bangladesh was 49 kg of coal equivalent; India, 210 kg; Tanzania, 69 kg; and China, 618 kg. For the purpose of comparison, consider 1980 data for the advanced countries: Sweden, 7971 kg; West Germany, 6053 kg; the US, 11 626 kg; and France, 5368 kg.

There is no need to cite more statistics, nor to belabour the obvious implication drawn from this way of thinking: the overriding need is to close the widening gap between the rich and the poor.

The existence of the gap is an indisputable datum. But that is not the heart of the matter. The point is: the gap between the advanced capitalist countries and the Third World is a *symptom*, not a *cause*, of what ails the world political economy. The manifest problems cannot be solved without remedying fundamental causes. The situation is much the same as treating a medical condition such as a chest pain. Before a prescription is given, it is essential to diagnose what is causing the ailment. The cure for indigestion is altogether different from the treatment for a heart attack. And an accurate diagnosis takes into account an individual's medical history, for what afflicts one part of the body affects the health of the entire organism. So too the position of a Third World country must be seen as a single limb of the whole, an organic segment of the world political economy.

If the challenges facing the Third World cannot be understood symptomatically, we must look beyond what meets the eye. If solving the problems of the Third World simply required closing a gap, the oil-exporting countries would now be advanced countries, given the massive transfer of capital and technology to them. Yet the member states of OPEC have been unable to digest the inflow. Clearly the matter is more involved than narrowing a gap.

Some observers say that the trouble in the Third World is the erratic, win-all-lose-all political process there. In many countries, coups beget counter-coups, with no end to this spree in sight. Political instability, it is believed, obstructs national development, especially when self-serving military juntas give priority to lavish expenditures on 'defence' and security.

This argument, like the other ones reviewed, is plausible. The difficulty with it lies in the distinctive experiences of certain stable countries like Zambia and Paraguay. Politically stable countries in the Third World have on the whole fared no better at development (if I dare use the word before defining it) than have politically unstable countries. Consequently, factors other than political stability and instability must be considered. Politics is not an autonomous sphere of activity. In politics the critical issues are heavily economic, as illustrated by an unhappy incident in southern Africa.

POLITICAL ECONOMY

Since it was likely that Ian Smith's bombers would attack guerrilla camps that night, I urged my driver to cover the distance between Chimoio, a town on the Mozambican side of the Rhodesian border, and the coastal city of Beira in the shortest time possible. At dusk we had a flat tyre. The driver was momentarily amused by my instructions to change it. 'There are no spare tyres in Mozambique,' he explained. I then understood that the parked vehicles strewn along the roadside had been abandoned. Suddenly my musings were interrupted by planes nose-diving overhead. Fear knifed through me. I felt utterly helpless. Would I become a hapless victim of the convulsions shaking the Third World?

The predicament in which I found myself provides a tip-off for understanding what ails the Third World. I was imperilled in rural Mozambique essentially because the sputtering economy lacked foreign exchange to import tyres. The reasons for Mozambique's chronic balance of payments problems lie in the intermeshing of politics and economics in the subcontinent of southern Africa.

Exactly what is the nexus between politics and economics? Controversies over this are legion. In the eighteenth and nineteenth centuries, an extraordinary lot of writers – among them Adam Smith, David Ricardo and John Stuart Mill – considered themselves political economists. Karl Marx, who wrote *A Contribution to the Critique of Political Economy*, was a part of this tradition. For these classical thinkers, political economy was the practical aspect of the study of moral philosophy. It developed as a single field of inquiry centring on the dynamics of civil society, including the social relations of production and the distribution of income. The classical writers primarily investigated national rather than international issues.

In the last quarter of the nineteenth century, economics became separated from political economy. Mainline economists became increasingly concerned with price and market theory, and less occupied with political phenomena. They focused on marginal techniques for making rational choices in a situation of market equilibrium.

In neo-classical economics, as this avenue of inquiry is called, the ideal is a perfect market, the allocator of scarce resources. Against this standard, market defects are gauged and explained. The manipulation of quantitative price models is an important element in this tradition. The concerns of classical economists with production relations and the conflicting interests of classes have been dismissed.

Meanwhile, in the twentieth century, political scientists have elaborated their own abstract models, chiefly concentrating on how social systems cohere and treating political behaviour as an activity separable from economics. They have sought to attain the high standard of empirical rigour characteristic of neo-classical economics, but have diverged sharply from the substantive concerns in that discipline. Whereas the two fields draw on a common fund of data and share research findings, they continue to formulate different sorts of questions in their compartmentalized areas.

Emblematic of this decoupling is the fact that the most recent edition of the highly touted *International Encyclopedia of the Social Sciences* contains not one entry under political economy. At the appropriate place for political economy, going by alphabetic order, there is an article on the well-trodden topic of political culture, after which the reader is referred to various other orthodox headings: culture, government and socialization, especially political socialization. Mention is made of related articles on modernization, national culture, political anthropology, political sociology and societal analysis. The index lists a single book on *Political Economy*, by a contemporary author, Oscar Lange, who taught at the University of Chicago before taking a senior position in the government of Poland. (Reviewing Lange's work for the *Encyclopedia* was a Polish immigrant to the US who chaired Columbia University's heavily neo-classical Department of Economics.)

Now there are forces pushing economics and politics back together, but analysts disagree over the meaning of political economy. In attempting to predict fluctuations of output (unemployment and business cycles), neo-classicals have developed a sophisticated understanding of market mechanisms. Nevertheless the limitations of deducing phenomena, such as the marginal efficiency of capital and the propensity to consume, from statistical observation of past behaviour are patent.

Added to this, in the aftermath of decolonization it has become increasingly evident that a host of factors, not least cultural practices, has considerable bearing on economic development. That the capacity to organize economic development is a political matter could no longer be denied. And of utmost importance in the 1970s and 1980s, worldwide economic tremors rekindled interest in the field of political economy.

The mainstream is at present storing a vast armoury of knowledge on the political dimensions of economics and vice versa. Politics and economics are said to be 'interdependent'. For, following John Maynard Keynes, who sought to substitute a steady level of employment for the historical pattern of boom–bust, recession–inflation, governments increasingly intervene in the economy through their policies of taxation, nationalization, agreements over prices and wages, and so on. It is also widely recognized that the strength or weakness of an economy may seal the fate of a particular government or administration. Given this acknowledged interplay, conventional political scientists and economists have adopted parallel procedures, but are loath to meld what they still see as their distinguishable areas of professional activity.

Unlike many liberal political economists, Marxists have steadfastly emphasized the social context of their studies: class *and* power. They have stuck to a holistic analysis. For Marxists, economics, politics and ideology are integrated levels of social structure. All three levels are deemed vitally important in history, economics being the major yet not the sole determinant in the capitalist mode of production. It is true, as its detractors claim, that some versions of Marxism are economistic. The crass view has it that 'politics is all economics'. Marx himself railed against this brand of reductionism, and the large majority of contemporary Marxists go to great lengths to scotch this way of thinking.

In keeping with the classical authors, then, political economy involves the social processes that differentially allocate produce among proprietors, holders of capital and labourers. It means the social laws that govern the production, distribution and consumption of goods. Additionally, political economy analysis must take into account the workings of the state, especially its ability to employ force against enemies, to broker class struggles and to exercise ideological hegemony. To summarize: *political economy refers to the social laws that govern the production, distribution and consumption of goods to satisfy human needs, as well as the state's capacity to organize and disorganize class forces, both within a social formation and at the global level.* Various elements of this definition will be examined in subsequent chapters (especially Chapter 4). But now it will be helpful to specify the object of the political economy analysis in this book: the Third World

HOW MANY WORLDS?

The Third World is easier to characterize than to define. In barest outline: (one-commodity economies, often small in size, abound.) Typically, (the majority of the population is engaged in agriculture.) This sector is usually marked by low levels of productivity and fails to meet the wants of the domestic market. The economies are oriented to the satisfaction of external needs, namely those of the advanced countries. Hence priority is often given to the production of cash crops – not food crops – and the extraction of raw materials for export. Manufacturing industry is limited, although some countries have shown phenomenal growth in this area: most notably, three in Latin America (Brazil, Mexico and, to a lesser extent, Argentina) and four in Asia (South Korea and Taiwan, plus the subcontracting economies of Hong Kong and Singapore). Foreign trade predominantly centres on a few advanced capitalist countries. The direction of trade is paralleled by the movement of skilled human resources, which is a major transference of wealth from the Third World to the West.

Equally important to consider are social elements. In most parts of the Third World, the receding colonial power sought to graft Western parliamentary and party institutions on to indigenous cultures, which are based on other historical realities. This implantation often aggravated existing class and ethnic rivalries. The apparent forms of conflict have varied enormously. What issues rent the social fabric – religion, language, regional disparities, and so forth – depended on the distinctive history and culture of a particular area. In all but a few cases, the replicas of Western polities could not withstand the swirl of these centrifugal forces. As often as not soldiers step into the political breach only to forget their promises to return willingly to the barracks. Unsurprisingly, there have been quite a few instances where politics have been awash with repression and no party systems, not to mention bulging bureaucracies. Popular discontent may then be vented in the form of riots, insurgency, secessionist movements and civil wars.

Beyond a brief mention of the broad characteristics of the political economies of the Third World, generalization is hazardous, lest one oversimplify a multifaceted phenomenon to which different definitions are assigned. As defined by the French authors who coined the term, the Third World – an analogy to the Third Estate before the French Revolution – meant specific strata not belonging to either of the most privileged groups of the day, the nobility and the clergy. The Third Estate was led by a non-commercial and professional bourgeoisie. Supported by the peasants, the Third Estate, unlike the other two orders, advocated vote by head. Even so, the deputies elected by all three orders argued that only men of property could qualify, thus excluding the common people.

A somewhat different notion assimilates the Third World to poverty in general. In World Bank parlance, the Third World comprises low-income countries. These may be subdivided according to GNP per person. But this definition is replete with empirical contradictions. Kuwait has a higher average per capita income than does the US, and there is a greater incidence of poverty in Harlem than in many parts of the Third World. Furthermore, at stake is a qualitative, not a quantitative, condition. From yet another angle, the term 'Third World' means the proletarian nations. It suggests the existence of states that are exploited and of others that are exploiters. The designation of proletarian and bourgeois nations has a certain cachet in some quarters because of its Marxist ring. But surely no present-day society is without classes; no social formation is composed entirely of the exploited masses or of their exploiters.

In common usage, the Third World encapsulates all countries not included in the First World and Second World. The First World alludes to the Western capitalist countries plus Japan, Australia and New Zealand. This grouping often finds room for Israel and South Africa as well. In the obvious sense, the Second World consists of the socialist countries of the East. These are sometimes called the Soviet bloc, but that rubric does not cover Albania and Yugoslavia. *The Third World encompasses the nations of Africa, Asia and Latin America, most of them former colonies which to varying degrees lack economic power.* This is even true of the oil-exporting countries. Unable to imbibe massive inflows of capital, these countries invested the lion's share of it in Western financial institutions. The banks recycled much of this capital in the form of commercial loans to oil-importing nations of the Third World. The oil importers are now repaying, on top of principal, staggering debt-servicing charges to Western moneylenders.

The ambiguities associated with the term 'Third World' are manifold. The term appears all too comprehensive. It can shroud the differences between and within the three continents in a mist of deceptive simplicity. Another complication is the role of oppressed peoples elsewhere in the world. Are black Americans part of the Third World? Native Americans? Australian aborigines? With immigrant workers in mind, Alain Geismar, a leader of the 1968 student uprising in France, asserted: 'The Third World starts in the suburbs.' (The suburbs around Paris are working-class districts.) Relatedly, ethnocentrism may be detected in assigning first place to the countries that rank ahead of the others according to an economic and technological yardstick. The Third World would be first if the criteria were the chronology of the human species (which begins with Africa) or total population.

Yet another snag is the disagreement over whether China belongs to the Third World. The Chinese position, called the theory of three worlds, holds that the US and the Soviet Union make up the First World. The other developed countries form the Second World. With the exception of Japan, the whole of Asia, Africa and Latin America comprise the Third World. China has proclaimed herself to be a socialist nation and part of the Third World, for she has suffered from imperialism, is not a superpower and shares common tasks with other oppressed nations.

Beijing's view of the matter has not been endorsed by Third World leaders. Despite all the accolades given to China for supporting Third World causes, hesitation to enlist her stems from the perception that while China may not qualify as a superpower, a country with one billion people, bountiful natural resources and nuclear hardware is, by any means of accounting, a big, big power. Hence at recent meetings of non-aligned nations, China has been an onlooker, not an invited participant.

Ambiguities aside, some observers reject the term 'Third World' altogether. The Brandt commissioners, among others, prefer a dichotomy, as indicated by the nomenclature of their report: *North–South: A Program for Survival*. The differentiation is between two hemispheres, the northern nations being more economically advanced than are their southern counterparts. The North includes well-to-do nations south of the equator: Australia, New Zealand, and more problematically South Africa. Located in the northern hemisphere, too, are India, with 700 million people – 15 per cent of the world's population – the rest of south Asia, most of south-east Asia, the Caribbean, Central America and the northern tier of South America.

However, the North–South distinction is not the only way to divide the world in two. In the twilight of his career, Kwame Nkrumah, Ghana's flamboyant head of state from 1957 to 1966, held that 'the "Third World" is neither a practical political concept nor a reality. It is merely a misused expression which has come to mean everything and nothing.' For him, the differentiation was ideological, tied to capitalism and scientific socialism. But surely this view is too rigid. It makes no allowance for a transition from capitalism to socialism. No attention is given to the process whereby a nationalist struggle converts to a socialist revolution. Socialism is seemingly a magic remedy for all the ills of capitalist life, without any consideration of the specific forces which might find expression in the transitional period.

Another viewpoint is that the world is one. To wit, former Indian Prime Minister Indira Gandhi claimed that it is wrong to slice up the world and to deny its unity, adding: 'We are responsible not to individual countries alone, but to peace and prosperity of the whole world.' A worthy goal that is! Yet Mrs Gandhi's imagery is devoid of power relations and social conflict, aspects of human existence that cannot be wished away simply because they are monstrous.

In a perceptive book, *The Capitalist World-Economy*, sociologist Immanuel Wallerstein also makes the entire world his unit of analysis, reasoning that there is a single world economy and it is capitalist. Like the Trotskyites who dismiss 'socialism in one country' as an impossibility, Wallerstein believes that socialism requires a new world system, which in turn necessitates a world government. The analysis that follows from this presupposition is useful in that it alerts us to an important dialectical process: while the internationalization of capital stirs unevenness among and within countries, it also acts as a homogenizing mechanism reducing national distinctiveness. On the one hand, economies (and sectors) develop and underdevelop at dramatically different rates. On the other, outside elements weighing on the Third World increasingly standardize commodities (witness consumption goods such as Coca-Cola and blue jeans); multinational corporations invite – even command – a large measure of uniformity in their management agreements as well as royalty and technology contracts; and international monetary institutions prescribe the same basic conditions, politely called 'adjustment policies', for diverse economies. The danger, however, in overemphasizing the broad strokes lies in omitting the fine detail, which is precisely what in substance must be discerned.

So where does this leave us? With one, two, three, four or five worlds?

The division of the world into three components is a reality. The Third World is a pivotal idea which has served as a focal point in such forums as the UN. It is an association of states, albeit not a unitary entity. However, to the extent that the Third World is a geographical category referring to the three continents, it is not an analytical concept. The drawback to Third Worldist thinking is sentimentality, the tendency to romanticize the struggles waged by 'the wretched of the earth'. A Third Worldist perspective gives the impression that only the advanced countries are the oppressors, neglects class differences within underdeveloped nations, and ignores the role of the locally dominant strata in these nations. In this book I will nonetheless continue to use the term Third World as a convenient shorthand to describe a critical and varied phenomenon. Despite its pitfalls, the convention is better than the other options. The phrases 'emerging areas', 'modernizing societies', 'developing nations' and 'less developed countries' are hollow euphemisms. The language adopted ought not be allowed to mask the struggles within societies, or to deflect attention from class alliances cross-cutting and transcending national borders. But what is the reality lying behind what I choose to call the Third World?

LEARNING FROM OUR CHILDREN

The question of terminology raises major substantive issues that form the core of this book. For now, I simply want to introduce the basic themes in this undertaking.

Volumes have been written about the meaning of development and underdevelopment. Within this compass are the master works of antiquity. Plato's *Republic* is a utopian schema for engineering distributive justice, and Aristotle conceived the polis as an agency to develop to the utmost the potential of humanity. According to the Greek doctrine *physis*, humans are in motion from a primary natural condition to a formed and finished completion. We will, says Aristotle, one day look back on the historic process, and observe the growth of institutions to discover their course and ultimate state. To this end, the philosophers of antiquity took it as their task to make value judgments about what constitutes the good society and about the institutions and processes through which the good life can be achieved.

Over the centuries the inherently ethical aspects of the development debate have endured. There is the story of the English administrator serving overseas in the early days of empire. He stumbled upon a 'native' lolling beside a lake and decided to do the chap a good turn. The colonizer gave the local a swift kick to the ribs, awakening him from a deep sleep, and demanded: 'Why are you idling with a dozen or so fish beside you instead of catching more?' The lackadaisical response was: 'I have caught all the fish that my family can eat today.' Unperturbed, the Englishman didactically informed his acquaintance: 'My good man, if you net another string of fish, you can sell it in the market place.' The local repeated his point: 'But we already have enough to eat.' So the English official persisted: 'With the proceeds of your sale, you can employ other fishermen.' By this time, the local was feeling quite dumbfounded. He asked: 'What then?' 'Why,' said the Englishman, 'then you can retire and sleep all day along this lovely waterfront.'

This apocryphal story not only raises the crucial ethical question 'development for what?' but also suggests deeper socio-economic processes. Clearly Third World producers are drawn into the cash economy in many ways. Demographic changes due to conquest or migration, the imposition of hut and poll taxes, the introduction of cheap manufactured goods, and the advent of wage labour flush peasants into production for exchange. All the same, the story reminds us to be aware of our values in arriving at judgments about development and underdevelopment; one must indeed guard against ethnocentrism. To do so in an area of inquiry which stirs sensibilities and emotion requires us to confront our own values. This leads to self-clarification and self-definition. In studying other cultures, we are the primary beneficiaries because we come to a better understanding of ourselves.

However, moral indignation, while understandable, will not solve the fundamental problems of underdevelopment which are deeply embedded in the political economy of the Third World. Let us avoid misunderstanding about the concept of underdevelopment. As employed by political economists, it is not an invidious term insinuating cultural deficiencies; neither is it virtually the same as undevelopment: objective shortfalls in production, organizational competence, technological know-how, and so on.

More properly, *underdevelopment* refers to the blockage which forestalls a rational transformation of the social structure in Third World countries: rational not in the commonsensical meaning that the options are deduced from reason alone, nor in the bureaucratic sense of a neat adjustment of means to ends. Rather, rational in that the interests and needs of the majority are increasingly dominant. What blocks development is an internal and external constellation of power and privilege.

Development entails but is not synonymous with economic growth. In my usage, *development* is the increasing capacity to make rational use of natural and human resources for social ends.

To create more goods and services, all peoples have sought to extend control over their environment. Thus development is a universal process, but the rates of development are highly uneven. Added to this, there is marked inequality in distribution.

In pre-capitalist, communal societies, economic productivity was of course low. The technological aspects of production were rudimentary. Property belonged to the collectivity, and work was done in common. People produced for their mutual needs, not for exchange with others. Commodities were not bought and sold on the market. There were social differences between the sexes and between elders and juniors. With growing specialization in production and the advent of long-distance trade, social differences became more pronounced. These undeveloped societies increasingly, albeit slowly, expanded control over their environment. The reversal of this condition through the withdrawal of the benefits of nature's bounty and human labour constitutes underdevelopment, a historical process which will be examined more fully in subsequent chapters.

Nowadays the most vexing matter, the terminus of the journey undertaken here, concerns the transition from underdevelopment to development. Third World – hereafter also called underdeveloped for reasons that will be explained – countries, from Afghanistan to Zambia, are all grappling with the question of how to engage the transition. Definitive answers are nowhere to be found. Yet novel experiments and new ideas bear careful examination.

These new forms are a response to the profound structural metamorphoses marking our era. It has become a cliché of late to note that the power of the US has taken a nose dive. There is more to this than the well-known reasons for the US' economic troubles: the *lowest* pace of domestic investment of all major industrial countries since 1960, the overvaluing of the dollar until the collapse of the Bretton Woods monetary system and depreciation of the dollar in the early 1970s, the heightened need for imported raw materials, sagging productivity, and decreasing federal support for non-military research and development. These woes cannot be chalked up solely to misguided government policies, for not only the US but the entire capitalist world is beset by deep-seated ills.

In the Western countries as a whole, the level of unemployment, gains in productivity and the rate of profit are causes of considerable concern. The retrenchment in the West edges into the Third World in a shrinkage in the volume of exports of primary commodities, while the price of most imports continues to mount. Meanwhile, the mature capitalist countries have lent the underdeveloped world over one-half trillion dollars. Debt service consumes an ever expanding share of export earnings. The greater the burden of debt service, the more the borrower's capacity to repay diminishes. Current borrowing continues at a gallop just to defray the cost of old loans, let alone to meet present needs. With good reason, then, creditors are jittery about the viability of a financial system of spiralling deficits, recycling and rescheduling. International bankers feel that they are held hostage. If one major borrower is not allowed to roll over a loan, or refuses to do so, then what? The whole system could cave in.

Is there a common thread to help us disentangle all this? A clue may be found by turning to children's ways. Children are intrigued by products discarded by the adult world: empty cartons, food containers, corks from wine bottles and so on. Not infrequently a young child prefers the box in which a present is packaged to the present itself. Children are known to have profound insights. However, much of this profundity is lost precisely because the socialization process hammers it out of existence. Then again, maybe not all qualities should be redeemed: children are often egocentric, intolerant and downright selfish.

We adults also waste products which ought to be preserved. I am suggesting that we should rehabilitate some of the wisdom lost from our intellectual heritage. Discarded alternatives may be detected in the classical theory of capital accumulation and usefully applied to fathom the political economy of the contemporary Third World. The key is to go back to the classical tradition in order to go forwards from it. Then we can adapt the old concepts to new problems, albeit ones for which they were not intended. To be sure, new problems require new answers. Eternal verities are not engraved in 'the great books', but these works do indicate a general direction in which to move and provide positive guidance.

This guidebook will stress that underdeveloped countries are in no sense impotent, mired in a hopeless situation. Underdevelopment is not an immutable fact. The foremost difficulty in attempting to snap out of this condition is to dismantle the mechanisms that reproduce it. Built-in features of the world political economy regenerate underdevelopment. This argument redoubles upon itself. For underdevelopment is renewed as ideology as well. Until now orthodox doctrines of development have been part of the problem. Our job here is to present an interpretation that will be part of the solution. Thus in Chapter 2 we will clear away the dead wood before charting another course.

Part II

Ideologies and Structures of Accumulation

2 Sources of Received Ideas about the Third World

The Acholi, a Nilotic people in northern Uganda, are wedged in a stretch between Zaire, Sudan and Kenya. The standard maps do not identify their locale as Acholi-land. I first encountered them when a fellow student invited me to his home, a mud-thatched hut, one among many surrounded by a makeshift thicket fence erected to keep out intruders, human or otherwise. Afterwards I discovered that the plight of the Acholi is told in a moving tale, *Song of Lawino*, by the late Okot p'Bitek, an Oxford-educated poet and novelist who directed the National Cultural Centre of Uganda. Indeed, the personal meaning of the changes stalking the Acholi, and the bulk of the Third World, is encapsulated in the lives of two fictional Ugandans; Lawino is a perceptive, uneducated woman who cries out in anguish over the new-found ways of her husband, Ocol:

> My husband
> Has read at Makerere University.
> He has read deeply and widely,
> But if you ask him a question
> He says
> You are insulting him;
> He opens up with a quarrel
> He begins to look down upon you
> Saying
> You ask questions
> That are a waste of time!
>
> He says
> My questions are silly questions,
> Typical questions from village girls,
> Questions of uneducated people,
> Useless questions from untutored minds.
> . . .

27

Ocol says
He has no time to waste
Discussing things with a thing like me
Who has not been to school.
He says
A university man
Can only have useful talk
With another university man or woman.
And that is funny,
That he should stoop so low
Even to listen
To my questions.

Ocol's altered attitudes are evident in his scorn for his people's religious practices, which he no longer observes.

My husband wears
A small crucifix
On his neck,
And all his daughters
Wear rosaries.

But he prohibits me
From wearing the elephant tail necklace,
He once beat me
For wearing the toe of the edible rat
And the horn of the rhinoceros
And the jaw-bone of the alligator.

A large snake
Once fell down from the roof
Of the cold hall!
The Nun who was teaching
The Evening Speakers' Class
Grabbed her large crucifix
And pressed it on her bosom,
Closed her eyes
And said something
We could not understand.

My husband says
The cowry shells.

The colobus-monkey hair,
The dog's horn charms
Are all useless things.

He says
Only foolish backward folk
Uneduated simple fellows
Who live in the shadow of fear
Carry these dirty things!

In the end, Lawino, grief-stricken, mourns the loss of her man. He has been mortified by wisdom, by the weighty knowledge of books. He is no more than a stump, thoroughly emasculated.

He borrows the clothes he wears
And the ideas in his head
And his actions and behaviour
Are to please somebody else.
Like a woman trying to please her husband!
My husband has become a woman!

Then why do you wear a shirt?
Why do you not tie
A sheet around your waist
As other women do?
Put on the string skirt
And some beads on your loin!
. . .

Bile burns my inside!
I feel like vomiting!

For all our young men
Were finished in the forest,
Their manhood was finished
In the class-rooms,
Their testicles
Were smashed
With large books!

When Lawino asks whether she must share her bed with a woman and whether the son of the Acholi can recapture his manhood, she does not plead for going back to the old ways. Rather, she implicitly raises the central question of how to escape the unsettling conditions in which her people are trapped. In fact, Lawino's lament is a condensation of the most basic human dimensions of development and underdevelopment. It is a clue for interpreting the whole.

In order better to understand the single instance, let us turn to the world of ideas and search for the precipice of new knowledge. Paradoxically, we are ultimately able to derive the utmost meaning from individual conditions by intially moving from the specific to the general. There are certainly different ways to traverse this course. The best known path has been staked out by liberal reformers who view modernization as, above all, a shift from a parochial fund of *traditional values* to an array of *new norms*.

LIBERAL REFORMISM

In the years immediately following the Second World War, a presentation of a thoroughgoing statement of the foremost theorizing about development and underdevelopment would not have required much space. It could have only been an embellishment of what the master philosophers had written about equality and inequality among peoples.

In the time of Plato and Aristotle, the Greek city-states increasingly came into contact with people who differed from the Hellenes in physique and culture. The leading minds of Athens attributed these differences not to race but to the effects of distinct environments on a stable human nature. In Greek eyes, it was the facts of geography that caused the tremendous variation in human culture.

For aeons the primary economic and social divisions of the world were understood as expressions of natural differences in climate, soil and rainfall. The eighteenth-century philosopher Montesquieu, for example, maintained that the immutability of culture and the low levels of income in southern nations result from a climate that saps the body of vigour and strength. Excessive heat, he argued, precipitates faintness of the mind. Under such conditions there is no enterprising spirit, no curiosity. Behaviour is passive. In India, even the children born of Europeans become indolent and lose the courage distinctive to their own climate, argued Montesquieu.

In the nineteenth and twentieth centuries, Western observers dismissed the environment theory and substituted a race theory to explain the diversity of humankind. It has been believed in some quarters that inherent differences among human species, identifiable in terms of skin colour, distinguish the achievements of societies. This way of thinking is so well known that we need not dwell on its tenets. A few graphic examples will suffice.

In a televised lecture delivered in 1963, Hugh Trevor-Roper, the Regius Professor of Modern History at Oxford University, maintained: 'Perhaps, in the future, there will be some African history . . . But at present there is none; there is only the history of Europeans in Africa. The rest is darkness, . . . and darkness is not a subject of history.' Similarly, Eric Severeid, the senior scholar of American television news, claimed: 'The truth is that there is very little in most of the new African and Asian nations worth anything in twentieth century terms that was not put there by westerners.' Adding to this, he commented: 'The truth is that in spite of talking about returning to their own cultural roots – remember Africanization – what they want to be is what the west already is.'

Such arrogance has often been carried over into American foreign policy. For example, in 1969 Henry Kissinger presented the then President, Richard Nixon, with five policy options in southern Africa, and Nixon chose the wrong one. He adopted the now famous Option 2, embodied in NSSM-39, based on the supposition that the liberation movements would fail: 'The whites are here to stay and the only way that constructive change can come about is through them. There is no hope for the blacks to gain the political rights they seek through violence, which will only lead to chaos and increased opportunities for the communists.' NSSM-39 Option 2 called for expanded communication with the white minority regimes. In practice, the policy meant closer economic and military cooperation.

Any remaining doubt about Kissinger's attitude toward the Third World was removed in the same year, when Gabriel Valdés, the foreign minister of Chile under the Eduardo Frei government, informed Nixon that Latin America was remitting $3.8 for every dollar in American aid. When Nixon questioned the statistic, Valdés pointed out that the figure had been borrowed from a study undertaken by a bank in the US. The next afternoon Kissinger requested a private meeting with Valdés. Kissinger opened the session with a salvo:

Mr. Minister, you made a strange speech. You come here speaking of Latin America, but this is not important. Nothing important can come from the South. History has never been produced in the

South. The axis of history starts in Moscow, goes to Bonn, crosses over to Washington, and then goes to Tokyo. What happens in the South is of no importance. You're wasting your time.

'I said,' Valdés recalls, 'Mr. Kissinger, you know nothing of the South.' 'No,' Kissinger answered, 'and I don't care.' Seymour M. Hersh, from whose book on Kissinger this illustration is drawn, concludes: 'The Valdés incident showed the White House attitude: like a child, Latin America was to be seen and not heard.'

The foregoing incidents are not harmless or isolated examples. They represent public or official behaviour by prominent scholars affiliated with top universities, Oxford and Harvard, an influential television commentator, and a former secretary of state. It is true to say that, nowadays, their statements run counter to a great deal of commentary in the media and a flurry of literature which attacks the race theory. Attitudes such as Kissinger's view of the Third World have come under fire on the grounds that they are factually wrong and morally repugnant. Contemporary liberal thinkers contend that it is not race but a lack of capital and technology that explains why the developing countries are lagging behind. External inputs, primarily investment and technical assistance, it is widely believed, are needed to modernize the flagging nations.

The term 'modernization' gained currency when it was trumpeted by American foreign policy makers as part of President Harry Truman's 1949 Point Four Program, which included assistance to transmit scientific and industrial knowledge to the underdeveloped countries. The term came into general usage in the age of decolonization, when most of the countries in Africa, Asia and the Caribbean graduated to political independence. The doctrine of modernization offered a palatable explanation for America's burgeoning role in the Third World. Its icy, analytical language called for a new world order, seemingly one without exploitation.

It is worth recalling that the naive optimism of the modernization school contrasted sharply with the canny *weltanschauung* touted in the old days before imperialism became a dirty word; the authors of imperialism had spoken unblushingly about a world of power. In 1895 Cecil Rhodes said:

I was in the East End of London [a working-class quarter] yesterday and attended a meeting of the unemployed. I listened to the wild speeches, which were just a cry for 'bread,' 'bread!' and on my way home I pondered over the scene and I became more than ever convinced of the importance of imperialism . . . My cherished idea is a solution for the social problem, i.e., in order to save the 40,000,000 inhabitants of the United Kingdom from a bloody civil war, we colonial statesmen must acquire new lands to settle the surplus population, to provide new markets for the goods produced in the factories and mines. The Empire, as I have always said, is a bread and butter question. If you want to avoid civil war, you must become imperialists.

For the architects of imperialism, power was empire, and empire was conquest. The vanquished, they claimed, would be better off living under the regency of the civilized rather than left to their own devices.

In time revolutionary nationalism increasingly challenged imperial doctrine. Battered by its Western critics as well, it slowly lost legitimacy. A theory was needed to replace the discredited notion of the 'white man's burden' and the *mission civilisatrice*. Attuned to the metamorphoses in an international system racked by two world wars, modernization theorists offered a vision of a restructured global order based upon universal processes of development. The alternative etched by these thinkers – most of them Americans – would be made possible by the spread of US economic muscle and military might. The new world powerhouse was portrayed as liberal, progressive and truly international. It had put in train international organizations – the UN and the Bretton Woods twins, the IMF and the World Bank – bent on curbing global war and helping all free nations to develop peacefully.

An avalanche of books and articles released by the acolytes of the modernization school descended upon our universities and libraries in the 1950s and 1960s, tunnelling the vision of an entire generation of thinkers, some of whom stepped into leading policy making positions. This much was brought home to me almost a decade ago when I was standing on the steps of the library at the London School of Economics engaged in lively conversation with a distinguished African writer and activist. In mid-sentence he nudged me and muttered, 'Look there'. I noticed a doting old man in a tweed jacket supported by a cane. My companion, a graduate of the London School of Economics, said, 'That chap set me back in my thinking by 20 years.' The old man was his former mentor, a specialist in the field of international development. The topic of conversation then shifted to an assessment of the foremost thinking about modernization conveyed to students and filtered to the general public.

Needless to say, as with other schools of thought we will examine, there are different versions and major debates among authors working within the compass of the modernization framework. Bibliographies and distinctions among individual writers, however, would be burdensome to follow and need not detain us. My concern here is to identify the mainstream of modernization analysis, not the tributaries.

In brief, modernization theory is an attempt to establish a model for understanding universal patterns of change. The starting gate for all nations embarking on a fast modernizing track is traditional society. In this stage, humans exercise little control over their environment. Traditional people lack the traits of modern individuals, whose culture is urban, literate and participant. Traditional society is not inscribed by political consciousness or active involvement in attempting to shape the future.

Not only can nations be distinguished in terms of the dichotomy between tradition and modernity, but also segments of a society and sectors of an economy reflect this split. The same duality is evident in the ambit of technology, where there is a changeover from age-old methods to the applications of scientific knowledge; in agriculture, a conversion from subsistence farming to the commercial production of crops; in industry, a turnabout from reliance on human labour and animal power to the use of machines; and in human ecology, a transformation from rural and village life to urban settlements. In all realms, tradition is staid and inhibiting, whereas modernity is vigorous and creative.

All societies progress through distinct phases on the road to modernization. In one formulation, the sequence consists of five categories: traditional society is said to be one with limited production functions based on pre-Newtonian science and technology, with a ceiling on attainable output per head. The second stage of growth satisfies the preconditions for the take-off to a modern economy: in a context rocked by the expansion of world markets and international competition, the insights of modern science are translated into increased production both in agriculture and industry. Then, in the third stage, comes the great turning point in this sequence. The take-off is the period when the obstacles to growth are transcended; the new technology becomes predominant in society and growth becomes self-generating.

In the drive to maturity, the economy converts to more refined and complex processes: for instance, from coal, iron and the heavy engineering industries of the railroad phase to machine tools, chemicals and electrical equipment; it moves beyond the original industries which propelled the take-off to absorb and to develop a wide range of resources. Finally, we reach the age of high mass consumption. The leading sectors of the economy now produce durable consumers' goods and services. The advancement of modern technology is not the sole objective, for at this ultimate stage societies choose to allocate additional resources to social welfare and security.

All societies, it is worth repeating, are thought to traverse this path. The progression is fixed and linear. The early modernizers (the Western countries) piloted the way; the late-comers will follow the same unswerving course.

What touches off the stirrings of modernization? Clearly no single element or agent spawns this process. Modernization is multidimensional, pluralist to the core, entailing a syndrome of impulses: as societies become increasingly complex, more specialized roles emerge. No longer does the chief represent the political executive, legislator and judge. Elaborate institutions evolve gradually. There are distinctive activities and functions to be carried out in order to solidify the nation-state; the gulf between castes, tribes, regions and religious groups must be bridged. Forging a national identity necessitates moulding new attitudes which centre on individual achievement and empathy for fellow citizens.

At the heart of modernization theory is evolutionary optimism. A fundamental premise is that this multifaceted process will correct the lag in development. This whole genre of thinking is permeated by a nineteenth-century belief in progress. Change is change for the better. The end point of the modernization vision approximates the traits of the present-day Western nations. The terminus of the journey is liberal democracy, a goal which all nations can attain.

This intellectual framework has had an enormous impact. To illustrate its practical consequences, consider the following application: in Bukoba, a district in north-western Tanzania, *matoke* bananas (the staple food) and coffee are interplanted because land is in short supply; the majority of producers, poor peasants, do not have access to sufficient acreage to grow the two crops in separate areas. The government's agricultural extension officers, however, have advised the small farmer to cultivate pure-stand coffee, since interplanted bananas draw nitrogen and water from the soil and shade the coffee crop. This advice is based on experiments performed under laboratory conditions. It benefits only the minority of well-to-do farmers with enough land to segregate bananas and coffee. The large land holder cultivates under conditions that resemble those of the research station. In addition, he is likely to mingle with the government experts in a social milieu that facilitates communication and hence adoption of the proposed changes.

The poor peasants resist the innovations suggested by the research team because its recommendations are useless or harmful to them. They have been known to fry cotton seeds before putting them in the ground or to plant cassava cuttings upside down. The government officers in turn regard the peasants as traditional: the stereotypical description is backward, irresponsible, lazy and stupid. The modernization thesis is then invoked to justify supporting the agents of change. These are deemed to be the rich farmers. The whole argument about modernization is often used to legitimize coercing the so-called traditional peasants.

This is not a random case. It typifies the way this armoury of knowledge is deployed. In fact, modernization theory informed US policy throughout Latin America during the 1960s. Known as the Green Revolution, it called for a large dose of foreign assistance to increase agricultural yields. Most observers believe that contrary to the rhetoric of the US AID, the overall impact of the policy was to entrench the powerful and the wealthy landowners in the Latin American countries at the expense of the small farmer.

Although the modernization school has contributed importantly to social science by extending its focus beyond the West to the Third World, there are a number of problems embedded in this way of thinking. To begin with, modernization theory is too general, too abstract, and without adequate grounding in history. The modern world, of course, did not come out of nowhere. The Western countries experienced a protracted and painful process disrupting older ways of life. In Britain in the eighteenth and nineteenth centuries, the enlargement of the market and the fanning out of wage labour entailed untold human suffering, including widespread violence and extensive pauperization. True, what was rational for an inventive bourgeoisie severed persistent bonds of exploitation, namely feudal servitude. But it is foolish to regard this process as progress for everyone and to sanctify its dynamics as the essential features of a model applicable to the development of the entire world.

Furthermore, the division of the world into traditional and modern societies implies that all peoples were alike at one stage. Thus bands of nomadic hunters, classical Greek city-states and bureaucratic empires of feudal times are placed in a single category. To term all of them traditional not only obscures the differences among them but also denies the unfolding history of peoples in the pre-modern, or pre-capitalist, era.

More problematically, modernization thinking lacks an explanation of the causes of underdevelopment. It is not that modernization theorists are wrong about the causes of underdevelopment: they do not even raise the question. They lead one to believe that underdevelopment is an original condition akin to original sin, and must be due to chance or bad luck.

The notion that underdevelopment can be chalked up to an (indeterminate) incapacity ingrained in Third World cultures gives the impression that these countries are autonomous, and that their leaders can really make fundamental decisions about their own destiny. This premise underrates external constraints on leadership; it is blind to the ways that Third World economies are tethered to the international market. This model of development, which defines Western values as universal values, deflects attention from the links between the underdeveloped countries and the mature capitalist countries.

These links are of course deeply rooted, going back to slavery, plunder and forced trade. Horrific tales of the kidnapping of about 20 million Africans, pillaging silver and gold from Latin America's ancient civilizations, and opening Asia's ports at the point of a gun are well known. What must be kept uppermost in mind is that the drain of resources from what is now called the Third World has fuelled the engines of capital accumulation in the advanced countries. An important aspect of this process was the enterprising ethic of a creative bourgeoisie in Europe. This ethic, dubbed an orientation to achievement, has been projected on to the Third World by modernization theorists.

An entrepreneurial spirit is indeed integral to an ideology of inequality wielded by the privileged. In the final analysis, modernization theory is an ideology of capitalist accumulation. We do not live in a modernizing world but in a capitalist world. What makes this world tick is not the need for achievement but the drive for profit. In the quest for profit, ideology poses as science. The primary targets for the ideas and symbols of modernization are the working class and peasant producers in the Third World. These ideas and symbols are transmitted by government programmes, bilateral aid projects and inter-

national lending agencies. Rationalized as the doctrine of modernization, government policies reinforce and extend inequalities, shoring
up a way of life in which certain groups predominate. Today, however, modernization theory is widely held in disrepute because of the
bruising charges levelled by its critics and its failures in practice.

WHERE HAVE ALL THE MODERNIZATION THINKERS GONE?

Stung by criticism from a variety of quarters, modernization theory
no longer knows what to make of itself. That modernization thinking
is fundamentally flawed is widely acknowledged, but liberals refuse to
choose among other options. All things considered, the conventional
approach finds itself at an impasse.

Modernization theory's intellectual crisis has engendered a more
empirical approach. The grand theory of the 1960s and early 1970s,
initially dominated by the work of the US Social Science Research
Council's Committee on Comparative Politics, gave way to a move
towards greater policy relevance and a rediscovery of the importance
of economics. Concepts like 'decisions', 'choice' and 'development
management' came into vogue in the 1970s. Theorists have often
failed to articulate what they mean by policy studies, but they refer to
values and social consequences as well as to processes and choices.
Sometimes policy is regarded as a synonym for state activity. Like
modernization theory's emphasis on elite maintenance, the focus of
policy studies is on the ruling elite who are deemed to act on behalf of
the general citizenry.

Such attempts to amend modernization theory have provoked
much discussion. Both strands of analysis fail to account for the
dynamics of global capitalism. Modernization theory and its progeny
neglect the underpinnings of state power and class formation. In fact,
public policy decisions reflect the efforts of elements within a class
structure to allocate state resources for their own or allies' benefit. In
this sense, policy analysis is thoroughly antiseptic and structurally
blind. Eddies in the mainstream have not achieved a breakthrough
but rather carry with them the flotsam of problems of modernization
theory.

In practice, the drive to modernize has reached a dead end. Take
Sri Lanka, known previously as Ceylon. This country has done
everything in the economic realm that modernization theorists could

hope for. The government, championing the virtues of free enterprise, abolished import and exchange controls, unified the exchange
rate, established free trade zones, opened the economy to foreign
banks and gave wide latitude to market forces. Domestically, the
authorities reduced food subsidies, scaled down the rate of unemployment and developed energy sources. Meanwhile, on the international market, rubber prices plummeted while petroleum costs
soared. Textile manufacturers encountered protectionism abroad,
resulting in a cutback in Sri Lanka's development programme. By the
beginning of the 1980s, 60 per cent of the country's capital budget
came from foreign donors.

Recognizing that without substantial foreign aid countries such as
Sri Lanka would sink, many influential commentators now claim that
the modernization vision can never be more than a pipe dream for
most of the developing world. Increasingly, a mood of despair about
the prospects for the Third World has set in. The unbridled optimism
of the modernization school has been supplanted by profound pessimism, as evidenced by the dependency approach.

THIRD WORLD RADICALISM

With the collapse of the liberal paradigm came the search for other
modes of inquiry. If Western liberal thought was marred by ethnocentrism, why not turn to the Third World itself for novel directions in
building an analysis of underdevelopment? Could the Third World
explain its own dilemmas?

In the 1950s and 1960s a new outlook known as the dependency
school emanated from Latin America. The dependency perspective,
while not monolithic, initially drew its inspiration from a UN agency,
ECLA, established in Santiago, Chile, in 1948. The technocrats and
intellectuals staffing ECLA offered a blistering critique of mainstream economics, arguing that its emphasis on the theory of prices
and general equilibrium failed to recognize the built-in features of the
global economy which disadvantage the underdeveloped countries. In
particular, ECLA highlighted the unequal terms of trade between the
exporters of raw materials and the exporters of manufactured goods,
resulting in chronic balance of payments problems. The first general
secretary of ECLA, an Argentine economist named Raúl Prebisch,
held that Latin America needs to industrialize behind high protective
barriers. He called for state planning and a common market to

achieve economy of scale. Most importantly, he proposed an inward-oriented development path known as import-substitution industrialization, which is based on manufacture to satisfy demand previously met by imports.

In addition to drawing on the work of ECLA, the dependency perspective gained strength as a result of the blossoming of leftist movements in the 1960s and 1970s. The Cuban Revolution, China's Cultural Revolution, the election of the Marxist government of Salvador Allende Gossens in Chile and the American debacle in Vietnam seemingly lent credibility to a radical analysis. Moreover, this was an era of aggressive economic nationalism in Latin America, creating a greater appreciation for the external constraints on development.

In Peru a nationalist military clique ousted the constitutional government of President Fernando Belaúnde Terry in 1968. The generals immediately extended state control over the economy. The government took over 75 per cent of banking, partially nationalized industry, organized an extensive agrarian reform programme and established procedures to give workers a 50 per cent share of their companies. But when the officers, led by President Juan Velasco, expropriated the holdings of the International Petroleum Company, a subsidiary of Exxon, and forced foreign concerns to relinquish mines that were not being developed, Peru entered a period of relative economic stagnation. There was little new private investment for five years. Although Washington officially denied placing a credit squeeze on Lima, the US government naturally sought to advance the interests of foreign investors. Hence the US Export–Import Bank provided no low-interest loans for projects in Peru. A number of loans from other sources were shelved until Washington and Lima reached an accord known as the Greene Agreement: the Peruvians were to pay $150 million in compensation to expropriated firms, $76 million to be allocated by Washington and $74 million to be distributed to companies by Lima.

Such examples are legion in the Third World. Many governments have initiated acts of economic nationalism only to erode the confidence of private investors and to set the nation on an unnavigable economic course that, in the end, is capped by a military incursion into politics or the assassination of the head of state.

Against this background, radical intellectuals in Latin America further refined the dependency approach. Their starting point is imperialism, viewed as an amalgam of economic expansion and political domination. Under imperialism, capital accumulation is based on the export of capital from the advanced countries to underdeveloped areas. Political and military might is used to assert control over the means of production in foreign lands, benefiting a segment of the citizenry in the advanced countries and their partners overseas.

Thus dependency denotes the effects of imperialism on under-developed countries. A special form of domination and subordination, dependency's defining characteristic is vulnerability: the limits on a collectivity's ability to determine its own response to social forces within the world economic order. External forces, the economies of the 'centre' (advanced capitalist nations), 'condition' the responses of the 'periphery' (Third World countries), limiting the options for independent development.

A country is dependent when the accumulation of capital cannot find its own dynamic within the national economy. The capacity to increase the scale of capital requires the creation of new technologies and the expanded production of capital goods (machinery and equipment). But peripheral economies are unable to alter the basic features of production because of the structure of relations between social groups within the underdeveloped countries. The groups hold-ing the reins of power are the chief beneficiaries of their ties to the centre and would be threatened by a realignment of political power. They have established through the political process a form of produc-tion consistent with their interests and objectives.

Clearly the dependency approach differs in essential respects from modernization thinking. Dependency analysis emerges from an explicit political position. And like Marxism, it takes the dynamics of capitalism to be the key to understanding development and under-development.

The major contribution of the dependency approach is to pinpoint the process whereby imperialism has incorporated Third World coun-tries into global capitalism, thereby underdeveloping the internal socio-economic structures within these countries. Theoretically, *dependentistas* have mounted a biting and effective critique of the modernization concept. For instance, they have debunked the dualist thesis, which holds that Third World economies are divided into a capitalist sector and a subsistence sector. On the contrary, commer-cialization and accumulation do occur in peasant enterprises and backward rural areas are yoked to the national economy as well as the world market. Practically, *dependentistas* have helped to muster support for liberation struggles in Indo-China and Africa.

Although *dependentistas* have assailed modernization authors for their lack of historical analysis, dependency writing itself tends to be historically weak. The centre–periphery distinction is based on existing market imbalances, not on unfolding social relations in the production system; thus, the concept of unequal exchange concerns trade between nations and does not address the question of class struggle. It is unclear how the imagery of centre and periphery is linked to class forces. Many writings within this framework say surprisingly little about the changing relations between peasants and workers on the one hand, and the dominant classes on the other, in a specific historical context.

One would like to know precisely which countries are dependent and which ones are not. President Charles de Gaulle, it will be recalled, charged that the US was a neo-colonial power subjecting France and other European countries to a subordinate position. More recently, Canadian officials have been galled by US dominance of their economy and, some say, of their culture and polity as well. Trade between the two nations exceeded $77 billion in 1980, representing 18 per cent of US trade and almost three-quarters of Canada's total international trade. In 1981, foreign investors – four-fifths of them US nationals – owned 65 per cent of Canadian energy industries.

Given the imbalance in trade and investment between the two countries, is it proper to assign dependent status to the US' northern neighbour? If so, is Canada therefore an underdeveloped country? Are dependency and underdevelopment one and the same? Obviously not, but what differentiates these concepts is murky.

Added to this problem are major omissions in the dependency framework: in the capitalist world economy, what role do the socialist countries play? Are they part of the centre, sharing in the exploitation of the periphery? If not, where do they fit into a world of central and peripheral countries? Not only do *dependentistas* neglect this issue, but they also fail to come to grips with how to eliminate dependency relations: how permanent and stable are these patterns? What is the way out? Seemingly the choices are either continued dependence or revolution. Some proponents of revolution also call for a strategy of self-reliance: an attempt to delink from the world economy and to follow a path of national autonomous development. But this strategy (which will be discussesd in Chapter 6) is not a panacea that cures all the ills of underdevelopment. There are no instantaneous solutions.

BEYOND ORTHODOXY

Clearly there is a wide choice in models of development, ranging from modes of analysis that are overly optimistic to avenues of inquiry that are unduly pessimistic. Notwithstanding the drawbacks to each model, the debates in recent years between divergent schools of thought are a significant advance beyond older, encrusted ideas which attribute a lack of development either to climatic factors or racial differences.

To recapitulate the key points: underdevelopment is not primarily a quantitative phenomenon (poverty), not merely falling behind and not by any stretch of the imagination an original condition; it is foolhardy to think that some countries suffer from a curse. Rather, underdevelopment may be best understood as a single chapter of the whole world political economy. Underdevelopment is a historical process. The same forces which generated development in the West engendered underdevelopment in the Third World. True, some aspects of a country's position in the international political economy, such as its resource endowment, have nothing whatsoever to do with external or social causes. But in the main the root problems of underdevelopment are not attributable to nature: they are man-made.

When Europeans first penetrated Africa, they encountered a medley of civilizations which were in no sense stagnant. In West Africa, there was a vigorous trans-Saharan trade, an exchange of scholars with North Africa, a gradual expansion of some centralized political systems, such as the Ashanti kingdom, and the extension of economic ties among previously disparate peoples. Similarly, in India the early Western explorers found highly advanced skills among artisans as well as sophisticated crafts. The colonizers introduced manufactured products, destroyed rural home industries, wielded superior military technology, and practised divide-and-rule tactics, pitting ethnic groups against each other. Some Third World peoples submitted to the indignities of imperialism, others actively collaborated and still others waged fierce resistance struggles.

In all cases, pre-capitalist economies changed dramatically. Indigenous skills were substantially eliminated. Cash crops were implanted, often replacing food crops, consequently altering dietary habits. To market these products new classes emerged, extending social differences. An ascendant merchant class played a vigorous role in corroding the home economy and paving the way for capitalist relations of production, in the absence of which it would have been impossible to install industrial capital. The colonial economy became increasingly oriented to export, rather than to local needs, catering as it did to the vagaries of foreign markets.

For centuries production and consumption had been in harmony but not unchanging. Subject to the pre-capitalist class structures and the limitations of their resource endowment, local peoples' produced what they consumed and consumed what they produced. With the injection of imperialism, however, production and consumption were disjoined. Hence nowadays local peoples largely produce what they do not consume and consume what they do not produce.

The Third World was undeveloped but not underdeveloped before the advent of imperialism. Imperialism reversed ongoing processes of pre-capitalist development in the Third World, contributing to class formation and hampering productive accumulation. In order better to comprehend the mechanisms that sustain imperialism in our time, let us briefly consider the transnational institutions which use to their advantage the ideas emerging from modernization and dependency analysis.

3 Received Ideas and International Institutions

Years ago, an African reminded fellow diplomats of the practical limitations of the UN in dealing with conflicts which the contestants do not wish to resolve: 'When there is a dispute between small countries,' he said, 'the dispute in question disappears. When there is a dispute between a large country and a small country, the small country disappears. When there is a dispute between two large countries, the United Nations disappears.'

The inability of the UN to solve such crises as the Indo-China War, the Nigerian–Biafran clash and the continuing strife in the Middle East has prompted much criticism of the organization, which goes to the heart of the nature of international institutions. What role do they really play in the global political economy? Insofar as they bear upon resource transfers, who benefits and who shoulders the burden?

INTERNATIONAL ORGANIZATION

For over a decade, various US permanent representatives to the UN have hurled a volley of attacks against the Third World voting majority in the General Assembly. Thus in 1974, President Nixon's representative to the UN, John A. Scali, warned that when majority rule becomes 'the tyranny of the majority, the minority will cease to respect or obey it'. Similarly, William F. Buckley, Jr, a US delegate to the twenty-eighth General Assembly, argued that the irresponsibility of the smaller nations of the world in the General Assembly is making the UN 'the most concentrated assault on moral reality in the history of free institutions'. Similarly, another US delegate, Daniel Patrick Moynihan, commented: 'the United Nations has become a locus of a general assault by the majority of the nations in the world on the principles of liberal democracy'. Numerous US ambassadors have intoned that it is hypocritical for Third World delegates to launch out at South Africa's policy of apartheid while turning a blind eye to genocide in their own countries.

In the face of this challenge to the world organization, compounded by the rhetoric of the Reagan administration and its 1984 decision to pull out of the UN Educational, Scientific and Cultural Organization, liberals rightly maintain that sovereignty does not lie with the organization but with its 159 member states. The main problem with the organization, the argument runs, rests in Washington, Moscow and the other capitals of the world, not at UN headquarters. Inasmuch as the cause of the world body's limited capacity to carry out the mandate inscribed in its charter is sovereignty, the solution frequently proposed by liberals is reform, particularly in the veto provision that permits any one of five powers to block action.

In the liberal perspective, the rationale for upgrading the UN, particularly its humanitarian activities and development programmes, centres on the important role the organization plays as a forum for exchanging ideas and learning from others' experiences. An oft-repeated justification for UN conferences on the environment, population, women and so on is that they help to raise people's consciousness about public issues and make politicians aware of their responsibilities. Even if the high-flown resolutions adopted at such conferences are unenforceable, it is said, these pronouncements educate the public and legitimize worthy goals set by the representatives of the majority of humankind.

The positions staked out by both conservatives and liberals are correct as far as they go: voting in the General Assembly *is* dominated by Third World countries, and in the implementation of Security Council decisions there is no way to override the will of the great powers. While bemoaning the gap between General Assembly resolutions and likely action, observers of varying hues frequently overlook the fact that international institutions are intended to distort the status quo. If they merely mirrored the distribution of power among member states, there would be little need for them. The key question – and a controversial one – is whether decisions made in the UN affect existing differences positively or negatively.

The claim that the gulf between lofty resolutions and effective implementation is due to automatic voting majorities underplays the responsibility of individual member states to honour the expressed will of the world body. It is not only those resolutions adopted at the behest of small states contrary to the intentions of the great powers that remain unimplemented. In the case of UN action against Rhodesia, for example, in 1968 the Security Council unanimously adopted Resolution 253 calling for mandatory sanctions. Yet the US, a permanent member of the Security Council, and hence with primary responsibility for the maintenance of international peace and security, wilfully violated sanctions by importing chrome.

The implications of the double-standards argument are unclear. Would the UN be in a better position if it did not take a stand on burning social issues? The response of most member states is that certain affronts to human dignity – namely, colonialism and apartheid – are so fundamental that the UN must seek to establish a climate of opinion favouring change, even if it is unable to provide a solution.

However, the contention that the UN's chief contribution is standard setting can be overemphasized. The beauty of the claim is that standard setting is an infinite process, one that is never completed, for there are always new objectives which avoid curtailment of the institution's programmes. The danger in the claim is that it can give the illusion of progress where there is none and deflect attention from the essential issues. The main point is that to make international institutions more viable, one must first understand history in terms of global processes.

Since capitalism is the first mode of production to encompass the entire globe, its architects require a universal vision, a picture of a globally conceived society, to join classes in different countries. The task of international organizations is to institutionalize global capital accumulation by setting general rules of behaviour and disseminating a developmentalist ideology to facilitate that process. Some international agencies in the UN system, such as the UN Development Program, still reflect the precepts of modernization thinking, whereas the newer agencies like the UN Conference on Trade and Development generally transmit the dependency perspective. All of these agencies, however, maintain the dominant world order by facilitating the internationalization of production. The main business of the international development establishment is to attend to the welfare aspects of global capital accumulation and to ensure compliance with the procedures codified in agreements among states. This broad claim can be best defended not by theoretical argument but through concrete investigation of foreign aid, technology, multinational corporations and international banking.

FOREIGN AID

Today welfare, sometimes known as aid, is a key element in global negotiations over a projected NIEO, originally proposed at the

Algiers Conference of Non-aligned Countries. Special sessions of the UN General Assembly promulgated the ideology of the NIEO in 1974 and 1975. The avowed purpose of the NIEO is to initiate processes of growth and diversification in Third World economies. It is to facilitate net inflows of real resources through trade and aid. In brief, the package of global reforms includes the removal of tariff and non-tariff barriers against imports, the expansion of the Generalized System of Preferences (temporary and limited safeguards to promote exports from underdeveloped countries), price indexation agreements, commodity management and stabilization schemes, the enlargement of processing and manufacturing for export in underdeveloped countries, the transfer of technology to low-income areas, product sharing and specialization arising from complementarity among Third World economies, and an increased official development assistance target.

Advocates of these resource transfers counsel that power and decision making within international institutions must be shared more broadly to reflect greater sensitivity to Third World problems. Various international commissions have called for an enlargement of 'mutual interests' of North and South, based on a common perception of the complex 'interdependence' in the contemporary world. This ideology is reflected in two reports, issued in 1980 and 1983, by a team of prominent commissioners headed by former West German Chancellor Willy Brandt:

> The valuable and unprecedented basis for consensus in the UN system, for communicating between North and South and between East and West, must be preserved. It is vital to get the best out of it, to strengthen it, and to build on it, utilizing the experience of the last three decades and the benefits of wide participation. An increasingly interdependent world must organize itself for the different and more difficult tasks of the future, which will call not only for political will and wisdom, but for a framework of institutions and negotiations which can convert policies and ideas into action.

The work of such commissions is useful inasmuch as it spotlights the external constraints on local initiatives in underdeveloped countries.

The calls for concessions to meet the demands for global reforms focus on market mechanisms. To be sure, if the international market operates more smoothly, the world economy will be more robust.

Underdeveloped countries stand to gain from greater purchasing power and increased savings. Even if state bureaucrats and large-scale traders were to consume much of the gains from tariff reductions and other aspects of a NIEO, there would still be an increment to feed into production. Gains in productivity may in turn filter down to the masses, thus contributing to capitalist development. The extent to which transfers of international capital actually augment production is contingent and varies from one context to another.

Whether such gains are deemed significant hinge on how the underlying problem is defined. If one posits, as does the Brandt Commission, that the root problem in 'North–South relations' is imbalance in the world economy, it follows that the solution is to establish balance. The problem may then be meaningfully addressed at the level of distribution (or redistribution) of wealth. But if one premises that a political economy analysis must spring from the level of production, then the redistribution of wealth, however far-reaching, cannot erase the structures of global inequality. As long as the social relations that underpin these structures remain intact, pouring capital and technology into underdeveloped countries, as the proponents of the NIEO prescribe, would at best be a palliative. The wealth funnelled into highly inegalitarian social structures has, in some countries, improved social services, but also has inflamed political tensions and has worsened economic polarities on the local level, thus deepening underdevelopment.

An ideology that espouses 'an increasingly interdependent world' diverts attention from the world economy's built-in biases which sustain underdevelopment. To issue moral injunctions is to ignore the limits to international reform. To call for 'power sharing' is to wish away differences and conflicts. To call for consensus through global negotiations evades the point that the negotiators would be statesmen (or stateswomen), most of whom have built their careers on forestalling fundamental change. It is preposterous to think that the Hassads, Zias, Stroessners, Mobutus and Kaundas of this world – those who have the most to lose from basic change – are going to restructure the global economy in the interests of the poor and downtrodden.

The ideology of the NIEO blends elements of the modernization school and dependency thinking. It is a hodgepodge. There is little that is new; many of its elements have been tried, unsuccessfully, in the past.

Foreign aid, or development assistance, was viewed as the solution to the Third World's problems in the late 1950s and the 1960s. It was thought that if the Marshall Plan had helped to put Western Europe back on its feet after the Second World War, why not do the same for the post-colonial countries? Today, this idea is outmoded if not downright naive. The purpose of the Marshall Plan was to strengthen Europe as a bastion against the Soviet Union, and the recipients of aid obtained non-repayable grants, not loans conditioned on bankers' criteria of creditworthiness. Donors know that debt-ridden borrowers are unlikely to repay new loans. And no one seriously believes that aid is a disinterested gift.

We understood the pitfalls of technical assistance in Uganda shortly after political independence in 1962. Ugandans, who in a short time had their fill of international experts, told the story of the two bulls. A young bull and an old bull eyed a herd of cows. The young bull said to his companion, 'Let's run over and get one.' The more experienced bull replied, 'No, let's walk in and get them all.' In this tale, the brash bull is the American bull who wants to charge forward and take over; the subtle bull is his British counterpart who knows how to control the situation.

In fact, many white settlers stayed behind after independence in East Africa. International aid agencies hired some of them because of their familiarity with local conditions. The 'experts', so-called local expatriates as well as foreign nationals, are often seconded – sent as technical assistants – to government ministries where they act as advisers and supposedly train counterpart personnel. But as numerous inter-agency reports show, few technical assistance projects actually build local institutional capacity; the experts rarely leave behind indigenous people with the know-how to carry on.

As a consultant to an international agency, I was asked to evaluate a UN project designed both to strengthen training in international law and to set up a doctoral programme in this field at a university in the Third World. By preparing students for teaching or work in such ministries as Foreign Affairs, Commerce, and Industries and Finance, the university would provide for the needs of the country as well as those throughout the region. Due to the time required for the university to select one of the three candidates named by the international agency, the expert, a professor of international law from Holland, started later than foreseen.

From the outset, problems impaired the implementation of the project. The dean of the Law Faculty who had initiated the project, an expatriate, left the country three days after the arrival of the Dutch expert, forgetting to consult the Faculty Board. The new dean, an indigenous scholar whose priorities fundamentally differed from his predecessor's, had major reservations about the orientation of the project. He suggested that the expert, an abrasive sort by all accounts, teach legal disciplines other than international law, a proposition that the expert was reluctant to accept. The dean's view of legal education reflected political and intellectual changes taking place in the faculty, leading to innovative approaches to teaching and research.

The expert's tenure was a stormy period, for other faculty members maintained that he was transmitting the very ideology which perpetuates underdevelopment. Under these trying conditions, the expert did accomplish the project's primary objective: the establishment of a postgraduate programme in international law. The expert also contributed to classroom teaching, developed syllabi and course materials for the LL M and PhD degrees, and helped to obtain from his agency the equipment and books that an international law programme requires. The main shortcoming, however, was the failure to train a counterpart. When the expert departed, no qualified national was available to replace him. At the close of the project, the options were to hire another foreign expert, again with the mandate to prepare at least one full-time, local counterpart, or to abandon the programme altogether.

Typically, there is inadequate coordination between international agencies and local training institutions. What needs to be ingrained, or restored, is local capacity for solving problems, implementing and evaluating projects, generating data, and analysing research findings. Central to these tasks is the development of training facilities.

The psychological effects of foreign technical assistance can be debilitating. A pervasive attitude in some parts of the Third World is that if a job is to be done properly, it must be assigned to outside experts. When skills and equipment are imported from one particular country, there is a tendency to continue to depend on that same source for future projects. In the long run, since technical assistance personnel implant certain practices and institutions, those ways of doing things become customary. Aid engenders reliance on foreign experts. It becomes a matter of habit.

Meanwhile, technical assistance personnel bring their life-style to the host country. By demonstration effect, they transfer consumer tastes. For instance, grocery stores in impoverished countries sell kosher foods, exquisite imported wines and books on how to prepare French cuisine. Other examples of taste creation are skin lighteners, cosmetics, soft drinks and powdered baby formulas. The tourism industry creates economic opportunities in the service sector for drivers, waiters, bellboys, guides, and the producers of artifacts facetiously known as airport art, but fails to build a resilient economy. A downswing in the metropolitan economies can have a devastating impact on a country dependent on tourist trade. Moreover, the wholesale importation of foreign customs can dilute the local culture and offend sensitivities. Cultural conflicts have arisen over Western ways such as nude bathing and, on the beaches of Gambia, the procurement of young male prostitutes by Nordic women: conduct regarded as distasteful by most people in the host countries.

Tourism may bolster a country's economic infrastructure by channelling foreign investment into airports, roads, hotels and so on. It does not, however, augment directly productive activities. Diverting development efforts from production oriented to local needs, and pumping capital into projects designed to show 'profitable' returns in the short run, is unrelated to, or antithetical to, long-run solutions.

The problems frequently encountered with external aid are apparent in Tanzania, the recipient of $3 billion in foreign largesse during the 1970s. In the decade since Tanzania pledged a policy of socialism and self-reliance, its foreign borrowing increased by a multiple of 21 and surpassed the domestic component of total development spending. Currently, aid accounts for about two-thirds of Tanzania's development budget. There has been a huge crop of economic blunders, often cultivated by foreign-aid agencies. So pervasive are the agencies that, as one US AID official told me, they simply divided the country among themselves, one taking Arusha Region, another Mwanza, a third Iringa, and so forth. When former President Julius Nyerere announced a policy of decentralization, the regional offices of government, lacking expertise in development planning, called on the international agency personnel based locally to help design the plan and thus to decide on basic priorities. In other words, the foreign experts do more than advise. They frequently make policy in such key ministries as planning.

Many aid projects only compound underdevelopment, for they lack a basis in the economy. Specifically, Tanzania does not produce spare parts for heavy-duty machines and equipment imported from abroad. Without foreign exchange, one cannot purchase these goods. Even so, to distribute food and other essential commodities, it is essential to maintain the transportation system. Tanzania's trains, buses and trucks come from such countries as Britain, Hungary and Norway. In an effort to keep these vehicles running, much of the aid that flows into Tanzania goes right back to the donor countries to pay for repairs, contractors, material and petroleum.

Britain agreed to build a $110 million highway in south-western Tanzania. London pledged to spend only $12 million locally and to employ a *total* of eight Tanzanians on the job. A railroad project, funded by Canada, was to provide 205 cattle cars and oil tankers, all from Canadian manufacturers. Meanwhile, a Dutch official remarked that he expected $51 million of Holland's $73 million in annual expenditure of aid to be remitted to Amsterdam.

Probing such loan agreements, a British economist uncovered the conditions for establishing a fully automated bread factory in Tanzania. Funded by the Canadian International Development Agency, the new factory would employ 60 workers and produce 100 000 loaves per day. There were several complications. One was that the cost far exceeded the original expectations. Critics of the project pointed out that 10 compact, semi-mechanized bakeries could each produce 10 000 loaves of high quality bread per day for much less. More than five times as many people would have worked in the small bakeries. With small units, the baking industry would have been less vulnerable to breakdowns. Since many of the spare parts for the automated factory are made only in Canada, Dar es Salaam's bread supply is subject to total disruption. The large bakery makes Tanzania dependent on a Canadian machine supplier and expertise; small-scale bakery equipment could have been produced in Tanzania. Because much of the wheat, which provides the flour used in baking the bread, is imported, the foreign exchange implications of the project are considerable. (Wheat, of which Canada is a major exporter, is a luxury food item in a maize-growing country.) All told, the decision to establish one large, foreign built, foreign maintained, and foreign supplied baking industry was directly contrary to the government's professed intention to nourish grass-roots self-reliance.

Given the drawbacks to foreign aid, should it be terminated or merely reformed? There is no doubt that such aid flows as refugee relief and food assistance are useful stopgap measures, particularly under emergency conditions. Development assistance can be improved through reforms, especially if greater emphasis is given to training local personnel. However, foreign aid does not begin to tug at the roots of underdevelopment: the blockage in the social system that limits the potential for advance. In fact, development assistance, granted to those who control state power, may strengthen locally dominant classes, thereby deepening underdevelopment. Thus foreign assistance can either facilitate in a very marginal way or impede the escape from underdevelopment; but aid flows are not an essential component of a strategy for eradicating underdevelopment.

TECHNOLOGY

Like foreign aid, technological change has a mixed character. It may either accelerate or hamper development. Technology is not a neutral element for attaining societal goals. Rather, it is both a commodity bought and sold on the world market and a cornerstone of the ideology of modernization.

One architect of the modernization school, W. W. Rostow (whose 1960 book, *The Stages of Economic Growth*, influenced a whole generation of scholars and policy makers), held that the fundamental turning points of history are the times of new scientific discoveries. As noted in Chapter 2, traditional society is said to be based on pre-Newtonian attitudes; it stands in sharp contrast to a Newtonian world subject to knowable laws and capable of systematic 'productive manipulation'. The central feature of traditional society, Rostow adds, is an upper limit on the level of attainable output, which reflects the absence of modern technology.

A widely accepted notion in modernization theory and neo-classical economics is the 'natural mobility of productive factors' within but not between nations: each national economy is to special-ize in the production of goods for which it is endowed with the more abundant factor (labour, capital or natural resources). All partners in exchange then share equally in the benefits of international trade. Dependency writers, however, reason somewhat differently. They emphasize the imperfect conditions in the international market for technology. The advanced countries account for 98 per cent of the total research and development of new technologies, according to UN reports. There is mounting sensitivity over who controls the technol-ogy, for Western-based multinational corporations hold 99 per cent of the patents on new technology.

In the face of rising Third World nationalism, increasing attention has been given to the transfer of technology. Transfer connotes the movement of knowledge, skill, organization, values and capital from the point of generation to the site of adaptation and application. There are several modes of transfer. One is direct foreign investment: the injection of technology with other critical inputs; another is purchasing machinery and other capital goods which embody technology; third is licensing and related contractual arrangements with foreign governments.

To correct the imbalances in the international economy, the proponents of modernization have stressed the importance of sharing knowledge. There has been no dearth of proposals: mechanisms for the exchange of scientific and technological information, International and regional centres, evaluation techniques and so on. International organizations have called for technical cooperation among developing countries, workshops, consultancy groups and codes of conduct. Integral to many UN recommendations is the idea that technological development requires building capability for the utilization of new knowledge.

Unfortunately this way of thinking is often confined to narrow problems and highly specialized issues concerning technical innovations. A technicist point of view is one that overemphasizes technical factors at the expense of non-technical considerations. Technology, after all, is a process, not a fixture: more like learning carpentry than purchasing a new drill. If one does not develop the skill to use the tool adeptly, and if one does not understand how one particular stage relates to other stages of production, one's product will be inferior and not sell. All stages of a technological venture are interrelated and must be comprehended. As two professors at Harvard's Graduate School of Business Administration put it: 'If the technology is imported from another company, even if the developers come with it, but the necessary support systems and understanding do not exist, then it is likely that the new products will be rejected as the human body rejects a heart transplant, though it is necessary for survival.' For technology to take root, it must become integrated in, or emerge from, the existing society. Social relations are more than a seedbed of technical processes. Changes in social relations have a reciprocal, or at times a decisive, influence on the course of development. Technological innovation requires that social relations be altered to allow for the potential for economic advance.

If technology does not exist in a free state, but is understood as a commodity like other commodities, then one should avoid the trap of technological determinism, the belief that changes in technique are the key to overcoming underdevelopment. This is a fallacy. There is no quick fix for the problems of underdevelopment. A technological fix does not address the underpinnings of underdevelopment.

It is frequently said that an appropriate technology is one that contributes the most to meet the objectives of development. The idea of the appropriateness of technology can help to expose the failings of a technology policy. Typically, commentators claim that too much emphasis is given to high-powered goods and services while the bulk of the population needs plain conveniences, such as pulleys for drawing water and simple stoves. But the criterion 'what technology?' must be linked to a consideration of 'technology for what?' Ultimately, this is a matter of 'whose objectives are to be met within a society?' Thus the appropriateness of a technology should be defined, in relation to its social, economic, and ecological context. In the end, science and technology must be understood in relation to educational and production systems. It is research and production that have the primary institutional capacity for learning and innovation.

As mentioned, investments in research and development are predominantly made by the advanced countries. Nonetheless it is true that US multinational corporations, for example, do spend around 1 per cent of their total research and development expenditure in the Third World. These multinational-driven research and development efforts are concentrated in a handful of countries, most notably Brazil and Mexico. Another facet of corporate-generated technological innovation is dumping old or obsolete equipment on the Third World. A changing international division of labour assigns higher technological tasks to the advanced countries and lower technological functions to the underdeveloped countries. Generally speaking, these functions involve the processing of goods and certain aspects of manufacturing, especially assembly operations.

In India, Brazil and East Asia, there have been real technological advances in textiles, steel and shipbuilding. India even exports consulting services and engineering goods. A country that is capable of producing its own engineering goods has extensive technological capacity. There is no doubt that local capital in the underdeveloped world has an internal dynamic. Capitalism in the Third World is not all externally driven. But once again the objectives of an underdeveloped country's technological capacity limit innovation. In India, a major concern with national prestige and regional competition with China and Pakistan put a premium on production of the atomic bomb, missiles and other military hardware. Also, India's industries imitate the consumer patterns of Western societies. Locally generated technology in the villages has been outstripped by Indian and foreign large-scale producers in such industries as soap, cooking oil, eating utensils, building materials and tyres. The great bulk of the technological system is not immediately relevant to the needs of most Indians.

Technological innovation in the Third World, while to some extent genuine and certainly important, should not deflect attention from the overall pattern: Not only is the lion's share of research and development carried out within multinational corporations (supposedly the conduit of technology transfer), but most technological knowledge remains within the corporations themselves. The putative flows between countries are really flows from corporate headquarters to the premises of a subsidiary. Innovative capacity is not transferred. In reality, the so-called transfer can become a substitute for innovation by indigenous people. Also, a bona fide transfer of the highest and most sophisticated technology can be at odds with the interests of the dominant classes in the heartlands of global capitalism. The transfer of technology, to the extent that it actually occurs, is nothing other than leakage from multinational corporations.

MULTINATIONAL CORPORATIONS

It is sometimes claimed that multinational corporations are a Trojan horse for neo-colonialism, betraying the promises of political independence in the underdeveloped world. On the other side of the ideological fence, multinational corporations (the bearers of capital and technology) are likened to Prometheus bringing light to the impoverished countries. As these images make clear, prevalent views of the impact of the large firms are highly polarized and, to avoid moral posturing, it is important to demythologize the issue.

The first step is to recognize that to abstract multinational corporations from their historical context would be a grave error. Properly understood, today's multinational corporations are but one facet of world industrial organization, a global structure in which the entrepreneur of yesteryear, the jack of all trades, is an anachronism. Formerly industries consisted largely of single function firms usually controlled by one owner or a small family who made all the decisions. In the contemporary multidivisional business, often a vertically integrated industry, a general office, hierarchically organized from top to bottom, carefully plans and coordinates the growth of corporate capital on a global scale. A firm which operates according to the principles of vertical integration joins under its auspices different phases of the production process, potentially ranging from sourcing raw materials and crude processing to marketing the final commodities.

As such, the multinational corporation is neither villain nor hero, as its detractors and apologists claim. True, as shall be shown, it is sometimes involved in crimes but, as with other types of criminal activity, one must search for both manifestations and underlying causes.

The multinational corporation is both an agent in and the result of the process of capital accumulation. It embodies the inner logic of the capitalist enterprise. So, too, it is an expression of the internationalization of production, a worldwide phenomenon which allows the politics, culture and ideology of one country to penetrate another. The dynamic is one of amassing capital, not of creating equality, and the benefits accrue unevenly.

From where do multinational corporations derive their power? Despite all the talk about free enterprise, multinational corporations seek to preserve a monopoly of technology. In theory, free competition would mean the perfect diffusion of technical information; every producer would have open and free access to technical innovation. In reality, technical knowledge is now a commodity produced by institutionalized activity, known as research and development, inside the big corporations. The ideas that scientific workers generate are owned by capitalists, whose patents help to ensure monopoly profits. What is more, multinational corporations seek to confine technological innovation to their home offices and plants, forestalling centres of innovation outside their immediate control. To do otherwise could reduce the profits garnered from the spread of their products and operations.

Another basis of multinational power is sheer size. The capital, market knowledge and access of the corporate giants are formidable assets compared with the resources commanded by an under-developed country. In some cases, the coffers of a single firm are much larger than the treasuries of entire countries. Moreover, the scope of multinational corporations has increased astronomically since 1960. Revenues of the top 200 firms have risen ten-fold, from about $200 billion to over $2 trillion in 1980. Mega-mergers and acquisitions – the corporate catchwords are 'restructuring' and 'maximizing shareholder value' – have become commonplace. The subsidiaries of huge companies now dispense entirely different product lines, with profits shifting from one to subsidize another so as to underprice competitors. Hence, using its profits from Marlboro cigarettes, the parent firm, Phillip Morris, adopted a strategy of low pricing and massive advertising to transform Miller, a small brewer it had purchased, into the second largest beer producer in the world.

Amid this concentration of capital, the position of US firms has declined. In 1960, 127 of the top 200 multinational corporations were US-based, accounting for 72.7 per cent of the group's revenue. Twenty years later, of the top 200 firms, 91 had their headquarters in the US, their revenue share having dropped to 50.1 per cent of the total (see Table 3.1).

Equally striking is the ascendance of Japanese-based multinational corporations in the top 200, from 5 to 20, with sales up from $2.9 billion to $155.2 billion. France, too, has moved up, its companies numbering 15 in the top 200, as against 7 in 1960. Their revenues have soared from $3.5 billion in 1960 to $161 billion in 1980. Clearly this increasing concentration of capital does not entail a reduction in competition. A multitude of disputes over international trade – the question of US protectionism against the influx of Japanese vehicles, a so-called pasta war to bar Italian products from the US and so on – indicate that the global capitalist economy still fosters rivalries between corporations and between governments.

The internationalization of production means that multinational corporations swiftly deploy resources across economic sectors and national boundaries. Companies manufacture parts of a commodity in one country, assemble it elsewhere, put on the finishing touches in some other place and sell it in yet another. To move goods along this production line multinational corporations often rely on joint ventures, licensing and subcontracting agreements, and free trade and export processing zones. Their market power derives from the mobility of capital, but also from the relative immobility of labour. For as capital encircles the globe in search of cheap labour and other favourable conditions, Third World countries must vie with each other. If workers protest the conditions of capital or go on strike, multinational corporations either pull out and dip into another labour reservoir or simply threaten to pull up stakes. Either way the post-colonial state will crack down on its labour movement, for those in power and their allies would be hurt the most by the withdrawal of their patrons.

More specifically, what is the impact of multinational corporations on underdeveloped countries? The relations between multinational and national interests have changed since the companies' initial incursions into the Third World, and now range from consensus to conflict over control.

When American corporations went abroad, many of them for the first time in the 1950s, they were an awesome force. Nationalist

Table 3.1 Top 200 companies by country, 1960–80

Countries	1960			1980		
	Number	Sales ($ billion)	Percentage of total sales	Number	Sales ($ billion)	Percentage of total sales
US	127	144.6	72.7	91	1080.4	50.1
West Germany	20	13.4	6.8	21	209.0	9.7
UK	24	19.6	9.9	16.5	199.5	9.2
France	7	3.5	1.8	15	161.0	7.5
Japan	5	2.9	1.5	20	155.2	7.2
Netherlands	3	6.4	3.2	5	89.6	4.2
Italy	3	1.9	0.9	4.5	69.5	3.2
Canada	5	2.6	1.3	5	32.5	1.5
Switzerland	2	2.0	1.0	4	31.9	1.5
Belgium	1	0.5	0.2	2	14.5	0.7
Sweden	1	0.4	0.2	2	11.0	0.5
Rep. of Korea	–	–	–	2	10.0	0.5
Others	2	1.1	0.5	12	91.1	4.2
Total (excluding US)	73	54.4*	27.3	109	1074.8	49.9
Total	200	199.0*	100.0	200	2155.2	100.0

Source: Calculated from *Fortune*'s listing of leading industrial corporations by John Cavanagh and Frederick F. Clairmonte, 'From corporations to conglomerates: a review of multinationals over the last twenty years', *Multinational Monitor*, January 1983, 17.
*The figures presumably intended here are 54.3 and 198.9, respectively.

leaders – Jawaharlal Nehru of India, Gamal Abdel Nasser of Egypt, Kwame Nkrumah of Ghana – accused American firms of interfering in local politics. It was no wonder. The big oil companies reportedly helped to topple Iranian Prime Minister Mohammed Mossadegh in 1953. Many observers claim that the United Fruit Company's quarrel with Guatemala's leftist head of state prompted the US-backed invasion there in 1954. And it is generally believed that in the early 1970s, ITT paved the way for a coup against Salvador Allende Gossens, Chile's socialist president.

The boldness of ITT's alleged venture shocked even the establishment in Washington, causing the Senate Foreign Relations Committee to investigate the influence of US multinational corporations on foreign policy. It will be recalled that Allende had been elected on a platform of nationalizing much of Chilean industry, especially copper, a sector controlled by a handful of firms such as Anaconda and Kennecot Copper. American firms operating in Chile accumulated huge profits: during the 1960s Anaconda made $500 million on a $300 million investment. ITT, with $200 million in diversified investments in Chile, urged the Nixon administration to safeguard US holdings there. The New York-based corporation's high-powered board of directors, which included the former head of the CIA, John McCone, found a sympathetic ear in Washington, where Kissinger exercised tight control over the intelligence agencies. Presented with a plan for anti-Allende activities, Kissinger remarked: 'I can't see why we need to stand by and watch a country go Communist due to the irresponsibility of its own people.'

Evidence compiled by investigative journalist and Pulitzer Prize winner Seymour Hersh, as well as by other researchers, suggests that the Nixon administration's policy against Allende was conditioned by an overriding concern for the future of American corporate assets in Chile. After much consultation, Nixon gave Richard Helms, the director of central intelligence, *carte blanche* to destabilize the Allende regime. All the while, McCone, an intermediary between ITT and Kissinger and Helms, relayed ITT pledges of assistance for getting rid of Allende. Acting independently, ITT subsidized members of the Chilean opposition, waged a propaganda campaign, and sought to convince Chileans that Allende's policies would mean economic chaos. There followed the killing of Allende during the military overthrow of his Marxist-oriented government in 1973.

Such marked divergence between multinational and national strategies of accumulation is unusual, however. The norm is for multinational corporations to reinforce local accumulation and to support the existing class structure. Broadly speaking, the partnership between multinationals and local entrepreneurs is based on a common interest in profits and accumulation. After all, the corporations are invited into host countries by the state and national capital, which expect to benefit materially from the connection. Within this framework of consensus is secondary conflict over the extent of local control.

Multinational drug firms, for example, have been pressed to decentralize their operations so that host countries retain a larger share of the profits. This has not caused a major problem. A sizeable portion of pharmaceutical production vested in multinational corporations now takes place in the Third World. But they still keep the generation of knowledge at home. Pharmaceutical executives claim that the environment in such countries as Brazil is unsuitable for research. They say that important economies of scale in research mean that shifting technologically innovative activities to another location would diminish efficiency.

Meanwhile, Third World peoples pay for a large portion of these research costs, often indirectly in the form of exorbitant promotional fees. According to a 1977 report prepared by a British physician, Dr John Yudkin, the 147 drug company representatives working in Tanzania, a country with 600 doctors, spend £1.07 million per year, more than the country's sole faculty of medicine's annual budget, to persuade these doctors to prescribe the company's products. Spending on drugs in Tanzania accounts for 22 per cent of the national health budget, a proportion twice as high as Britain's.

Drug purchasing in Tanzania is in the hands of a small group of people beset by drug sales representatives offering free gifts, parties, drug samples, help in ordering and support for medical research and equipment. In a variety of Third World countries where legislation is inadequate and medical literature scarce, Dr Yudkin notes, some companies suggest that 'potentially hazardous drugs be used for minor modifications and they play down the risks of side effects'. Central medical stores have enough drugs to last from 5 to 50 years, whereas their shelf-life is less than two years and may be no more than six months under tropical conditions.

In the face of the drug companies' anti-social tendencies, host countries have adopted legislation to regulate, though not ban, the firms. A growing number of underdeveloped countries has initiated policies aimed at curbing the excesses of pharmaceutical companies and attaining control over the health care sector.

Still, there is a broad range of unresolved issues concerning local regulations, monitoring, education, cultural differences and corporate behaviour. The tragic leak of poison gas from a chemical plant in Bhopal, India, in 1984, killing more than 2000 people and injuring 200 000, brings these issues into sharp relief. The Union Carbide plant did not meet American standards and had not been visited by auditors from headquarters for 2½ years. It is not clear whether the company violated local laws, but many experts believe that corporations have a responsibility to live up to high standards, especially where the work-force is unskilled and the populace unaware of the risks presented by such plants. For the most part, the law in underdeveloped countries is not yet equipped for high technology. Regulation in these nations lags behind the introduction of new technologies. In the absence of an industrial culture, the testing practices prescribed by Union Carbide could not be used. Workers memorized what they were supposed to do without understanding the reasoning involved in safety procedures. Maintenance people signed what they could not read, and critical pressure gauges for toxic chemicals were in disrepair. Training and education programmes were lacking and sorely deficient in respect to cultural differences. In fact, in some parts of the world, pesticides are widely regarded as medicine because they kill worms and insects and help subsistence farming. Thus workers in Latin America have been known to come home with their woollen parkas soaked with pesticides and to sleep in them.

Most recently the emphasis on controlling multinationals has changed to channelling direct foreign investment into designated sectors or areas. Many Third World countries now offer the multinationals such incentives as low taxes, import privileges and market advantages. At the same time, they set performance standards, including the establishment of training programmes, the development of forward and backward linkages, export percentages and import ceilings. Notwithstanding the companies' interventions in local politics and the questions posed by the Bhopal disaster, underdeveloped countries, including the ones aiming at socialism, are increasingly trying to attract external capital and, in some cases, allowing more generous terms for foreign enterprise. In this context, industrial capital and loan capital go hand-in-hand, the latter often securing the conditions for the former.

MULTINATIONAL BANKS

David Rockefeller and other financial tycoons insist that ideological considerations do not determine their loan policies, but conservative business practice dictates that funds for Chile dry up when an Allende is in power and are plentiful for undemocratic regimes such as General Augusto Pinochet's. Quite clearly the political power wielded by the moneylenders is formidable. Like other multinational organizations, the banks eagerly dispatch their representatives to pursue Third World clients. Flush with OPEC deposits, they finance such strongmen as Zaire's General Mobutu Sese-Seko, a large measure of the monies going into the hands of his corrupt accomplices and their private accounts in Switzerland.

The growth of international lending to underdeveloped countries is a recent phenomenon. Before the onrush to independence in Africa in the 1960s, market surpluses and deposits mobilized locally were stored for safekeeping in Europe and far exceeded the volume of loans to the colonies. By lending money to the colonizers, the colonies helped to finance development in Western Europe. Similarly, the private banks did not channel loans to Latin America before the mid-1960s. Historically, the movement of gold and silver flowed in the opposite direction. However, large-scale industrial expansion in Latin America in the 1950s and 1960s, the rise of Euromarkets accompanied by the search for new customers and the oil shocks of the 1970s all made overseas borrowing a booming business.

In 1971 the lion's share of the outstanding debt of the Third World came from governments, while most credit from private sources emanated from commodity suppliers, not banks. At the end of 1980, loans from official sources had dropped to 37 per cent of unpaid debt, and bank loans had jumped to more than 60 per cent of uncollected private credits. In fact, the banks have become so highly exposed that it is difficult for them to avoid involvement in political crises in the Third World.

In the face of a trillion dollars of Third World debt to private foreign banks, governments and international agencies, no one really believes that the principal will be repaid. It is widely recognized that interest payments are a political problem within underdeveloped countries, not strictly a technical economic matter. To expect Third World countries to make huge debt payments each year, to achieve economic growth, and to maintain political stability – all at the same time – is utterly unrealistic.

The immense debt owed to the banks is a storm cloud that threatens to burst. Each of the nine largest US banks has more than 100 per cent of shareholders' equity at risk in four countries: Mexico, Brazil, Venezuela and Argentina. Taking a single bank as an example, Citicorp, with $119 billion in assets in 1982, maintains offices in more than 100 countries. It earns the bulk of its before-tax income from overseas operations. The bank's statements note that its loans to Brazil in one year exceed the total equity of the Citicorp's shareholders. Now, what would happen if the four superdebtor countries defaulted on their payments? Obviously the banks would have negative net equity, requiring their shareholders to absorb the losses. In the US, as well as in other Western countries, the state would then have to choose between allowing the major banks to collapse or intervening to keep them afloat. Notwithstanding their free market ideology, the Republicans in Washington could be compelled to support a *de facto* nationalization.

How did the banks, presumably expert at assessing risk, let loans to underdeveloped countries reach gargantuan proportions?

The crisis of indebtedness emerges from a mix of causes. With massive injections of petro-dollars, the banks sought new customers. Third World countries promised high interest returns. As competitors, the banks did not share information with each other about the level of lending to the debt-laden countries. Deregulation in the US pushed this tendency to an extreme, impelling the transnational banking industry to evade the strictures of federal agencies. Besides, the regulatory agencies could not keep up with the quickening pace of lending. The bankers did not understand the root cause of the problem, for they were part of it. At bottom, the crisis reflects the *incoherence* of Third World economies. When the debt piled up in the 1970s, the bourgeoisies of the Third World thought that they could rely on external loan capital to sustain accumulation. There followed not an accumulation of capital but an accumulation of errors. The contradiction between the consumption patterns of the bourgeoisie and the need for the internal generation of savings is glaring. So drained are Third World economies that debtor countries borrow just to repay a portion of the interest due. Prior indebtedness thereby eats up current export earnings. The debt-ridden countries are caught between the demands of their overseas creditors and the needs of ordinary people at home.

The banks are also in a fix. They must provide new money just so that their borrowers can pay interest on old debt. The problem redoubles upon itself: if a bank wants to stay on the top echelon of world finance, it must continue to attract deposits; yet the crisis in the world economy has limited the number of creditworthy countries capable of generating these deposits.

Impaled on the horns of this dilemma, some private banks seek relief through a multibillion dollar secondary market which enables them to swap the troubled loans or to sell them. An investor, for example, can buy a Bolivian loan for about 20 cents on each dollar of face value or an Argentine loan for around 70 cents on the dollar. Most of this discount purchasing is done by corporations with business interests in a particular country, by investors who thrive on risks and by the debtors themselves who reclaim their loans at a discount. Volume on this market, believed to have begun in 1982 during the Falklands War, is fairly small: about $3 billion in 1984.

More consequentially, the private banks have forged a symbiotic alliance with international monetary institutions. The commercial banks increasingly rely on the IMF's 'stabilization program' for assurance that a country is a good credit risk. To Citicorp, Chase Manhattan and the other multinational banks seeking an outlet for their surplus petro-dollars, the IMF seal of good housekeeping on the financial policies of a member state indicates that the debtor country has accepted the fund's stringent formula. For the borrower, the IMF imprimatur means that private bank loans and development assistance, of a magnitude far larger than the fund's largesse, are likely to flow.

To comprehend the fund's current impact on underdeveloped economies, it is essential to recall why it was established and how it has evolved. The IMF was launched at the 1944 Bretton Woods monetary conference in order to encourage free trade and investment between capitalist countries. The vast majority of underdeveloped countries were colonies in 1944 and hence were not involved in designing the IMF. Based in Washington, DC, near the US Department of Treasury, the fund was organized to allow an American veto on any major policy issue. A lender of last resort, it was created to provide short-term financing for temporary balance of payments relief, not to redress deep-seated ills in the world economy.

Since 1944, almost all of the underdeveloped world has gained political independence and has joined the IMF. Nowadays the deficits of the underdeveloped countries differ in essential respects from those of the developed countries: underdeveloped economies are structurally weak, subject to declining terms of trade and afflicted by wild fluctuations in the prices for primary commodities on the world market. The very attempt to restructure an economy – to develop – is likely to create a deficit because of inevitable short-term dislocations. The IMF was not set up to deal with this *development deficit*.

Increasingly the financially strapped members of the IMF require emergency loans. The fund, however, does not command huge resources. Rather, its power stems from its role as a coordinator among the advanced capitalist countries and as a go-between with the underdeveloped economies. To secure an IMF loan, a borrower must accede to a set of conditions: policies which ensure reliance on market mechanisms and which impose austerity measures. Specifically, the fund's standard formula, known as conditionality, calls for retrenchment in the public sector, including cuts in social programmes and the reduction or elimination of subsidies (on food, for example) to diminish government expenditure further and to heighten use of the market; increases in taxes so as to decrease the overall deficit and to hold down consumption; restrictions on domestic credit and money supply, particularly in countries that produce a great deal of currency; devaluation, which raises the prices of imports to local consumers and lowers the cost of exports for foreign buyers; and higher interest rates, which put a damper on borrowing, deflate the economy and constrain imports. The objective is to liberalize capital flows and to promote export-oriented growth.

The problem with this prescription is that there is little evidence that it works. In terms of balance of payments, growth, savings and investment in the 1970s, the economic performance of Third World countries with IMF programmes was no better than for the countries without them. This is apparent even if the criterion is the fund's own targets, as shown in careful research by the Canadian economist John Loxley. Why else would there be a multitude of debt reschedulings for IMF members who borrow heavily? Although official creditors claim that they will negotiate debt relief arrangements only when a debtor country is in a state of 'imminent default', postponements have become increasingly frequent. According to the State Department, the US participated in 76 multilateral debt negotiations from 1956 to 1983, 24 of these reschedulings in the period 1980–3.

Borrowing countries apply for IMF loans because they lack other sources of foreign exchange. But if a debtor enters a pact with the fund, it must take the pain along with the cash. The burden of adjustment is borne unevenly by local classes. It falls most heavily on urban wage earners. The belt-tightening exercise administered by the state invites social protest, often followed by a wave of repression. So-called IMF riots have swept such countries as Peru and the Dominican Republic.

Perhaps prosperous societies that have developed social security and unemployment insurance can make the sacrifices mandated by IMF structural adjustments. Underdeveloped countries, however, do not have the socio-economic infrastructure to relieve the destitute who are called upon to reduce their standard of living.

The IMF's export-oriented model accentuates the problems endemic to disjointed, outward-looking economies originally fashioned by colonialism to meet the needs of the metropolitan market. This is how the seeds of indebtedness were planted in the first place. IMF interventions cannot remedy the crisis, for the fund's framework reflects a view of modernization that is a product of the advanced capitalist countries. The concept of squeezing local demand in order to force production into exports may achieve the goals set by policy makers if the factors of production are highly mobile, or can be mobilized, in response to monetary manipulation. But in an under-developed economy, the mobilization of factors of production is prob-lematic. As noted, one cannot count on the willingness of rural dwellers to adopt a sophisticated technology to increase production. The explanation pertains to the dynamics of social structure at a level that does not enter into the IMF framework. Insofar as fund interven-tions permit the local ruling class to consume loan capital and require that peasant surplus flows back to the advanced capitalist economies in the form of interest on old debt, the direct producers will actively or passively resist IMF policies.

Although the IMF was designed to bridge short-term problems of payments imbalance, the crisis in underdeveloped economies is not of a short-term nature. It is structural; a worldwide financial crack-up is a real possibility. All the great banks of the world are involved, and the structure of debt cannot be effectively tackled by ramshackle arrangements. Bail-outs and infusions of more money – global wel-fare – do not go to the heart of the problem. Resolution of the world economic crisis lies outside institutional control. The story of debt is no more and no less than the problem of underdevelopment itself. Patchwork measures beg the question, 'in whose interests will the international monetary system be reformed?' Adjustments will con-tinue, but in the end, what will be left to adjust? In this vein, former Brazilian President João Baptista Figueiredo's 1984 comments give pause. He reportedly declared: 'When I took office in 1979, Brazil stood at the brink of an abyss. But in the last five years, we have taken a great leap forward.'

Like Brazil, many Third World countries have encountered the predicament of how to generate capital accumulation at home while participating in the global political economy, a network of structures (some of them enshrined as formal institutions) that disadvantage the underdeveloped world. These institutions embody the rules of the game. The main function of international organizations is to look after the welfare aspects of global capital accumulation. Owing to the effects of superpower competition, the importance of UN security provisions pales in comparison. In the final analysis, the web of international organizations, aid agencies, technological agreements, multinational corporations and banking concerns presents a formidable challenge to the Third World: how to amass an investable surplus while reducing global inequality?

4 Back to the Nineteenth Century for New Ideas

Saudi Arabia's royal family is trying to spearhead an advanced industrial economy while inoculating against a social upheaval. Given the surge in the price of oil from about $3.50 a barrel in 1973 to a peak of $34 in 1981 and 1982, billions of petro-dollars have been available to plough back into development projects and private industry. The sum accumulated in one year alone (1981) – a $30 billion excess of income over expenditure – is truly colossal.

The signs of material growth, while diminished after the oil glut in the early 1980s, are evident everywhere in the desert kingdom. A flashy superhighway – as yet leading to no apparent destination – sweeps by a clatter of donkey carts, herders and their camels. A glittery airport (the world's largest), massive bulldozers, and burly cranes deck the landscape around Jedda, the ancient port on the Red Sea. Jutting boldly out of the sand are the elegant edifices of Jubail and Yanbu, fledgeling industrial cities built by the government.

State involvement in the economy is extensive. Bloated state agencies are responsible for the construction of roads and housing, electrification and the establishment of private companies, particularly in agribusiness. Public agencies provide subsidies for food and free medical care, offer many types of interest-free loans, and dole out $300 per month to university students to supplement lavish stipends which cover the full cost of books, tuition, and room and board. The gush of oil is so prodigious that income tax is deemed unnecessary.

The state is attempting to inaugurate a work ethic. A network of recently constructed schools is trying to speed the training of locals to replace foreigners in order to increase the Saudi influence. The teachers propagate new values centred on success and mobility. In rural areas nomads are given incentives to settle down and farm according to the prescribed procedures.

Yet the obstacles to development are formidable. Between 8 and 9 million Bedouins are spread across a gigantic sandbox. About four-fifths of the population is illiterate. The ten-fold hike in oil revenue did not commensurably buoy the non-oil sectors of the economy. The theocrats-cum-business executives who run the show are forcing rapid social and economic change but, as the Iranians found out, there is no sure-fire way to control it: a swift shift in the mode of social relations can unsaddle an entire political system. In light of the upward spiral of fierce competition in the national marketplace, what haunts many Saudis today are the prospects for their own rock-bottom economic survival. There is tremendous pressure to dodge the throng, to avoid being obliterated by the rash of new companies spawned by the state, and above all to accumulate capital.

Saudi Arabia is an exceptional case in that it is the world's largest oil-exporting country. Still, even in the poorest countries, a *surplus product* – the end-result of human labour expended for goods which are not immediately consumed – is available for productive invest-ment. Typically, what is in dispute are the uses of the surplus product: how are savings for investment disposed in new methods of produc-tion? This question gives rise to contending ideas about how to achieve development. These ideas in turn help to shape the policies aimed at conquering underdevelopment. Thus *the current challenge in the Third World is not to eliminate poverty but first to create new knowledge to build the capacity to develop natural and human resources.*

In this chapter we turn to the key building blocks for analysing development and underdevelopment in particular countries. The place to begin is with the cornerstone of all strategies of development: capital accumulation.

CAPITAL ACCUMULATION

Why is capital accumulation the port of entry to understanding the dynamics of the Third World? First, in most contemporary Third World societies, the primary political debates do not so much concern political institutions – elections, representation in Parliament, party responsibilities, and so on – as the generation and allocation of capital: how to wrench limited resources from the existing units of production and channel them so as to uplift the national economy? From whence is a surplus product to be roused if a country is going to industrialize? Will the peasant sector permit a transfer of resources to the more advanced sectors of the economy? In the countryside, what units of production – privately-owned estates, state farms, cooperatives, communes or families – merit government support so that a nation can feed itself and not drain precious resources from other worthy activities or go into hock to international banks?

Second, notwithstanding the passionate tug-of-war between them, Marxists and non-Marxists alike regard the question of capital accumulation as central to economic development. In the mainstream view, capital accumulates when some quantum of current income is saved and invested in order to elevate further outputs and income. New factories, machinery, plants and equipment augment the 'capital stock' of an economy, making it possible to expand output. These are investments in 'directly productive' activities. They must be accompanied by investments in 'infrastructure', which facilitate other economic measures. Infrastructure has both social (for example, health care and education) and economic (for example, feeder roads, railways and harbours) components. Whatever the form of investment, and irrespective of the type of resources, capital accumulation involves a trade-off between present and future consumption: sacrificing something now for more later.

In the Marxist view, capital accumulation is the process of profit making and reinvestment. A successful capitalist enterprise gathers a portion of its profits and pumps it back into production in order to enlarge the scope and improve the efficiency of the operation. A well-known tenet in Marxism is that a capitalist economy must expand; it cannot stand still. (As Walter Wriston, who reigned for 14 years as chairman and chief executive officer of Citicorp, the biggest banking organization in the world, gleefully expressed his Darwinian philosophy of how business works: 'You either move forward, or you die; it's true in all biology.') A stalled capitalist enterprise will be devoured by large, dynamic corporations. Moreover, continuous expansion is forced by labour market competition; collective working-class actions have resulted not only in labour unions but also in organized political activity.

To come to grips with accumulation in a Third World country, it is essential to inspect the system of production. *The starting point is production* because consumption is necessary for human life, and to consume, humans must produce. Put simply, goods must be produced before they can be distributed and converted to use. Production, distribution, exchange and consumption are interrelated aspects of a cycle. The sequence among them is crucial, as the following parable shows.

Isaac and Levy own jewellery stores opposite each other. Isaac buys a decorative pearl necklace for only $10. He shares the news with Levy, who is spellbound. 'Sell me this necklace,' he pleads, 'I was just promising one like it to Rebecca, my wife. She'll love it. Here's $11.' Isaac gives in. Later he informs his wife, Sarah, about the deal. 'At 10 this morning,' he says, 'I bought a necklace for $10, and five minutes later I sold it to Levy for $11. A dollar made in five minutes!'

'You idiot,' answers Sarah. 'It's always the same with you. If Levy paid you $11 for that necklace, it was because he realized it's worth much more. Hurry up and buy it back from him.'

A few hours hence, Isaac visits Levy. 'Levy,' he implores, 'if you are a friend of mine, sell me back that necklace. Sarah made one of her scenes about it . . . Here is $12.'

Levy hands it over, and at dusk tells Rebecca about it. 'This morning Isaac came over to sell me a necklace for $11 and this afternoon he bought it back from me for $12. I made a dollar without stirring from my counter.'

'You idiot,' declares Rebecca. 'It's always the same with you. If Isaac came in to see you again, to buy back that necklace for a dollar more than he sold it to you, it must have been because he'd found out meanwhile that it's worth much more. Go and get it back from him.'

Next day, Levy proposes $13 for the necklace and takes it back to his shop. Then Isaac recovers the necklace at a cost of $14 and on they go.

Two weeks later, the necklace had gone up in price to $24 and is on Isaac's counter. Levy comes in and slaps down $25. 'The necklace,' he commands.

'The necklace isn't here any more,' Isaac responds. 'Last night, just before I closed, an American woman looked in. I offered it to her for $30, and she bought it.'

Levy falls into a chair. 'You've sold our necklace? But, you idiot, thanks to that necklace we were quietly, easily making a dollar a day each. And you've sold it – our livelihood.'

There is something amusing about this story. But what? It seems absurd to think that someone makes money without adding value to a product. This is precisely the point. First goods must be produced before they are worth swapping. Then a profit is realized in exchange between buyers and sellers, as on the stock exchange. A profit accrues to an individual when he (or she) outsmarts competitors by buying cheap and selling dear. This activity occurs in the orbit of circulation. Society as a whole has not gained, the commodity has only moved about. In order for society to gain, production must mount.

Now production, an interchange between humans and nature, must be considered in terms of both its physical and social facets. The *physical organization of production* means the technical units and instruments (tools or machinery) applied by human labour to transform nature into commodities for distribution and consumption. The *social organization of production* refers to the relations between groups of people in the national and international division of labour. By knitting together the physical and social aspects of production, one avoids adopting a mechanical and overly economic view of capital accumulation. Crucial to political economy is to know who controls production and to what end.

The social aspects of the expansion of capital are bound up with the whole question of the *exploitation* of labour. In common parlance, exploitation means utilization for profit. Whether exploitation is sinister is not at issue here. Ethics is an important aspect of political economy, but moralizing about societal ills is beside the point, for our objective is to understand social forces. Exploitation may take many forms and may be sanctioned by law. The following vignette, related by one of the first Zimbabweans to go abroad for military training during the anti-colonial campaign, graphically illustrates the process of exploitation.

The main issue giving rise to the armed struggle in Zimbabwe was land hunger among the rapidly growing black population. Peasant producers were deprived of their land by the colonial state, especially after the Second World War, with the large influx of white farmers, who cultivated only a tiny portion of the areas reserved for Europeans. In 1951, when the Native Land Husbandry Act (which reduced Africans' entitlement to land and cattle) was passed, a young herder who was to become a guerrilla received one shilling in return for a cow which had been a gift from his father. Thereafter, the father repeatedly asked his son whether the shilling had turned into a larger sum, and the boy, puzzled by the question, answered that it had not. This procedure continued for weeks until the father explained that the shilling had not expanded in value because Africans were oppressed. Meanwhile the cow, now the property of the white man, was producing calves and hence wealth for the farmer, but the shilling would remain a shilling, the father added, for the Act was simply a means to impoverish Africans and enrich Europeans. The father rightly perceived that expansion is the key to exploitation.

However, the central question in political economy is, expansion of what? Not of cows but human labour, which is the source of all value.

That being the case, capitalist exploitation may be regarded as the value added by the worker beyond the sum needed to cover his (or her) means of subsistence. The incremental value is wrested from the worker by the capitalist in the process of production.

This principle is a bedrock of the trail blazed by Karl Marx. No understanding of current writing in political economy is possible without grasping the major tenets set forth in *Capital*. Examining Marx's theory of capitalism is the basis for resurrecting the concept of capital accumulation as well as for considering reformulations and extensions of this theory in respect to the Third World.

THE ENIGMAS IN MARX'S VIEW OF HISTORY

The young Marx became embroiled in the great philosophical debates of his day. At the universities of Bonn and Berlin, the radical current in German philosophy turned the tide in Marx's life. He chose a revolutionary path, leading him into exile. This bearded foreigner lived a spartan existence in one of London's darkest slums. Marx, his wife and children were often gravely ill. Hounded by bill collectors, he beseeched his lifelong friend and collaborator Friedrich Engels for assistance from his family's textile industry. There were times when this strange man in tattered clothing could not go to his work-place, the British Museum, to pore over tomes of documents and statistics because his shoes and overcoat were at the pawnbroker's. Poking his nose out one day, he aptly commented: 'Never has anyone written about "money in general" amidst such total lack of money in particular.'

Throughout his life, Marx was preoccupied with the question of the interplay between economics and society. First and foremost, he viewed people as productive creatures. Production is the expenditure of labour power, the capacity for work. Production creates the objects which correspond to human needs, whereas consumption satisfies these needs. Between production and consumption are distribution and exchange. Distribution divides social products, and exchange further apportions the shares to individuals.

A familiar tenet in Marxism is that in the development of a society, its mode of production is decisive. A mode of production is a combination of forces of production and social relations of production. Forces of production means the mode of appropriation of nature; relations of production, the mode of appropriation of labour.

For Marx, appropriation entails 'transformation'. Tools, for example, are used to transform natural substances into value.

Of course Marx was not primarily concerned with stringing together definitions. Rather, by enlisting the power of abstraction, he unfurled a bold working hypothesis to explain emerging historical patterns: people are always adapting their relations of production to their forces of production to suit their needs.

One of these elements, by itself, cannot constitute a mode of production. Machines and the other means of production are instrumentalities but not a social process. Marx recalls the experience of Mr Peel, an English manufacturer, who set out for Swan River, West Australia. No mere tourist was he. Mr Peel brought with him means of subsistence and of production to the tune of £50 000, as well as 3000 working-class men, women and children. As soon as he reached Australia's bountiful shores, Mr Peel no longer had a servant 'to make his bed or fetch him water from the river'. 'Unhappy Mr. Peel who provided for everything except the export of English modes of production to Swan River!' In effect, he found himself without a class of wage labourers. In England, Mr Peel had owned and controlled the means of production. In budding Australia, however, labourers could accumulate for themselves. They were no longer for hire. The old social relations of British capitalism did not obtain.

Capitalism differs from other class societies in one vital respect: exploitation takes the form not of bondage or serfdom but wage labour. The surplus coaxed out of labour is surplus value, which is realized as profit and is systematically ploughed back into production. The concept of surplus value is based on a distinction between two types of value, use value and exchange value. A commodity's use value is simply its utility, its usefulness. Use value is realized only through the consumption of a commodity. But a commodity is produced not only for use but also for exchange for another use value. Put differently, commodity production has both a qualitative and a quantitative dimension.

The quantitative relation between things is in reality only an outward form of social relations. What is embodied in the commodity is human labour. Both living labour and dead labour are congealed in machines and materials. Under capitalism, the qualitative transformation of use value is replaced by the quantitative expansion of exchange value as the object of production.

The capitalist buys the proletariat's labour power at its full exchange value. All the while members of the proletariat are deluded into thinking that they are free because they can sell their labour power to whichever capitalist employer they choose. The capitalist class as a whole administers the use value of the labour power it has purchased. This useful labour creates an exchange value of the labour power contracted. Here lies the key to profit making.

Surplus value cannot derive from lifeless materials, and neither can it arise from a mere exchange of commodities: as we have seen, if everyone were to attempt to land a profit by hiking prices 10 per cent, what one gained as a seller would be lost as a buyer. Hence the expansion of capital springs only from the value that labour imparts.

For his (or her) contribution, the labourer expects to receive a wage. The actual wage depends on the number of working hours the labourer needs to subsist. If it takes five hours of labour per day to keep the worker alive, his (or her) worth is $5 (at $1 per hour). But a whole working day is not five hours. At present it is eight hours. Hence today's labourer provides eight hours of value a day, although he (or she) is paid for merely five hours. Wages cover subsistence and not more (in the absence of collective working-class action). Meanwhile, the labourer has sold the value which he (or she) produced in an entire working day. This differential is the source of surplus value.

Inasmuch as the value of the labourer's wages, computed in hours of labour time, is less than the number of hours the labourer works for the capitalist, the labourer surrenders a share of his (or her) creative power. This is surplus value: the overall value churned out less the wages paid to the labourer.

Thus the capitalist skims additional value in the production process. No one is swindled. These are the rules of the game. The capitalist appropriates surplus value not because of greed or an innate profit 'motive'. The non-labour components of the production process must be purchased, and the capitalist must receive compensation. Moreover, the capitalist makes decisions within a structure of accumulation over which an individual exercises little control.

All the choices concern how most profitably to redirect a chunk of surplus value in production in the form of capital. The capitalist may convert a portion of surplus value into means of production, referred to by Marx as *constant capital*, or may designate a larger or smaller segment for the means of subsistence, which Marx termed *variable capital*. In so doing, the capitalist can hire additional labourers or intensify the pumping out of surplus value from labourers whose labour power has already been contracted. A combination of these techniques is the structure of accumulation characteristic of capitalism.

It is possible to accumulate a limited amount of capital without converting surplus value into additional capital. This may be accomplished by extending the length of the working day or by increasing the productivity of labour through an improvement in technology (exclusive of a supplementary outlay of capital). Unsurprisingly, the capitalist will try to jack up the number of hours which the labourer spends producing surplus value relative to those required to generate subsistence wages. Over the long haul, however, the restless forces of accumulation, driven by intercapitalist competition and the labour–capital conflict, necessitate the conversion of surplus value into productive capital.

With the snatching of more and more surplus value, accumulation brings about a concentration of wealth in the clutches of the capitalist class. The owners of capital extend the scale of their operations, speeding, amplifying and homogenizing the accumulation process. In the meantime bigger units of capital devour smaller ones. Acting in their individual capacities, the captains of the railroad industry, for example, could not have sent their steam engines whistling around the globe in the nineteenth century. Centralization of capital, along with technical know-how, made this feat possible.

The further application of machinery to the labour process means, by definition, that constant capital expands faster than does variable capital. Capitalism provides more labour power than it can absorb, thus establishing an 'industrial reserve army of labour'. The reservoir of labour performs a double service for the capitalist. It furnishes both a potential pool of labour power and pressure on the proletariat in the form of a lever to lessen wages and heighten exploitation.

If surplus value is extracted from an ever-declining amount of variable capital, relative to the amount of constant capital, then the rate of profit is likely to fall. This is a tendency, not a law. There is a host of countervailing factors. These include cheapening the elements of constant capital, intensifying exploitation, depressing wages below their value, making adjustments in foreign trade and investing capital abroad where rates of profit are higher than at home. Even if an individual capitalist enterprise adopts techniques such as speed-up and stretch-out to augment exploitation, its competitors have recourse to the same methods. Hence the rate of profit may fall irrespective of the will of the individual capitalist. To counteract this tendency, and to replenish the reserve army of labour, capitalism periodically erupts in crises. Typically, capitalist production then inclines towards further centralization and concentration while readying for the next crisis. Once again, productive forces are spastic and expansive. Labouring producers are rendered increasingly super-fluous. The technical calibre of production exceeds the capacity for social control.

This logic led Marx to deny the possibility of infinite capitalist expansion, but he failed to map the intricacies of the breakdown of capitalism. Moreover, he had limited knowledge of economically and technologically backward areas outside Europe. By current standards, relatively few sources of information were available to him. This is especially true with respect to Africa. It will be recalled that Marx wrote before the partition of Africa at the Berlin Conference of 1884–5. And unlike the pattern in Europe, the capitalist mode of production did not completely replace pre-capitalist modes in the Third World. The low level of productive forces in Africa would not permit class formation along the lines of European feudalism. Owing to a lack of advanced technology and the insubstantial productivity of labour, there was a meagre surplus for an African appropriating class.

Although Marx studied the period of primitive accumulation in which the Western bourgeoisie amassed capital by plundering Africa, Asia and Latin America, he nevertheless had little to say about underdevelopment. Moreover, his central supposition about it was wrong. Marx foresaw not underdevelopment but development in what is now known as the Third World. In the *Communist Manifesto*, he seemed to anticipate that advanced capitalism would spread throughout the world. He expressed this theme in the following terms in 1867 in the preface to the first edition of *Capital*: 'The country that is more developed industrially only shows, to the less developed, the image of its own future.' But as we know, this is far from what actually happened. Advanced capitalism did not replicate the European, North American and Japanese pattern whereby surplus generated in agriculture is reinvested internally to stimulate the growth of industry and hence to elevate demand for the production of mass consumption goods and capital goods. Rather, it created dependent, export-oriented economies in the Third World.

There have been many transcendental developments thoroughly unforeseen by Marx. Capitalism is remarkably adaptable. Today, many savants are returning to the unsettled questions in political economy. In particular, they are bringing to light the nature of the state and contemporary class conflict. Rather than copying the paragons of the nineteenth century, the task before us is to enrich these concepts creatively.

BEYOND CLASSICAL AND NEO-CLASSICAL THOUGHT

Capital accumulation, the state and class forces are interwoven aspects of the political economy of development and underdevelopment. They are themes suffused throughout classical political economy. We might visualize their relationship as a triangle much like that shown in Figure 4.1.

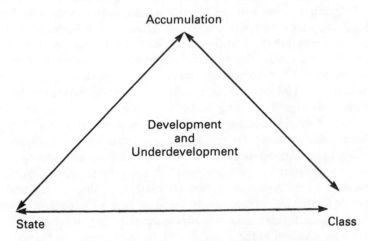

Figure 4.1   The dynamics of development and underdevelopment

The internal space delimited is development and underdevelopment. The opening allows for specific conditions: social dynamics cannot be fully explained without reference to particular cultures and historical trajectories. A new accumulation strategy corresponds to a realignment of class forces. A reconfiguration of social forces means an alteration in state power. An alteration in the social composition of the state is the basis for an innovative policy of accumulation.

On the one hand, thinking of development primarily as a strategy of capital accumulation, understood in its social and political context, has prima-facie plausibility. Contemplate the acquisitiveness of capitalist culture in the West, which is familiar to all of us. In addition, mull over the crass materialism in many Third World countries. For example, Nigeria during its period of oil opulence was awash with a surfeit of commodities. Even with the tightening of the spigot, there were so many vehicles in Lagos that the authorities adopted a licensing system to reduce traffic; each private vehicle was permitted on the road only on alternate days. It was still impossible to travel at more than a snail's pace, making midtown Manhattan's gridlocked streets look like expressways in comparison. Driving to the airport in Lagos, one was solicited by a horde of aggressive entrepreneurs hawking their wares, a surprising stock of goods pirated from the far reaches of the earth: Japanese radios, Italian shoes, American tool kits, French linens, English sweets, and so on.

At government officials' homes, a visitor's request for water was greeted by the sound of popping corks released from champagne bottles. Some of these houses have upwards of 20 bedrooms and are adorned with Victorian antiques galore imported directly from London. The owners believe that they are living in mansions, but they are fooling themselves. In fact, the huge, surrounding cement walls laced on top with broken glass give the impression of prisons.

At a gala luncheon at the home of a former vice-president of Nigeria, a chief dressed in a snazzy Western business suit was seated opposite me. Asked his occupation, he said, 'A real estate agent'. It seemed reasonable to presume that the dapper gent traded in expensive property in Ikoyi, a swanky section of Lagos. 'No,' he responded, 'I deal in Beverly Hills, Scarsdale and Kensington.' Overheard at the same state function was a warm personal greeting, meant flatteringly, exchanged among officials: 'You smell of money.'

So it seems safe to say that the theory of accumulation passes the inter-ocular test: it hits you right between the eyes. But we have seen the limits of commonsensical explanations of social behaviour. Clearly, accumulation in the present-day Third World is of a different order from that in the time of Karl Marx.

For one thing, industrialization is firmly implanted in such countries as South Korea and India. This entails a complex division of labour and gains in productivity. Second, foreign capital is heavily involved in local manufacturing. Foreign interests may indeed be a decisive political element. Third, the state plays a major role in organizing the local economy. In most parts of the underdeveloped world there has been a pronounced inflation of state power in recent years. State power has often meant only executive power.

Whereas the state is a set of political institutions, it is not most useful to describe these institutions. Rather, the telling question is, whose interest does state power serve? In the liberal view of things, the state supposedly acts in the interests of society as a whole. It is a referee, a neutral arbiter, among competing groups. The state ought to pursue policies which benefit the bulk of the citizenry, widening the middle classes and providing stability, a vital condition for economic growth.

From a decidedly more critical perspective, the state is an agent of capital accumulation. Officeholders seek to consolidate the accumulation process. They erect a bureaucracy and a civil and military technocracy to smooth the process. Political institutions are thus a means whereby dominance is maintained. Rarely is there dominance by a single class. Typically in Latin America, domination is maintained by the allied interests of the *latifundia* (large landed estates), the Church, the army, local industry and multinational corporations. Just as the capitalist state unites these diverse elements, so too it disunites the groups at the bottom of the heap, namely workers and peasants.

Given its pivotal position in organizing and disorganizing class conflict, the state is a prize contested by competing groups. It is also an arena of political struggle, the site at which major societal conflicts are fought out. But it seldom comes down to all-out class warfare.

Usually the state need not resort to draconian measures because it projects an ideology to legitimize the interests of the dominant classes. These interests are presented as the interests of society as a whole, or the national interest, which is a device for muting class conflict. The state furthers the position of its dominant classes by melding consensus and coercion.

A telling example of this use of ideology may be drawn from Henrik Ibsen's *An Enemy of the People*. The play centres on a small town economically dependent on tourists who are attracted to the area by springs with reputed curative powers. The town's doctor discovers that the water supply is infected by organic matter from a nearby tannery, also a mainstay of the local economy. The mayor – the doctor's brother – warns him not to disclose this information, couching the issue in terms of 'moral authority', while imploring: 'The public doesn't need new ideas – the public is much better off with the old ideas.' Having failed to persuade the town elders of the impending danger, the doctor appeals to the public to take decisive action. In the end, the liberal press and the townspeople, along with the business community and the politicians, heap scorn upon the doctor. Dominant interests and the collective ideology are one.

The process portrayed in Ibsen's native Norway is similar to what transpires in the Third World. The leadership propounds an ideology of 'modernization', which, the general public believes, serves the national interest. Politics in Mexico, for instance, is dominated by the

PRI. This party controls all major positions within the federal, state and municipal governments. The PRI is a corporate organism enveloping organized labour, peasant associations and the so-called popular sector, which includes congeries of small landowners, teachers and state employees. The leading elements in the PRI form a coalition of major private interests, powerful groups within the state and foreign capital. (This is not to overlook secondary conflicts among them.) The dominant sectors of national private capital are highly concentrated: vertically integrated industries, commercial houses, transportation firms and financial institutions. Ownership is in the hands of an oligarchy of about 2000 wealthy families. The state guides the accumulation process, commanding resources and key sectors, investing directly in industries such as chemicals and iron and steel, and establishing tariff and fiscal policies which channel the inflow of external capital.

Meanwhile, the PRI brooks no opposition from left-wing movements. The left is either coopted or repressed. Cooptation, the preferred option, is largely an ideological process. The PRI claims the legacy of the Mexican Revolution of 1910. The state vaunts the image of defender of the labouring and marginalized classes as well as opponent of the privileged classes and the monopolies. To maintain this image, state agencies diffuse populist ideas and practices. These are rituals thoroughly detached from their original historical significance.

To the extent that subtle forms of social control fail, outright repression is used. The armed forces are unleashed to enforce 'law and order' and to neutralize dissident groups. In an acute crisis of accumulation, the soldiers are apt to move into politics and topple the civilians who hold the reins of power. Ordinarily it makes little difference which are the officers staging the coups. There are numerous reshufflings among military officers that change the style but not the substance of politics. In Guatemala, for example, rightist generals ran the country for three decades. General Efraín Ríos Montt came to power in March 1982 by a coup supposedly because he and his supporters regarded that year's presidential contest to be rigged. Yet he refused to schedule elections for the presidency in 1983, postponing them until 1985. His sad human rights record drove the economy near bankruptcy. The apparent potential for instability troubled many foreign investors. Also bothersome to the small crew of rich landowners, military men and conservative bureaucrats who really dominate the country was General Ríos Montt's religious fanaticism.

A born-again Christian from a small California sect, the Church of the Word, he openly aided the campaign to proselytize within Catholic Guatemala. He lectured Guatemalans about repenting their sinful ways, and gave unintelligible interviews to the media. Hence it was not surprising when he was ousted in April 1983 by Brigadier-General Oscar Humberto Mejía Victores.

The coup was launched because Guatemala's leader had come to be seen as a liability to the landowners, officers and bureaucrats who sought to establish a propitious climate for foreign investment and social stability. There and elsewhere, the soldiers' underlying mission in seizing state power was to stabilize the process of extraction and investment of surplus. Military intervention, however, did not solve Guatemala's problems. In 1985, the military rulers were replaced by civilians. The new regime continued to terrorize the society by brutal repression, disappearances, torture and murder.

The role of the state in the underdeveloped world is of course not precisely the same as it is in the West. In the Third World, political power is a major means of appropriation of surplus. There is a win-all-lose-all philosophy because political power is the route to the accumulation of wealth.

This attitude is vividly dramatized by Chinua Achebe, one of Nigeria's best known novelists, in *Man of the People*. The corrupt politician Nanga shrewdly understands that the voters will respect his self-interest if he honours his promise to benefit them. Odili, a young intellectual bitterly opposed to the Chief Nangas, summarizes this outlook:

> We ignore man's basic nature if we say, as some critics do, that because a man like Nanga had risen overnight from poverty and insignificance to his present opulence he could be persuaded without much trouble to give it up again and return to his original state.
>
> A man who has just come in from the rain and dried his body and put on dry clothes is more reluctant to go out again than another who has been indoors all the time. The trouble with our new nation . . . was that none of us had been indoors long enough to be able to say 'To hell with it.' We had all been in the rain together until yesterday. Then a handful of us – the smart and the lucky and hardly ever the best – had scrambled for the one shelter our former rulers left, and had taken it over and barricaded themselves in. And from within they sought to persuade the rest through numerous loudspeakers, that the first phase of the struggle had been won and

that the next phase – the extension of our house – was even more important and called for new and original tactics; it required that all argument should cease and the whole people speak with one voice and that any more dissent and argument outside the door of the shelter would subvert and bring down the whole house.

Speaking through Odili, Achebe articulates the frustrations of the first post-colonial generation in Africa. He recounts the large sums of money piled up by a government of corrupt politicians and their betrayal of the dreams of independence. But dreams cannot suffice.

If independence is to become a reality, one must begin with an acute understanding of the social forces which are expressed through the political realm. The key factor is the nexus between social classes in the establishment of a system of accumulation.

Class is an elusive concept, one that has been subject to much dispute. Marx did not assign a formal definition to it. The critical last chapter of volume 3 of *Capital*, entitled 'Classes', was interrupted by Marx's death. The chapter breaks off just where he begins to delineate the concept. To this day, there are several unsettled questions about class precisely because it is a dynamic construct: since classes are always being born and are always dying, they defy precise boundaries.

There are a number of common confusions about the concept. One is to view class as merely a statistical category. The press in the US, for example, uses the term class to designate an income level or a conglomerate of occupations. Thus 'the middle class' is a residual, catch-all of everyone between the very rich and the very poor. In this usage, description is a low-grade substitute for explanation. Second, class is often understood in strictly economic terms. The trouble with this singular way of thinking is that the class struggle is ultimately fought out by political means. And as we have seen, classes propagate ideologies. Ideologies can convince people to embrace a position that does not correspond to their interests. Workers, for instance, sometimes espouse a bourgeois position, as did the 'hard hats' in the US who supported the war in Vietman. Third and closely related, class is not primarily a matter of social origins. In contrast to belonging to a class, caste membership is ascribed by birth. You cannot switch from being an untouchable to being a Brahmin. But if you are born into the working class, you can become a capitalist.

While there is some mobility, class membership is not primarily a matter of individual experience and choice. For an overwhelming majority, class place is determined by underlying societal conditions. That a minority escapes its social origins legitimates the ideological myth 'from rags to riches'. Even if all the individuals who comprise classes were to switch places overnight, fundamental social structures would still remain. Only the members would change. Irrespective of whether the owner of a firm is a Rockefeller or someone born in a ghetto who then 'made it big', class exploitation is a basic dynamic of capitalist life.

Properly understood, class is a grouping of agents who occupy a definite place in the social division of labour. In other words, classes must be seen in reference to the means of production. And it makes no sense to speak of a single class. The concept denotes opposition. Classes must be discerned in regard to their ever-changing relations with each other.

The interplay of class, the state and a strategy of accumulation suggests a basic set of relationships. A coalition of local propertied classes, the military and multinational interests supports an authoritarian, non-popular state bent on a dependent capitalist strategy: massive government intervention in the economy, severe exploitation of the labour force, and a substantial inflow of foreign investment accompanied by the outflow of national capital. Alternatively, in the afterglow of a revolution, a worker–peasant alliance spawns a bureaucratic ruling class whose strategy of accumulation emphasizes autonomous national development and withdrawal from the world capitalist economy. A worker–peasant alliance can also bequeath state power to its agents. Labourers, bureaucrats and revolutionary intellectuals imperfectly represent the alliance and manage the ties of dependency by simultaneously bolstering and undermining global capitalism. What are the successes and failures of each strategy? What are the trade-offs? Who benefits and who loses?

The varying relationships among class, the state, and accumulation rivet our gaze on efforts to remove the blockage which is at the core of underdevelopment. This explanatory framework requires continuous updating. What is needed is creative and original thinking in different historical contexts. In the next three chapters, we will see the extent to which distinct strategies adopted by Third World countries have lifted or reinforced the blockade restraining development.

Part III
Strategies of Accumulation

5 The Conventional Route, Joining Global Capitalism: Brazil

Formulating a strategy of development requires looking back over the trails Third World countries have already trod in their quest to accumulate capital. The real choices in the current world system are quite limited. One is to join the lane of traffic headed for capitalist development. A second is to leave the mainstream and aim for another destination. Third is to weave through the congestion, exploring an alternative passage, forcing an opening to the other end of the tunnel. Each route is a risky venture.

On the main thoroughfare, the police are tough; they are strict about enforcing the highway code, imposing it on all travellers. For those who choose the exit option, there are the twin dangers of coming up against a dead end and being run off the road by police with licence to patrol any territory. The other possibility, mindfully threading through dense traffic in search of an uncharted diversion, may wind up as a circuitous and harrowing path back to the capitalist lane. These journeys mark the entire range of options. Each one leads to distinctive fortunes and misfortunes, as Chapters 5-7 on Brazil, China and Mozambique illustrate.

BRAZIL IN THE LIMELIGHT

In April 1975 two businessmen met in a posh New York hotel to strike a deal which would allow an American firm to distribute the ambrosial coffee beans produced by a Brazilian enterprise. One of the men, well heeled and expert in the ways of high finance, sensed that his counterpart was in a weak position, his company ripe for the taking. Flush with himself after the meeting, the urbane financier confided in an associate, 'I'm going to buy this company.' Within one year, he made good on his pledge!

A typical case of *yanqui* imperialism quenching its thirst by lapping up the resources of the Third World? Not at all. Corpersucar, a Brazilian-based multinational titan, had swallowed up Hills Brothers, the fourth largest coffee producer in the US. When the deal was consummated, Brazilian well-wishers let fly a barrage of telegrams deluging the offices of the financier who had made the purchase. The local press treated the transaction as a sign of Brazil's destiny: a Latin American powerhouse among the handful of industrial countries that dominate the world of international capital.

Indeed, observers have dubbed Brazil's meteoric rise to fortune and fame in the period 1968–74 as nothing less than a miracle. The country's performance during those years is often touted as a model for other nations aiming at rapid economic development. By any standard, Brazil is an extraordinary land, a mosaic of African, native American, Lusitanian and other European cultures. The largest country in Latin America and the fifth in size in the world, Brazil has a population of 135 million: one out of every three Latin Americans is a Brazilian. Its borders touch all the South American countries save Chile and Ecuador. Not only is the GNP on a par with Canada's, but also the resource endowment is truly colossal: 16 per cent of the world's reserves of lumber; 25 per cent of the iron ore; and 60 per cent of the niobium, which is used for making jet engines, gas turbines and rockets. Compared to other national producers, Brazil ranks number one in its stock of tin, and number three in bauxite and manganese, the latter being an essential ingredient in the manufacture of warships, tanks and armour plating.

Given its strategic importance and vast resources, Brazil's chances of pulling out of the quagmire of underdevelopment are seemingly greater than are those of other Third World countries. If the state capitalist model of development – now widely adopted in the underdeveloped world – is to make good anywhere, it should score a success in Brazil. The fate of the Brazilian model has major implications for dozens of nations if not for all of us.

Stripped to its essential features, the Brazilian strategy of development is to embrace global capitalism; extend state control of the economy; accumulate capital from above and outside in order to expand the stock of machinery and other productive equipment; and concentrate income in the fists of the upper echelon of society and major foreign investors while promising that wealth will ultimately percolate down to the needy. Of course this development strategy cannot be properly understood without reference to how present patterns came to be.

THE BACKDROP

From the advent of Portuguese colonialism in the sixteenth century until the world depression of the 1930s, a bevy of local landowners and large merchant concerns, mainly English firms, dominated the economic and political life of Brazil. The planter oligarchy exported primary products – sugar, precious metals and coffee – to the burgeoning European market and imported manufactured products. These were mostly luxury goods. In the mid-1600s, for example, one-quarter of all profits generated from the export of Brazilian sugar was spent on imported wine.

The plantation owners and the European merchants sought to thwart the emergence of a manufacturing sector in Brazil and forestall diversification of the local economy. Both groups wanted to ensure a steady supply of cheap labour and the flow of inexpensive goods from overseas. To meet their needs, the colonial government allowed slave traders to import between four and five million Africans and banned the manufacture of products which would be competitive with finished goods produced in Europe.

The lion's share of the capital accumulated in Brazil was ploughed back into the production of primary goods for sale in overseas markets. Export earnings were used either for luxury consumption or the purchase of manufactured goods. Coffee, Brazil's major export crop, is especially susceptible to the vagaries of the international market. A rapid downturn in the price of coffee coupled with slack foreign demand could cripple the Brazilian economy, since the domestic market is too scant to cushion external shocks.

When the big shock came in the 1930s, the worldwide depression jolted the social order of Brazil. The economic convulsion set loose new class interests. A nascent, profit-minded bourgeoisie had already sunk its savings into maiden industries. Railroads were an especially lucrative investment given the interest of the planter oligarchy and merchants in transporting coffee to the ports. The entrepreneurs who built the railways required the services of an expanded proletariat, for which they had to compete with a lingering class whose strength had waned. The heady days of the planter-dominated agro-export economy were over.

With the industrialists in the driver's seat, the old economic vehicle was abandoned and replaced by a more dynamic model of capital accumulation. The new model, known as import substitution, was designed to develop Brazilian industries capable of producing basic manufactured items previously purchased abroad. Locally produced goods were to substitute for foreign imports, thereby lessening Brazil's reliance on external markets. Multinational corporations would provide the capital and technology to establish modern industries. The state was supposed to regulate these activities in order to ensure that foreign capital would not stall domestic capital accumulation.

Whereas local industrialists stood to gain the most from the new system, they could not ignore the demands of other classes. The rural bourgeoisie had not been totally disarmed. It tacitly agreed to go along with import substitution as long as the state maintained the price of coffee and pledged not to upset the system of land tenure from which the landlords benefited so handsomely. The urban petty bourgeoisie received government jobs and positions in public enterprises. The industrial proletariat was coopted by state-run unions and through fringe benefits, mainly social services and retirement packages. The huge mass of rural labourers continued to produce agricultural goods for export without deriving any concessions from the new corporate order.

An authoritarian regime ushered in import substitution during the 1930s and 1940s. Although the pro-fascist politicians were ousted from office following the Second World War, their populist successors similarly promoted rapid industrialization, quadrupling Brazil's production of manufactured goods in the period from 1930 to 1964. Also notable during this period was the expansion of the state's role in the economy. The government sought to channel foreign capital into designated sectors and to reserve critical areas for direct public investment.

To achieve success, an import substitution policy must foster capital accumulation based on a growing internal market and must increase the production of domestically manufactured goods. Yet in Brazil, the rural bourgeoisie's dogged control over an exploited work-force, combined with the political weight of an industrial bourgeoisie whose rate of profit hinged on keeping wages at a subsistence level, deformed and constricted the domestic market. Added to this, the decision to rely on foreign investors to 'rev up' the fledgeling industries put multinational corporations in a dominant position in some of the most dynamic sectors. By the late 1950s, Volkswagen, Mercedes, Willys, Ford and General Motors had established motor vehicle manufacture as the leading industry in Brazil. Other foreign firms set the pace in the production of refrigerators, locomotives, radios and washing machines.

The industries which sold the bulk of their goods in the advanced capitalist countries realized the highest profit margins. The external orientation of industries driven by capital-intensive technology plus cheap labour reinforced the tendency of an underdeveloped economy to satisfy the wants of the well-to-do rather than the needs of the people of humble origins. This conjunction of interests was not the result of conscious political decisions, but rather reflected the logic of the market. Since the poor had no money, capitalists could not profit from producing for them. All in all, an import substitution policy caused some inefficiencies, created relatively few jobs, and stymied the growth of the domestic market. The policy was, however, proceeding into investment in capital goods, the technologies required to turn out finished products. This important move was interrupted by the economic crisis of the early 1960s. Triggered by a drop in prices for raw materials on the international market, the crisis coincided with political instability in Brazil.

The populist presidents of the post-1945 period rode to power on the back of multiclass electoral alliances. To form winning coalitions, the populist leaders made honeyed promises, all of which could not possibly be honoured. The pledge to provide price supports and to fund industrial projects laid excessive claims on the treasury. The professed commitment to increase wages on a par with the rate of inflation could not be reconciled with the economic stabilization measures enjoined by both domestic and foreign industrialists.

Brazil's leaders postponed a political breakdown for two decades, adroitly combining economic growth, partly based on a chronic trade deficit, and high inflation rates. But one impressario after another found it impossible to run the show. Getulio Vargas committed suicide in office in 1953. His successor, Juscelino Kubitschek, completed a full term but bequeathed a major crisis to Jânio Quadros, who resigned after only eight months at the helm. Three years later João Goulart, formerly Quadros' vice-president, was deposed in a military coup.

THE STAGE IS SET

At a historic rally in Rio de Janeiro on 13 March 1964, President Goulart stood nervously behind a speaker's platform. Facing him were 150 000 workers flanked by several rows of plumed fighting cocks: white-helmeted army officers, their machine guns at the ready. Goulart was apprehensive because he feared the day of reckoning his predecessors had so resolutely postponed.

Perhaps the president briefly contemplated the course of events that led him to the dais on this day: the economic engine serving as the motor force of the populist programme had run out of steam. The only real option was to ask Washington to provide the means to rejuvenate Brazil's efforts to achieve industrialization. But the IMF and the US, wary of a president who was a wealthy rancher but soft on 'the Communist threat', had laid down harsh terms for a loan. Stung by the monetary fund's conditions, Goulart then contemplated walking out on the talks and declaring a unilateral default.

There was no easy answer to the question he undoubtedly pondered: was the government's popular base sufficiently large and adequately organized to enable the regime to weather the political storm which would erupt if Brazil refused to take shelter under the IMF's umbrella? Brazilians of various ideological hues called for a clear-cut decision: either cope with the tumultuous elements generated by the international market or pay the price and pull out of the storm. When faced with this dilemma, Goulart vacillated. He played for time, initially agreeing to the conditions set by the IMF and later balking at implementing them. Consequently, in March 1964, enraged foreign creditors curtailed assistance to Brazil. At the same time, all parties to the populist pact impatiently demanded that the government honour its end of the bargain. Everyone knew that the cupboard was bare, but nobody was prepared to walk away hungry. Goulart had to decide whose stomach to feed.

At this point, perspiring profusely, the president grasped the dais. The enthusiastic applause of the assembled workers rose to an ear-splitting crescendo. Goulart dramatically signed two decrees that buried Brazil's post-war *modus vivendi*. The first one called for the nationalization of all private oil refineries operating in Brazil. The second bill announced the expropriation of large tracts of land, the oligarchy's massive holdings. In addition, Goulart proposed to enfranchise illiterate workers and *favelados*, the inhabitants of sprawling slums and jerry-built squatter settlements, massive appendages of untold misery and human despair surrounding Brazilian cities.

These moves irrevocably violated the class truce of the last two decades, burning the regime's few remaining bridges to international capital and alienating domestic capital, especially the rural bourgeoisie. Some military officers already favoured deposing the president. He had antagonized officers by siding with subaltern ranks in a dispute with their superiors. Thus the military establishment claimed that Goulart was an enemy of the constitution; he had initiated the takeovers and land reform measures by presidential decree, not by legal process. Dutifully noting their responsibility to defend the constitution, the armed forces promptly ousted the civilian-politicians.

With hindsight, it is clear that Goulart played the card he should have held for another hand. He gambled on the poorly organized and deeply divided working class against the allied forces of domestic and international capital, which put their money on the odds: the Brazilian armed forces. Goulart made a fool's bet. The soldiers, holding all the aces, marched on the capital unopposed. Having tempted fortune, a bad wager under the circumstances, Goulart made his last move as president when he slipped over the border into exile in Uruguay.

SAME CAST, NEW CHARACTERS

Central to the Brazilian drama was the Johnson administration's decision to cut off all financial assistance to the national authorities (but not to politically acceptable state governors), deeming the Goulart government as 'the most serious problem for us in Latin America – more serious in fact than Cuba since the missile crisis'. Thus when the generals staged the coup on 1 April 1964, US naval and airborne units were immediately mobilized to support their fellow soldiers. Although foreign military intervention was not required, the US opened the economic pipeline, pumping aid as quickly as the spigot had been turned off. The US AID dished out $50 million to the new regime within hours of the soldiers grabbing state power. From the vantage point of policy makers in Washington during the Cold War era, not only was Brazil the strategic linchpin of the South Atlantic, but also the soldier-politicians' ideological outlook dovetailed with the American national interest.

The generals called for a rapid expansion of industry driven by a massive infusion of direct foreign investment and foreign borrowing. Low wages and high productivity could ensure substantial profit rates in the new industries. Admittedly, this strategy would not remedy the perennial problem of the constricted internal market. Although the economy would maintain its export orientation, the low cost of labour would convince investors that Brazilian exports could be priced competitively in world markets. Export earnings would be used to repay the debts incurred in the new wave of industrialization, leaving Brazil with a modern industrial base and placing the economy in a strong position in the global pecking order. At that point, wages could be raised so as to allow all Brazilians to share the growing wealth. The curse of underdevelopment would be but a relic, a legacy shorn of its most odious aspects.

In this cheerful script, each class was cast in a specific part. Playing a premier role, the military provided ideological leadership, forging cohesion in the new order, partly by embellishing their self-seeking policies with modernization lingo. The coup was not a coup but a 'democratic revolution'. Bureaucrats were not bureaucrats but 'technocrats'. Hard political choices were to be made not through political competition but by the 'scientific methods' deployed by technocrats who would render 'fair and impartial' judgments in a backward society lacking 'the discipline' to advance itself. Although the power behind the technocrats was evident, the ranking officers were said to be 'above politics', representing no one class or faction but rather 'the national interest'.

If the populace failed to understand the logic of modernization, there were other ways to convince people of their true interests. The military found Brazil's labour law, a copy of Mussolini's, a handy instrument. It was basically unchanged since Vargas had introduced the legislation. Under its provisions, military rulers unleashed repression against rural organizations. Additionally, the Ministry of Labour exercised close control over union operations. Worker organizations outside official structures were banned. In deciding upon union recognition, the ministry stressed social welfare programmes, not the unions' role in representing workers' interests. Budgets were monitored and strike funds proscribed. The ministry reserved the right to approve slates of candidates for office. It supervised the election process and vetoed winners whom it deemed unacceptable. The ministry took over the administration of unions, seizing monies and occupying labour organizations' headquarters. If these techniques were unsuccessful, the military politicians relied on brute force. Amnesty International reported that the Brazilian authorities frequently inflicted torture: electric shocks, near drownings, simulated execution, *Pau de Arara* (hanging from a parrot's perch or rack), sexual abuse and detention in refrigerated cells.

On the front stage, too, the multinational corporations were supposed to provide essential ingredients in the Brazilian strategy of development. The legacy of import substitution under the populist government was a demonstrated capacity to produce manufactured goods but not capital goods. Brazil needed computers for automation and quality control in mass production as well as state-of-the-art mechanisms for extraction in the country's huge petro-chemical industry. The multinational corporations were the only possible source of these much sought-after capital goods, technologies whose utilization require skills usually furnished by foreign experts. Powerful corporations generated the capital to finance the technology and skilled personnel, both directly through the investment of their own funds and indirectly by their very presence in Brazil, which the big banks viewed as a green light to go ahead. Added to this, corporate collaboration facilitated access to foreign markets: an essential element in the government's plan to sell the new products abroad. Without participation by multinational corporations, this whole scheme would have been unworkable.

Although Brazilian capitalists were to be among the main beneficiaries of the miracle plan, they were assigned a supporting, not a starring, role. Their part was to provide practical information about the political and economic climate in their home country and to whip up popular enthusiasm for the performance. In Brazil, as elsewhere in the Third World, nationalist sentiment against multinational penetration runs high. In fact, Brazilians of diverse classes have backed legislation enacted to regulate the multinational firms. Military might notwithstanding, economic policies without a veneer of nationalist respectability are politically unwise. Nationalist appeals, nonetheless, have their limits since they may spotlight social inequalities.

The working class was cast in the role of the fall guy. Punished by wage cuts, the chosen weapon in the fight against inflation, workers were required to produce goods cheaply enough to guarantee the nation's export earnings. Moreover, the regime banned working-class political activity because it could threaten the stability needed to attract foreign investors. The generals sought to silence the workers by promising to house and feed them if they would only sacrifice current consumption for a secure future.

Backstage, the rural bourgeoisie would go along with the show provided that the large agricultural estates were left intact. The deal struck by the landlords in the 1930s was still in effect. Behind the scenes as well, the *favelados* were marginal to the political economy of Brazil. They produced little and consumed less. Thus when the curtain rose on the Brazilian miracle, the underclass was decidedly off-stage and was assigned no role in the prepared script.

ACT ONE: THE DRAMA UNFOLDS

After a marked slump from 1964 to 1967, when policy makers crafted a new strategy, the Brazilian economy inaugurated a remarkable six-year boom. Showered with accolades, government planners were dubbed 'wizards' and Brazil was touted as 'the Latin American darling of the international business community'. Academic pundits celebrated the technocrats' policies, sanctifying them as a general economic doctrine and proliferating theories on why military rule lends itself to conquering underdevelopment.

There is no mistaking Brazil's economic achievements during the period 1968–74. The GNP ballooned at the rate of 10 per cent per year, the highest in Latin America. The industrial sector enlarged even faster, 11 per cent per year. True, the full-throttle expansion of international investment and the carefree disregard for society's poor made the meekest observers a bit queasy, prompting one journalist to comment ruefully, 'The Brazilian economy has grown . . . in much the same way as a Brazilian drives his car. That is extremely fast, disregarding everyone else on the road, narrowly avoiding accidents, and not stopping to consider whether his passengers have been left behind.' But during the miracle years, such criticism was rarely heard.

The government barred open questioning of the rocketing foreign borrowing. Acting without scrutiny by the press, the flamboyant Minister of Planning, Antônio Delfim Netto, repeatedly expressed unwavering conviction in his own course of action: 'We know 100 per cent of the population are getting 100 per cent of the national income: the distribution is not important.' This posture, characteristic of Mr Delfim's aggressive personality, led local commentators to quip that the minister's spherical physique illustrates that the distribution of national income is no problem for at least one citizen.

Turning to the evidence for Mr Delfim's claims: under military tutelage, the authorities stepped up domestic production of weapons. Brazil, which has the Third World's biggest arms factory, exceeded the $1 billion mark in export sales per year. Government patronage extended into this realm and others as well. The state served as a forum in which local and foreign capital could set the terms of joint ventures. To the extent that Brazilian capitalists lacked the muscle to vie with multinational corporations, the government served as the primary Brazilian participant in these ventures. The state, drawing on the country's vast resources, acted as an agent of capital accumulation.

High-tech, high-profit enterprises spawned by the alliance between state and multinational capital quickly outstripped the capacity of Brazil's creaky infrastructure. The state reacted by expanding its direct investment in basic industries, especially steel, fuel and power as well as in such related activities as communications and transportation. Ungrudgingly, the military-politicians and bureaucrats abandoned their conservative notions of free enterprise, sanctioning instead government ownership of a major portion of the assets of the 100 top firms in the country. In 1972, the state controlled 46 per cent of the assets of the largest 100 non-financial corporations in Brazil; foreign companies accounted for 31 per cent, and local private interests held 23 per cent.

In the 1970s a welter of state companies was established with catchy titles usually ending in 'brás', signifying Brazil in Portuguese: Electrobrás, Portobrás, Siderbrás, Nuclebrás, and a few hundred others. These state companies have consumed the largest portion of the federal budget. Their payrolls currently carry 1.4 million employees who enjoy lifetime job security. The ranks of the state-run enterprises are filled with retired military officers who are offered bonuses for showing up for work and a share of annual profits even in firms which generate no profit. Researchers have found that Brazil's state-run corporations are 50 per cent as efficient in their use of capital for productivity and job creation as are private domestic and foreign firms.

Massive state involvement in the economy made some business people squeamish. The head of one foreign concern regretted that Brazil had joined the socialist camp. Another executive, who also confounded socialism and statism, remarked: 'It's like doing business with the Russians: you have to play by their rules.' These misgivings, however, were uncustomary. US-based multinational corporations increased their direct investment in Brazilian manufacturing from $846 million in 1966 to over $2 billion in 1973. Large investments poured in from West Germany, France, England and Japan as well.

By the late 1970s, multinational corporations held predominant interests in over half of Brazil's 100 largest private manufacturing enterprises and accounted for about 50 per cent of manufacturing sales. Forty per cent of Brazil's biggest corporations were subsidiaries of multinational concerns. These concerns controlled all of Brazil's production of automotive materials and rubber goods, 94 per cent of pharmaceuticals, 55 per cent of machinery, 32 per cent of foodstuffs, 32 per cent of aluminium, 32 per cent of pulp and paper and 80 per cent of chemicals.

From the vantage point of the state, what the multinational corporations did with their profits was their own business. Tax regulations drawn up by the generals left the state with a small cut. Foreign investors remitted the lion's share of the profits to their home countries. There was no legal requirement to do otherwise ever since the military government nullified a law enacted during Goulart's tenure stipulating that foreign concerns must plough a large measure of locally earned profits back into the host economy. Thus in the mid-1970s, the Brazilian Congress reported that the 11 multinational corporations most active in the country had invested a total of $238 million in the economy over the last half-century and had exported $744.5 million in profits during the past decade.

The Brazilian capitalists with a foot in the door of the massive multinational and state projects reaped something of a bonanza. Their compatriots who retained control of their own operations also cashed in on the booming economy. But many small and medium-sized businesses went bankrupt. In an attempt to drive down inflation, the state adopted tight credit policies, which took a toll on all but the largest entrepreneurs.

Local business people could have questioned the extensiveness of foreign capital in the Brazilian economy, but to raise doubts about the legitimacy of the multinational corporations would have meant challenging the very basis of the generals' development strategy and indeed of the regime itself. Rendering such demands effective would have required mobilizing a constituency to support them. The working class was the only candidate for this role. Yet the spectre of a mobilized proletariat rallying against the big corporations was as frightening to Brazilian capitalists as it was to their foreign counterparts.

For the common people, conditions worsened considerably during the miracle years. By 1970 the real minimum wage had plummeted to 50 per cent of its value of a decade before. Nearly 60 per cent of Brazilians working in industry received only the official minimum wage or less. And they had little to consume. Despite the profusion of such luxury items as passenger cars, the production of staples – rice and beans, the bulk of the working-class diet – declined precipitously during the early 1970s. Moreover, the diminishing amount of affordable food had to be divided among more people: Brazil's population was growing at the brisk pace of 3 per cent per year.

In greater São Paulo, the largest industrial centre in the country, the proportion of houses with access to piped water fell from 61 per cent in 1950 to 56 per cent in 1973. After six years of military rule, 52 per cent of Brazilians suffered from malnutrition: an increase of 7 per cent from the time of the coup. In addition, the infant mortality rate rose a staggering 45 per cent in the period from 1960 to 1973, climbing to a level exceeded in Latin America only by that of Haiti. In terms of its social effect, the miracle years meant that the majority of Brazilians were hungrier, sicker, dying younger and paid less than in the placid days before the wonder plan.

At the same time that its inadequate standard of living declined, the working class was stripped of its political rights. Apart from exercising tight control of electoral politics, the military brought organized labour to heel by dismissing union leaders and handpicking new ones. The government unilaterally determined wages. Negotiations between workers and management were proscribed. Workers who sought to spark 'illegal' strikes were incarcerated for a minimum of four years. We have already noted what a labour organizer could expect during the period of incarceration.

ACT TWO: A FAILED MIRACLE

Suddenly, in 1974, as quickly as the economy had boomed six years before, the growth rate declined. Domestic consumption plunged and inventories piled up. A mounting deficit in trade and in balance of payments caused financial loans to dwindle. New international loans failed to pick up the slack. In 1975 inflation rose 20 per cent and the cost of living index climbed 32 per cent. When the curtain dropped on the miracle period, a former cabinet minister uttered: 'We are at a dead end, trapped, and so is [President João Baptista] Figueiredo, even if he doesn't know it.' There is no doubt about how quickly the tide turned, but what explains the sudden ebbing?

The greater the expansion of the pace-setting sector during the boom – high-tech, high-profit manufacturing – the greater the need to import capital goods. Brazil could pay for capital goods only by exporting its manufactured products. But Brazil's finished products – television sets, for example – are sold in highly competitive markets.

Not only did an export-oriented economy generate an increasing need for imported technology, but also many of Brazil's leading enterprises, subsidiaries of foreign-based corporations, transferred abroad mushrooming profits made on the sale of export products.

A sky-high growth rate, which attracted foreign investment and loans to cover the mounting deficit, was the glue which held the whole lopsided package together. In a heady economic climate, government planners envisaged a happy future in which strong demand and easy credit would be around forever. Their projections came to naught, however. The onset of the world recession in 1975 restrained the customers who purchased Brazilian goods and slammed the brakes on domestic economic growth. Policy makers debated how to compensate for the shrinkage of worldwide demand.

The obvious solution was to offset the contraction of foreign markets with increased domestic sales. But to stimulate domestic sales, a nation's industries must produce goods which satisfy the needs of the people. In addition, wages must be sufficient to enable the masses to buy these goods. In Brazil in the mid-1970s, the realization of one or both of these conditions would have knocked the legs out from under the entire development strategy. After all, the shopping basket from which Brazilians could choose their goods was not the result of mere happenstance. The economic menu served up to society at large reflected the tastes of Brazil's upper crust and the appetite of foreign capital. The delicacies gobbled up by these prosperous consumers were obviously not the common people's pickings. Wages were depressed expressly to court foreign investment and to fetch high profits in export markets. In effect, the allied interests of the locally dominant classes and international capital formed an economy dangerously exposed to external shocks.

In the late 1970s Brazil's foreign exchange reserves dipped to dangerously low levels. The rates of inflation and unemployment soared. Many businesses folded. The generals' only real option was to enter secret negotiations with the US government and the IMF. Finally, in November 1982, an official from the central bank of Brazil visited Washington to deliver a letter of intent to the fund. In such a document, the sending government indicates the steps that it is prepared to take to set its economic house in order. Adoption is contingent upon the application of stiff austerity measures. If IMF officials deem the proposed measures adequate, a rescue package is normally provided.

Two weeks after Brazil filed its letter of intent, US President

Ronald Reagan sought to add a touch of personal warmth to the already cosy relationship between the two countries. He visited Brazil, meeting President Figueiredo, the country's fifth consecutive military ruler. In the midst of a sumptuous feast at a formal state dinner, Mr Reagan rose, lifted a glass of Brazil's finest wine, and invited those present 'to join me in a toast to President Figueiredo and the people of Bolivia'. When an aide discreetly pointed out his gaffe, Mr Reagan corrected himself: 'That's where I'm going.' Wrong again. His itinerary included Bogotá, the capital of Columbia, not Bolivia.

No matter. The president was preoccupied with other business. He announced that the US would grant a jumbo loan of $1.2 billion to keep the Brazilian economy afloat during the coming weeks. But he did not mention that negotiations over the loan had begun in October and had been hushed up so as not to embarrass the military regime before elections were staged. Instead, he applauded the government's pledge to institute austerity measures – a reduction in the spending of state-controlled enterprises, slashes in social programmes, increased taxes and further restrictions on wages – in exchange for an injection of international finance.

At the close of the state dinner, President Reagan again hoisted a glittering wine glass and offered to allow a Brazilian astronaut to ride on a US space shuttle. The offer startled his hosts since there are no Brazilian astronauts. A local commentator twitted the politicians, suggesting that planning minister Delfim Netto should be the first Brazilian put into orbit. Had he not sent Brazil's inflation rate, then over 100 per cent, skyrocketing? Had he not launched the foreign debt, already $83 billion, into outer space? Coming down to earth, a practical observer noted that a relaxation of US import controls on Brazilian shoes would make the people happier than a free ride on a guided missile.

A fortnight after Mr Reagan's goodwill mission, the store of funds supplied by the US government was depleted. Brasília immediately announced that it was seeking an additional $1.5 billion in emergency loans. The *New York Times* declared that Brazil was on the verge of financial collapse. Similar crises in Mexico and Argentina had shaken the confidence of the international banks in investment in Latin America. No loan officer, explained the *Times*, wanted to be the last one to extend credit to Brazil before the country went bankrupt.

After a spree of negotiations dragged on for two months, the international banking community mounted a massive rescue operation. Finished in late 1983, its dimensions were staggering. Designed to put Humpty Dumpty together again, a cornucopia of loans, credits and refinancing provided Brazil with an infusion of over $30 billion. The agreement called on Brazil to implement a stiff austerity programme, cut its budget deficit in half by 1984, and again divide it by a factor of two in 1985.

The IMF declared that the crisis was resolved, but for many Brazilians it meant climbing down to the bottom of the ladder. Typical is the deteriorating situation that Luiz Antônio Pereira and his wife Vinhais have faced. They live in a *favela* in Rio de Janeiro with their two sons, aged 10 and 12. Still employed as a delivery man, Mr Pereira is more fortunate than many of his compatriots. Galloping inflation, however, has changed the Pereiras' life-style dramatically. 'We're restricting ourselves to staples,' Mrs Pereira told a *Wall Street Journal* correspondent. 'Last year our main dish was soup. We can't do that anymore,' she added. The interview in the *Journal*, however, did not recount what remained on the table when soup was beyond the family's means.

Also worrisome for the Pereiras is medical care. To pay for emergency dental treatment, Mrs Pereira sold her sewing machine. Root canal work and glasses for the children are out of the question. Yet unlike most *favelados*, Mr Pereira is bringing home some money. His job is all that separates the Pereira family from the untold misery and abject fear that haunts the teeming mass of unemployed Brazilians.

The Pereiras and their cohorts on the lower rung of the social ladder immediately felt the effects of the austerity formula prescribed by the IMF. Two months after the deal with the fund had been sealed, the unemployment problem reached explosive proportions. Out of a total work force of 5.2 million in São Paulo, for example, 800 000 people were jobless. Each week 1500 more workers joined the ranks of the idle. Added to this, the rate of inflation rose to 210 per cent in 1983.

Against this background, desperate groups of homeless persons seized public lands in Rio de Janeiro, housewives in areas adjoining Brasília burned utility bills, and frustrated youths in Rio and São Paulo stoned and axed public buses. The political climate was increasingly feverish. President Figueiredo rushed a note to Delfim Netto asking, 'Is it possible to endure this?' According to *Time* magazine, what perturbed the president was not the inflationary spiral or unemployment but the climbing interest rates, which upset the business community.

The April 1983 march of unemployed workers lit the fuse that ignited a keg of political dynamite. Hordes of disgruntled labourers romped through the streets, pillaging shops and desecrating hallowed symbols of authority, including a governor's mansion. Storming major arteries in city centres, the rioters chanted, 'Stop unemployment or we will stop Brazil.' A European ambassador, possibly recalling President Reagan's difficulties in uncurling the names of Latin American countries, offered to translate the grievance to outsiders: 'The riots could be a message from the people that they're not willing to accept the conditions that foreign bankers and the International Monetary Fund are imposing on the country.' Not only the downtrodden but also the well-to-do chafed on account of the economic crisis. As a prominent Brazilian lawyer put it, 'Before, every Brazilian was an expert on soccer; now we've become a nation of economists.' For Brazilians of all classes, the suture joining hunger and international capital is not an imperceptible stitch sewn into the minds of a long-haired intelligentsia but a nasty scar apparent to all save the most undiscerning bystanders.

ACT THREE: THE GRAND FINALE

To sustain the marriage between the state and global capitalism, Brazil has continued to borrow heavily from both international public and private banks. In 1964, the Brazilian foreign debt came to $3 billion; by 1974, with the onset of the world petroleum crisis, it reached $17 billion. By 1982, the debt oscillated between $80 billion and $88 billion. Upon last sighting, it was running at $93 billion, the highest in the world.

A wide range of solutions has been proffered. In-house technocrats have favoured the voluntary renegotiation of the debt to allow breathing space. Some economists have held that Brazil should reduce its economic dependence on foreign markets by adopting a modified model of expanded domestic consumption of agricultural and industrial products. More recently, members of the opposition party have discussed the possibility of the wholesale cancellation of foreign debts, claiming that the advanced capitalist countries have exploited the Third World and have recycled the profits in the form of loans. Taking this logic one step further, critics have called for the creation of a debtors' cartel to prevail upon the North for easier repayment terms.

The chances that the regime will default or declare a moratorium on loan repayment are practically nil. Not only would external finance be cut off, but also heavy pressure by unrequited creditors could block participation in international commerce. Given Brazil's geopolitical importance to the US and other lending countries, it is not unlikely that financial measures imposed by the banks would be accompanied by a strong pull on the political ripsaw of destabilization.

To contend with the tilt toward the conventions of international finance, a government must exercise an ironclad political will and enjoy the unwavering support of the popular classes. It must rest assured of its ability to inspire the masses to withstand a Niagara of pressure. The ability of a government to mobilize the general populace implies deliberate and effective mass organization, which is a far cry from the actual situation in contemporary Brazil. Until a regime with these attributes comes to power, the vaunted debt threat emanating from this potential strongman in the Third World is nothing more than a pipe dream.

In the meantime, which could be a long time, the current plans for bailing out Brazil are untenable. If the government actually plays the game by the bankers' rules, the stiff conditions for debt repayment will mire Brazil in deeper recession. The debt will not peter out in the near future, and whether it will ever be cleared up is a $93 billion question. No one is more acutely aware of the intractability of the problem than are the foreign bankers. On the one hand, they reap whopping profits in Brazil: up 126 per cent from 1981 to 1982, including 20 per cent of Citibank's worldwide net earnings in the latter year. On the other, the banks are trapped in a debt structure with no escape hatch in sight. Citibank and some other large US banks increased their loan loss reserves in 1987. In fact, this policy represents an internal transfer of funds, and does not relieve the burden on the debtor countries. The banks will still attempt to recover the interest and principal outstanding on their loans.

Thus in the revised script, we are witness to – nay, actors in – an unfolding drama of debt peonage in which the big banks and multinational corporations portray the plantation owner, the Brazilian bourgeoisie is the foreman, and the labouring classes are the serfs. The *dénouement* is a failed miracle, a modern day Third World tragedy. It is a melancholy conclusion to an economic *tour de force* once touted as a magic cure for the ills of underdevelopment.

More specifically, the difficulty is that Brazil's tight-fisted military rulers turned a blind eye to the nation's domestic market, taking at face value the World Bank's claim that export earnings would filter down to all reaches of society. This strategy was shipwrecked on the torrents of external markets and the government's own miscalculations, particularly overinvestment in glamorous, state-run, and inefficient development projects. Aware of the shortage of fuel, Mr Delfim tried to stoke these enterprises, but Brazil's economic furnaces would not heat up. The country was caught between high interest rates and weak overseas demand. Hectored by his critics, Mr Delfim, not one to mince his words, angrily snapped: 'Of course we have a neo-capitalist economy – no denying it – with all of its errors and all its faults. It's an unstable economy and, what is more serious, no mechanism is provided for redistribution of national income. But I would like to know in which capitalist country things are any different.'

CURTAIN CALL: THE DEBT NOOSE TIGHTENS

Whatever the shortcomings of Brazil's economic performance, Mr Delfim should be given a fair hearing. The government's chief planning expert never looked upon development as the national use of resources for the benefit of the majority. His is a narrower concept centring on sheer economic growth. Judged on this basis, Brazil's rapid industrialization is a truly impressive feat. Under Mr Delfim, the miracle plan certainly did achieve six years of real growth averaging 10 per cent per annum. One facet of this growth is the export of national capital to other countries. Brazilian construction firms have established subsidiaries in Africa and the Middle East, and a government-owned petroleum corporation is active in oil exploration abroad. What is more, Brazil's new-found capacity to produce steel outpaces domestic demand. Siderbrás steel company is negotiating to export semi-finished steel slabs to corporations in the US despite the objections of American labour and the doubts of Washington.

Brazil's economic accomplishments during the miracle period suggest that in the underdeveloped world, the most expedient way to accumulate capital rapidly is to woo foreign investment and to exploit thoroughly the domestic labour force. This strategy is usually the work of the military and the propertied classes led by a non-popular client state. This species of capitalism is propagating, displacing the old-fashioned neo-colonial regimes, and challenging socialist advances.

In the dependent statist variant of capitalism, accumulation falls more to the public sector. Compared to Chile and Guatemala, Brazil has relied heavily on gigantic state-owned enterprises and the regulation of much of the economy. To be sure, Brazil sustained respectable growth rates after the miracle period. In 1985, the country's first civilian president in 21 years took office, and the economy grew at an astonishing rate of 8 per cent, the world's fastest. The recovery, however, was accomplished by inflationary means: a vast increase in the money supply, a hike in the government's internal debt (what it owed to Brazilians), and high interest rates.

In its attempt to amass funds to service a huge foreign debt, an externally-oriented economy must rely on its export earnings. The logical move is to make exports cheaper in order to increase sales. This is achieved by devaluing the currency. Devaluation, however, causes imports to become more expensive. The rub is that imported goods are essential to production. Falling production levels lead to diminishing revenues. Then when the value of the currency drops, debt servicing is more expensive. The debt noose tightens as a result of a policy designed to loosen it. The more an impoverished nation thrashes about trying to escape, the tighter the knot.

Is there a way to slip out of the debt noose? With a resolute political will, which would require a different social configuration in power, Brazil could seriously challenge the foreign banks. Of critical importance are the country's bounteous resources, the scale of the economy (the ninth largest in the world), and the near balance between its exports and imports ($23 172 million versus $24 007 million in 1981). If Brazil were to declare a moratorium on debt repayment, Western concerns could of course withhold credit and refuse to trade. But Brazil produces almost everything it needs except oil. Even a lack of oil could be overcome, for the country's sugar plantations are providing alcohol, which is already being used as fuel, and other Third World countries would continue to sell petroleum to Brazil.

The country must choose between two options: servicing the debt means hardship in order to fill the pockets of Western bankers. Declaring a moratorium means hardship in order to realign the home economy and to release funds for internal development. Either way Brazilians are going to take the pain. Having already suffered on account of bloated debt servicing costs, the majority of Brazilians would choose the second option, if only their voices were heard.

6 The Exit Option, Withdrawing from Global Capitalism: China under Mao

In recent years, the People's Republic of China, like many under-developed countries, has sought to industrialize and to sell more of its manufactured products overseas. Thus China's exports of textiles to the US increased dramatically after 1980, reaching a value of $500 million in 1982, when the US was mired in a severe recession. With American textile producers idled and workers laid off, pressure mounted to restrict China's access to the US market. Washington responded by cutting Beijing's textile quota in half, whereupon China reduced its purchases of American grain by more than $500 million.

With an eye to China's enormous market, Washington relented and granted Beijing a modest 4 per cent increase in its textile quota. The agreement pleased American grain producers, who stood to gain from expanded sales to China, but rankled American textile manufac-turers, who faced growing competition from Chinese enterprises. Weighing heavily in the political decision on US trade policy were a desire to outpace Western European businesses and the Reagan administration's determination to outflank the Soviet 'evil empire'. The administration thus accorded privileges to China normally reserved for the other major Asian textile producers, all staunch members of the capitalist camp.

That China succeeded in winning concessions from the US is striking, for the underdeveloped countries have triumphed infre-quently in their economic dealings with the West. Not only is the textile agreement an emblem of China's re-emergence in the world political economy, but also it gives pause to consider that nation's industrial and agricultural development. Viewed historically, the

109

contradictory nature of China's agricultural and industrial policies is the key to understanding the achievements and failures of an inward-looking development strategy.

'THE EAST IS RED'

A shortage of arable land and extreme inequality in property ownership stalled capital accumulation in pre-revolutionary China. Whereas landlords and wealthy peasants owned the best land, animals and tools, the bulk of the population rented their fields and implements or worked as wage labourers. In bad times peasants had little protection from the ravages of floods and droughts. In good times dilapidated infrastructure kept rural dwellers from marketing their crops save through unscrupulous merchants. Constantly threatened by indebtedness and foreclosure, peasants lacked the power and resources to develop rural society.

Urban industry was no more advanced than the agricultural sector. Fighting during the Japanese occupation of the Second World War and the Civil War between Nationalist and Communist forces devastated the budding industrial economy. In 1949, industrial output and grain production amounted to half of the pre-war peak level. Transportation networks were destroyed. The Guomindang (the National People's Party that had ruled from 1928 to 1949) looted the state treasury, stripping the country of its foreign exchange reserves. The Soviet Union, seeking war spoils, commandeered over half of the industrial capital in Manchuria, a major centre of manufacturing and transportation.

China's nascent manufacturing sector included a textile industry, electrical power plants and steel mills. Adept at absorbing foreign technology, a bevy of scientists, engineers and skilled workers spearheaded this small but vibrant sector. Concentrated in a few coastal cities, its products (mostly consumer goods) were largely for export. Clearly a minuscule export-oriented manufacturing sector, alongside rural impoverishment, could not sustain a national economy. The abject state of capital accumulation in China in 1949 was not only a catalyst for revolution but also a formidable challenge for the Communists who seized power.

OUT OF THE ASHES

At the time of the Chinese Revolution, the US held a commanding position in worldwide production and trade. Washington sought to enforce 'a multilateral and competitive trading system in which American goods would enjoy the widest possible access'. Old policies on import controls and other protectionist measures were renegotiated through a new complex of international organizations to harmonize with US interests. Pre-revolutionary China was to be part of this system: in 1948, the US provided 48.4 per cent of China's imports, approximately 250 per cent more than in the years immediately before the war.

The US had furnished large amounts of military and development aid to the Nationalist regime in pre-revolutionary China. In 1950 the Truman administration decided to support the defeated Guomindang as the sole legitimate government of China. Moreover, the administration sought to isolate the new regime by adopting a two-pronged policy of international trade embargo and military containment. The US had already applied extensive controls to the Eastern European countries and had attempted to ensure compliance by its Western allies. The Western powers followed suit but not always to the letter. Britain and Portugal, for example, maintained indirect contact with China through their colonies, Hong Kong and Macao.

To enforce the boycott against China and other socialist countries, the US set up an international coordinating committee in 1952. The CCP, in turn, threatened to nationalize foreign holdings. Adamant in its stand, Washington showed no willingness to end the boycott and blocked Chinese assets in the US. Beijing retaliated by seizing American property and assets in China. The US repeatedly wielded its veto and influence in order to exclude China from the UN and other international agencies. Aid was denied, and China was barred from multilateral agreements on development, trade and finance. Meanwhile, the US concluded a series of bilateral and multilateral military agreements in Asia. The Truman administration proclaimed its commitment to defend Japan, Korea, Taiwan and Indo-China.

Although some Western countries violated the trade embargo, China had already turned to the Soviet Union and Eastern Europe for economic assistance. In the military realm, China faced the US-led effort to subdue Korea's communist north. In October 1950, Chinese forces blocked General Douglas MacArthur's attempt to cross the thirty-eighth parallel, and then checked his campaign aimed at the Manchurian border. Three years of war had not ended or weakened communist rule in North Korea and China.

Isolated from the West and assisted by the East, the CCP sought to convert China's weaknesses into strengths. As noted, the vast population engaged in inefficient, labour-intensive agriculture, and a minute manufacturing sector was limited to a few urban areas. China lacked essential agricultural inputs, and a capital-intensive policy would surely have driven people from the land. The CCP therefore planned to utilize the existing basis of agriculture as a source of surplus. The state would buy grain from peasant producers and sell it at a higher price in urban areas. A large measure of the difference between producer prices and consumer prices would be channelled into the industrial sector and targeted according to the national development plan.

When the Soviet Union introduced a similar strategy in the period after 1928, the authorities often relied on coercion in the countryside. The Russian Revolution had originated in the cities, and the Bolsheviks lacked long involvement in the peasant sector. By contrast, the CCP had experimented with reforms to supplant landlord power in its northern China base areas, in some cases satisfying claims by poor peasants for redistribution without alienating middle peasants.

The CCP could not have adopted the coercive measures practised in the Soviet Union. Grain consumption in China after 1949 verged on bare subsistence. However meagre, the Soviet peasantry's standard of living in the 1920s hovered above subsistence, allowing the state to skim surplus for investment in industry. China had no such room for manoeuvre. A policy of cutting peasant consumption would have caused massive starvation. Internal capital accumulation required increasing the rate of savings by expanding, not merely redistributing, agricultural output. The problem, of course, was not simply to amass surplus but to generate it in the first place. The task was to increase peasant production, hold down consumption and deliver surplus to the state. For those in power, the key question was how to stimulate productive forces both in industry and agriculture in a manner that improved the material conditions of the working classes.

During the era of post-war reconstruction, vast new territories came under the control of the CCP, often in areas where the party lacked organizational structure. While the CCP faced the challenges of economic development, it had to lay its political foundations in central and southern China. Mobilizing its cadres, the party instructed the villages to assort the local populace into classes, separating the rich from the poor, the exploited from the exploiters, the landlords from the peasants. This process was meant to raise class consciousness and to establish the party's legitimacy by empowering the peasantry.

To generate revenue for the state, the CCP introduced tax reforms with exemptions for the downtrodden. The authorities kept average tax rates below the levels set by the Guomindang. In addition to cancelling all back rent owed to landlords and the credit institutions, the CCP reduced interest rates by 25 per cent. The new tax and interest rate policies were accompanied by land reform, a programme which aimed to sever feudal landlords' control of agriculture.

Government policy stipulated that all peasants had the right to work a plot of land without infringement by landlords. In some villages, however, there were no landlords. The overzealous implementation of government policy thus deprived rich and middle peasants of their land, alienating them from the worker–peasant alliance. In other villages, redistribution was carried out smoothly, but the amount of land transferred to peasant households was relatively small. In Hunan and Hupei, a family of five generally received between one and two acres.

At the same time that the CCP restructured rural property relations, it increased agricultural output beyond pre-war peak levels and attained greater political legitimacy. One obstacle, however, was the lack of trained cadres to implement policy, particularly outside the party's base areas. New recruits, many of them unschooled in Marxism and without technical know-how, were responsible for instituting state programmes at the local level. Learning their jobs by trial-and-error, they provided leadership, channelled state policies to the village and conveyed information to the party hierarchy about local conditions. Partly owing to its weak foundation in many villages, the party allowed new recruits great latitude in interpreting policy. They were encouraged, for example, to launch bold attacks on counter-revolutionary elements. Unsurprisingly, abuses of power often resulted. In such cases, the people were supposed to have recourse through 'rectification' campaigns: public criticism of the performance of party cadres, who could be held responsible for their action. These campaigns actually served as a group-pressure method of regulating behaviour within the party.

The political and economic reforms established new mechanisms for capital accumulation. Most importantly, the reorganization of the agricultural sector provided the conditions under which peasants could produce a larger surplus for investment. Without swelling government expenditure, this policy allowed the CCP to pump a small supply of capital into the industrial sector.

In industry, the state sought not only to complete the tasks of reconstruction but also to control private enterprise. Whereas the state took over large enterprises owned by 'bureaucratic capitalists' and the former government, it preserved a sphere for the market economy and permitted private concerns to do business. Even so, with the expansion of the state sector, an increasing amount of revenue flowed into public enterprise. State companies dominated trading in key commodities. The CCP nationalized extensively but steered clear of across-the-board expropriation and refrained from introducing wage and price controls.

In foreign economic relations, ties to the Soviet Union were crucial in the reconstruction period. Faced with Western intransigence, Beijing and Moscow signed a 'Treaty of Friendship Alliance and Mutual Assistance' in 1950, followed by agreements on long-term credits and defence. COMECON's share of China's trade increased from 29 per cent in 1950 to 70 per cent in 1952, the end of the recovery period. Soviet loans, heavy industrial equipment and advisers played an increasingly important role in China's effort to overcome underdevelopment.

In 1952, prices stabilized, marking an end to the runaway inflation of the immediate post-war period. After three years of rehabilitation, annual output of grain and cotton rose 11.3 per cent and 53.6 per cent respectively over the pre-revolutionary peak. Steel production jumped 46 per cent above the previous record. Coal increased 7 per cent above the highest pre-liberation level. Further, the state restored transportation networks, with all pre-war rail lines in operation by 1951. Remarkably, China completed the reconstruction process while embroiled in the Korean War and in the throes of a rural transformation.

THE FIRST STATE PLAN

In 1952–3, Chinese planners prepared the First Five Year Plan. They faced awesome challenges in the countryside, where class antagonisms raged. Poor peasants were still insecure and feared that their land would be reclaimed. Centralized control over land could reverse egalitarian reforms and redound to the advantage of rich peasants. Similarly, in manufacturing, a capitalist class could rear its head and find new opportunities for accumulation. Various restrictions on business would probably hamper growth, but successful capitalist ventures could jeopardize socialism.

The First Five Year Plan, operative in 1953, gave new direction to China's development strategy. The plan called for increasingly advanced forms of cooperative farming. Typically Chinese peasants cultivated fragmented plots far from each other. Noting the vast amount of non-productive labour power devoted to transporting tools and workers, the state decided to consolidate agricultural units into larger and more rationally organized enterprises.

As a first step toward collectivization, MATs – small units in which a handful of peasant households pooled their labour – encouraged peasants to help each other with the harvest, furthering what had previously been an informal practice in the countryside. While materially helping the poor peasants, the MATs roused the communal impulses of the peasantry without attempting to convert private land ownership. There was no attempt to collectivize in one fell swoop. The plan called for gradual change, with several phases in which each step followed on the heels of the previous one. Seasonal MATs were to be replaced by permanent teams, which would share land and tools. In time, teams would merge, forming larger work units and evolving into more comprehensive collectives.

The party envisaged that cooperatives would be the main vehicle for transforming the countryside. They were to mobilize labour for such projects as irrigation works and land reclamation. By amassing the savings of peasant households into a general fund, the cooperative could provide the basis for productive investment. Risk would thereby be spread, easing the burden of failure by individuals or enterprises. The cooperatives, each one encompassing a cluster of farms, would also offer economies of scale in the use of machinery, seed and irrigation schemes. Finally, the cooperatives furnished an improved social security system: a welfare fund to protect peasants when times were bad.

Among the many problems in installing the cooperatives was the peasantry's ingrained attitude of self-interest. Smallholders with relatively good land were sometimes unwilling to pool their plots with those of poor peasants, since transfer of property disproportionately benefited the latter. Skilful farmers hesitated to work hard when their reward was commensurate with that of their less productive team members. At issue were incentives: how to persuade peasants to transcend self-interest for the common good?

Peasants would develop cooperative attitudes only if the new units could demonstrate their superiority as a system of agricultural production. This was a tall order: nothing less than new technology, improved management, reduced expenditures and higher levels of output. To entice peasants, a network of people's banks offered savings programmes and low-interest loans to the cooperatives, facilitating transactions with state trading companies. While granting preferential rates to the cooperatives and to poor peasants, the banks siphoned domestic capital, funnelling it to high-priority productive structures. The expansion of the banking system brought an end to the private moneylender market. The state's interlocking policies in the areas of price, trade and finance closed off unregulated private accumulation, but did not entail direct expropriation (save part of the property of the landlord class). In the peasant sector, one could no longer amass wealth by renting land, hiring labour, lending money or buying cheap and selling dear. Income would accrue only through expanded production. In theory, increasing numbers of peasants would prefer cooperative agriculture, because more surplus could be generated at less risk through joint efforts.

As before, surplus from the agricultural sector was to be diverted to urban industry, particularly to capital-intensive enterprises. In industry, the CCP squeezed private concerns. State enterprises sold their products below market value until competitors went out of business, levied exorbitant taxes on certain commercial activities and purchased shares in private companies. Thus government ownership of industrial enterprises snowballed from 34.7 per cent in 1949 to 67.5 per cent in 1956; the remaining firms in the latter year were joint (public–private) concerns. Under the First Five Year Plan, the state unswervingly directed over three-quarters of capital investment into a core of heavy industries, including a nucleus of 156 fully equipped factories imported from the Soviet Union. During the plan, agriculture contributed from 37 per cent to 46 per cent of total gross domestic profit but received only 8.6 per cent of total investment.

With the quickening pace of collectivization in 1954–5, agricultural output fell below the party's expectations. Despite the CCP's efforts to serve the interest of poor and middle peasants, the privileges of many wealthy peasants were intact, betokening renewed class conflict. Meanwhile, industrial output slackened. Worse yet, the imbalance between sectors caused unprecedented problems. Sluggish performance in the agricultural sector doubly threatened industry; lower agricultural output reduces investment and lessens peasants' capacity to purchase goods produced by local enterprises. This tendency is compounded when faltering industries are unable to provide the necessary inputs to fuel the agricultural sector. A decline in both sectors makes it even more difficult to motivate workers to meet production targets, for the people fail to reap rewards from the system.

By 1955, the Chinese economy was on a downward course. The First Five Year Plan called for 4.6 per cent growth per year between 1953 and 1957, but actual growth in 1953–4 came to only 1.7 per cent, a decrease from the previous year. In industry, growth in the production of consumer goods reached 26.7 per cent in 1953, then slipped to 14.2 per cent in 1954, and registered a negative percentage in 1955. Similarly in producer goods, 36.5 per cent growth in 1953 receded to 17.8 per cent in 1954 and to 14.5 per cent in 1955. These shortfalls were shocking because they occurred in the very sectors earmarked for substantial investment.

Equally troublesome was the repolarization of wealth in the countryside, weakening the position of the productive middle peasantry. The party sought to strengthen the relationship between this class fraction and the poor peasants, both indispensable elements in the effort to augment agricultural production.

According to Vivienne Shue's data on agricultural income in 1954, productivity per *mou* (one-sixth of an acre) of cultivated land was higher among middle peasants than among poor peasants. In fact, the average household income of middle peasants per *mou* approximated that of rich peasants. However, on average, rich peasants' overall household income far exceeded middle peasants' household earnings. The rich peasants generated a higher level of income less by elevating their rate of productivity and more by virtue of owning and controlling the means of production, especially land, tools and wage-labour. The relative deterioration of conditions for middle peasants thereby offset the state's egalitarian reforms and eroded the support of a key class fraction for the new agricultural policies.

In June 1955, Mao Zedong admitted the failings of agricultural policy and advocated a stepped-up pace of collectivization. Although his fellow party leaders and state officials in Beijing did not wholeheartedly embrace Mao's position, the bulk of the peasantry supported his initiative. Yet, as Shue notes: 'in the provinces and rural counties they [the local leaders] leapt at his words as the solution to their problems of rural investment capital seepage'.

The wave of collectivization swept through the countryside. In March 1955, only 14.2 per cent of peasant households belonged to Agricultural Producer Cooperatives. By May 1956, 91.2 per cent joined, manifesting the end of private agricultural production in China.

Mao repeatedly emphasized that channelling peasant resources into large units and developing them at a rapid pace would be the catalyst for a radical transformation in the countryside. Critics have assailed his policy on the ground that it marked both the abandonment of efforts to accommodate gradual transition and the denial of democratic participation in the socialist project. In response Shue explains that, 'Mao accurately perceived the precariousness of the shifting balance of power in the villages.' She adds: 'The peasant constituency for a swifter transition was clearly in place; the demand for it was voiced by a restless village cadre force.' Given the currents that backed collectivization, the difficulties with the policies emanating from the First Five Year Plan signalled the need for a dramatic change in the agricultural sector.

In industry, the wages of industrial workers rose 19 per cent between 1954 and 1956; however, feeble output prompted a review of policy. The difficulties may be traced to the organization of production at the factory level. China imported not only factories from the Soviet Union, but also borrowed Moscow's system of industrial relations, which tied rewards (wages and promotion) to performance. In nearly one-quarter of China's industries in 1956, wages were determined by piece-rate: the volume of a worker's output governed his remuneration according to standards set by managerial specialists. The system pitted line workers against managers; the former sought to hike wages by pushing for changes in rates. In the face of budding protests, the CCP installed small worker-administered teams to organize and discipline their cohorts. Management groups continued to determine wages according to piece-rate calculations.

The piece-rate system circumscribed the authority of the small groups, denying the party a base in the factories for motivating workers. Workers thus channelled their grievances to factory-level management, increasing the probability of factory-wide protest. Group leaders found themselves in an ambivalent position, upholding management policy and sympathizing with workers' grievances about piece-rates. These leaders were placed in a potentially adversarial relationship with workers and exercised little influence over the setting of rates. The reward system, according to Andrew Walder, 'directly undermined Party efforts to establish political and social control in industry at precisely the time they were forced to extend it over a rapidly expanding state sector'.

In addition, the system of wage determination was ill-suited to the vagaries of an underdeveloped economy undergoing a radical transformation. Geared to worker effort, the piece-rate method provided no means to compensate workers when production halted through no fault of their own. The Chinese economy did not yet run according to plan: goods were frequently delivered late, in insufficient quantities, or in substandard condition. When machines broke down, spare parts were in short supply. The reward system could not respond to such complications, thus worsening other industrial problems.

In both industry and agriculture, discontent among the rank and file threatened to distance the party from its principal support base. Clearly the CCP had reaped the benefits of reconstruction and land reform. But following the redistribution of wealth, it was human labour that had to produce greater value. The CCP still faced the fundamental problem of how to build a self-sustaining economy.

'MASS PRODUCTION OF USELESS PRODUCTS'

Against a backdrop of a rapidly changing international environment, central planners reassessed the strategy of accumulation adopted under the First Five Year Plan. Imports from the COMECON countries cushioned China against the effects of the US-led trade embargo. With the recovery of the Western economies in the mid-1950s, an increasing number of European countries violated the embargo. Ultimately, the US alone remained adamant about maintaining the boycott of certain commodities. Meanwhile, China developed ties with the embryonic non-aligned movement. Premier Zhou Enlai played a key role in the 1955 Afro–Asian conference in Bandung, and China promptly established diplomatic and trade relations with such newly independent countries as Ghana and Guinea.

In 1956 Nikita Khrushchev shocked the outside world by attacking Joseph Stalin's strategy of 'Industry First' and his abuses of power. Given their own experience with Soviet industry, the Chinese were familiar with its shortcomings and wary of domination by a powerful neighbour. While Moscow wanted Beijing to develop as part of a socialist commonwealth, in which the Soviet Union was the senior partner, China sought Soviet aid to boost national industrial development. Following differences over the impending offshore islands crisis and the Soviet Union's hesitancy to bolster China's fledgeling industries, Beijing moved towards self-reliance on defence questions in 1958. Moscow then withdrew its atomic assistance in 1959. In addition, the Soviet Union called home many advisers. Trainloads of Soviet equipment and supplies were halted, slowing China's industrial recovery.

In the light of these international pressures and recurrent failings in domestic economic policy, the CCP reconsidered the lofty growth targets inscribed in the Second Five Year Plan, which began in 1958. China embarked on the Great Leap Forward: a mass mobilization to raise industrial and agricultural production. This campaign emphasized the simultaneous development of industry and agriculture, or 'walking on two legs'. Age-old methods of production were to be used alongside new technologies. The campaign was to be spearheaded by novel forms of social organization, with renewed ideological consciousness.

The state would direct added inputs into agriculture and assign priority to the mobilization of labour in the countryside. Central planners called for new vehicles to enlist underemployed and off-season labourers. Thus peasant communes, established in the period 1958–60, were to serve as the nucleus of administration and decision making in rural areas. Planners reasoned that the communes could make extensive use of labour-intensive techniques and raise the level of productive forces in the countryside without requiring vast inputs from the industrial sector. Then expanded agricultural output would produce surpluses for investment in the cities. Productivity in the agricultural sector could be enhanced with little supplemental cost.

The revised plan also stressed small-scale industry. The party exhorted peasants to expand local operations which provided inputs into the farm economy: cement works, iron foundries, fertilizer plants and so on. The urban industrial sector would maintain its large-scale, capital-intensive basis, fed by redirected farm surplus. The state aimed to bring select industrial projects closer to the communes, in the locale of raw materials and large markets, thereby spreading employment opportunities and reducing transportation costs.

Central planners believed that in one intense effort, a great leap, China could realize its latent potential. They set new production targets and, initially, the country's teeming population made impressive gains. Steel production more than doubled, from 5.35 metric tons in 1957 to 11.08 metric tons in 1958. Total grain output rose from 191 metric tons to 206 metric tons during the same period. The targets, however, were later revised downwards because of falsified reporting at the beginning. Successive years of drought and flooding followed the excellent harvest of 1958. Equally nettlesome were the human errors of poor planning, overzealousness in the execution of policy, and breakdowns in communication. Although such difficulties were not new, the Great Leap Forward heightened uncertainty and accentuated tensions.

In the 1959–60 period, the economy entered a depression. While industry grew slightly, agricultural production dropped precipitously, reducing per capita grain output to its lowest level since 1949. Aside from the overall decline, the problem was that the party had established a new social structure of accumulation without eliminating powerful vestiges of the old structure. Within the worker–peasant alliance, conflicts developed between industrial labourers and factory leaders, between peasant and collective, and among fractions of the peasantry. As was to be expected, counter-revolutionary tendencies among former landlords and the capitalist classes were rife.

The party gradually consolidated power and extended its reach, but at considerable cost. Generally speaking, local leaders were creative, flexible and adept at matching the central government's policies with community needs. However, as the party sought to increase agricultural output and to appropriate surplus at higher, assured levels, central officials became less tolerant of partial compliance with their policies. The authorities in Beijing came to view local leaders as untrustworthy aides and as rivals. No longer was the rural party a basis for, and an extension of, central authority, bringing government to the people and facilitating communication with leaders at the top. Now the party sought to diminish the power wielded by local cadres.

Local leaders became increasingly guarded and less candid in dealing with the centre for fear that they would be blamed for deviations from policy. They began to regard their relationship with the government as competitive.

Similarly, in industry, the problems of planning and party power caused a shift in policy. In the late 1950s, the party instituted a work-group system to replace Soviet-style piece-rates. Under the new system, a small number of workers and a leader evaluated performance and determined rewards, including wages, promotions, food ration stamps and medical care. The work-groups considered not only output but also an employee's attitudes toward his colleagues, the factory and socialism. This system reduced the power of technical personnel formerly responsible for setting piece-rate quotas, giving the impression of redistribution of power in the factory.

However, the redistribution was lateral, not vertical; group leaders assumed power in the factories. The new leaders dominated the evaluation process and hence the allocation of rewards. In sectors where work-groups were most important, principally in state-owned heavy industries, jobs were few and the remuneration generous by Chinese standards. Workers coveted these jobs, knowing that their economic standing hinged on maintaining employment in the same sector, which invariably meant in the same factory. Rewards were tied to one's performance evaluation by fellow workers and especially by the group leader. The locus of conflict over wages and working conditions thus shifted from the relations between labourers and factory-level management to the arena of small groups. This system enabled the party to prevent factory-wide and industry-wide opposition. Activist workers could be coopted by granting rewards tying the most articulate and politically engaged employees to the power structure; and disgruntled workers could be brought into line by actual or threatened sanctions.

The party paid a political cost for effective control of the shop floor. Factory workers were called upon to direct their grievances to the very individuals who determined their wages, thus impeding genuine communication. Leaders and workers engaged in a ritual wherein employees were supposed to raise criticism while the group sought to achieve consensus. This exercise was something less than democratic and participatory: while leaders attempted to enforce directives, workers conformed to standards during structured political activities. Like their rural counterparts, urban workers looked out for their own security and avoided politically sensitive issues.

The CCP exhorted workers to adopt innovative techniques which would enable Chinese industry to overcome the 'superstitions' of Western productive methods. Workers were to increase production without additional capital investment. The labour force thus responded by making shortcuts to meet quotas. In steel mills, for example, workers cut heating time in half by doubling temperature. The new procedure had a disastrous effect on quality. Factories produced 'steel that was like butter' and machines that did not work.

Such problems could not be candidly broached at group meetings, for workers feared receiving a poor evaluation.

During the Great Leap Forward, the CCP dismissed technological constraints and proven engineering practices, applying instead untested production methods in vast areas without regard for differences in local conditions. In the new rural industries, unschooled cadres and inexperienced workers were unfamiliar with the notions of inspection and quality control. Industries lacked essential inputs, primarily because of recurrent shortfalls in the agricultural sector. Food supplies were inadequate in the cities and the countryside. In the face of impending famine and widespread opposition to the Great Leap Forward, the party again reappraised its strategy of accumulation.

READJUSTMENT

The failure of the Great Leap Forward demonstrated the futility of attempting to develop the agricultural sector without a sizeable investment in the countryside. Little uncultivated land remained, and the labour-intensive land reclamation efforts had apparently reached their limit. Further expansion of agriculture depended not only on mobilizing labour, but also on scientific advancement and substantial expenditure.

While internal sources failed to furnish an accumulation fund, tensions with Moscow continued to mount, culminating in the public expression of the Sino–Soviet split in 1960. That year 11 000 Soviet technicians went home, causing major disruptions in Chinese industry. Imports from the COMECON countries, which represented between 60 per cent and 80 per cent of total purchases in the 1950s, were drastically reduced.

In the period from its break with the Soviet Union in 1960 to Mao's death in 1976, China adopted a strategy known as self-reliance. In principle, this strategy entails an attempt to minimize participation in the global economy and to mobilize domestic resources. In fact, China's international options were limited, for it brooked opposition from both superpowers. China received no long-term commercial loans, foreign assistance or credit from international monetary institutions. The country by and large spurned tourism, private foreign investment, imported consumer goods and academic training in most Western countries. However, China did not totally withdraw from the international political economy. After an initial decline, foreign trade grew. The trade profile changed: large quantities of grain, not inputs for heavy industry, dominated imports. Additionally, in its quest for self-reliance, China exported capital in the form of loan repayments to the Soviet Union and aid programmes for underdeveloped countries.

At home, in a startling reversal of policy in 1961, the CCP assigned priority to agriculture as the foundation of the economy. Next in order, light industry took precedence over heavy industry. Rejecting a strategy of rapid industrialization, planners held that the growth of industry would ultimately follow upon increasing extraction of raw materials in the rural sector. Although these shifts in policy were clearly articulated, there is little reliable information concerning actual allocations to respective sectors.

Without dismantling the infrastructure set up in the 1950s, the authorities decentralized communes so that smaller production teams would decide issues of management and decentralization. To provide incentive for increased production, the state relaxed grain quotas. Most importantly, the state invested substantially in new agricultural inputs, authorizing long-term, interest-free loans to stimulate the production of chemical fertilizer, tools and equipment such as electric water pumps.

Not only did the state invest in communes, but it also provided material incentives for individual peasant producers. Private plots, eliminated during the Great Leap Forward, were restored, allowing independent accumulation and household consumption outside the network of cooperatives. The state thus tolerated a very limited role for the market economy.

In the industrial sphere, planners called for the consolidation of all installations. The nucleus comprised factories inherited from the pre-1949 capitalist period, large plants supplied by the Soviet Union during the 1950s and small rural industries inaugurated during the Great Leap Forward. A major problem was the lack of linkages between these disparate industries. Now planners sought to lay the groundwork for the sharing of technical know-how and administrative skill. Unlike the old formula of expanding investment in industry with little consideration for quality, the new pattern was to synchronize and improve existing facilities.

Novel policies in agriculture and industry emphasized coordination, better management and streamlined administration. The economists and technical specialists demoted during the antisuperstition campaigns and the Great Leap Forward regained positions of authority in the planning process. In factories, the influence of technical experts increased relative to that of work-group leaders. Central officials assumed greater power over planning, provincial economic matters and even individual enterprises. They sought to impart discipline in industry by introducing austerity measures, closing non-competitive factories and restraining workers' wages to cut costs. Undertaken to promote efficiency, implementation of the new policies sometimes required the application of brute force. The state pushed educated, urban youth out of the cities into the countryside, thereby shifting the burden of supply to the rural communes.

The readjustment reforms effected some savings, but an inept swollen bureaucracy swallowed up surpluses, preventing the state from substantially building its accumulation fund through a range of policies. Enterprise managers, struggling to meet output quotas, adopted devious tactics. From a manager's vantage point, underproduction jeopardized one's position while overproduction caused the next quota to increase. Managers, therefore, concealed excess output. Goods were left unfinished in one production period so that they could be added to the quota in the next period. To avoid coming in under quota, managers hoarded spare parts and raw materials. Such practices enabled factories to achieve their targets, but the waste and inefficiency drained China's industrial sector.

To remedy similar problems, most Eastern European countries have introduced market forces in the state sector. Chinese officials in the 1960s, however, considered this course 'revisionist', and inveighed against the capitalist road.

CAPITALIST ROAD OR SOCIALIST ROAD?

The lesson Mao drew from the Soviet experience and the problems besetting the Chinese Revolution was that a one-sided emphasis on productive forces could not transform society. The greatest danger to revolution comes from above, Mao attested in 1966 on the eve of the Great Proletarian Cultural Revolution. He admonished leaders who failed to honour the principles and values of the revolution, dubbing them 'capitalist roaders', and called for the continuous involvement of peasants and workers in the management of their own affairs. Mao described the immediate aim of the Great Proletarian Cultural Revolution as the removal of the capitalist roaders.

The campaign to reduce bureaucratic privilege began with the promotion of egalitarianism in production units. All workers received 'supplementary wages' of about 5 *yuan* per month irrespective of how hard they laboured or what their group achieved. No amount of effort could increase their wages. Without the power to manipulate wage rewards, the group leaders relied on hortatory appeals, political education and group criticism. In place of work-group evaluations, study meetings and self-criticism sessions were supposed to provide collectivist incentives.

However, the living standards of industrial workers as a class did not improve during the 1960s. The state appropriated a large share of the margin between subsistence and total production as surplus for investment. Moreover, the changes in the incentive system introduced completely new forms of inequality. In the eight-grade scale of industrial wages, workers at the top earned three times as much as those at the bottom. Whereas in the past increasing seniority meant higher wages, the abolition of upward wage adjustments ended remuneration for seniority. However, the termination of adjustments meant that a worker who had received periodic bonuses now collected double or triple the wage of a recently hired worker equally skilled at the same job. The skilled worker recruited after the adoption of the new policy had no hope of closing the gap. Similarly, employees enlisted under the new policy in the 1960s earned the same amount as novices hired in the 1970s. The older worker was likely to have a family to support, but drew the same wage as a young, single employee. In wholly unanticipated ways, the new system failed to promote egalitarianism among workers.

Apart from changing the incentive system, the state reduced the power of technical experts in industry. As many as 80 per cent of them were cut in some plants. These technicians received new assignments as production workers on the shop floor. Power devolved to line managers, who gained control over the allocation of resources in individual shops. The problems that afflicted management at the factory level – hoarding of spare parts, working to quota and avoiding novel experiments – contributed to a worsening performance on the shop floor.

The campaign against bureaucracy backfired, contradicting the plans of its architects. Faced with unprecedented levels of inefficiency in the 1970s, the state finally reinstated many technical experts, but the political cadres who had assumed responsibility for technical tasks during the 1960s often remained in place. Bureaucracies thus snowballed in size without any real change in incentives for direct producers.

The Great Proletarian Cultural Revolution failed to alter the basis of capital accumulation. There was not a great deal of rural mobilization, and the displacement of party leadership in the countryside, fundamentally disrupted agricultural production. The shift from material incentives to intensified political education and appeals to Maoist values did not motivate peasants to increase output. At the local level, the shift engendered confusion, resistance and overzealousness. In one case, village elder Old Guo saved his family from starvation by selling a steady supply of duck eggs. The brigade leader viewed the private ownership of ducks as a 'sign of rotten capitalism', and he ordered Guo to cut the tail of capitalism by slaughtering the six ducks. Guo could either do as told or appear at a criticism session before the commune. He risked being branded as an opponent of the will of Mao, a grave offence. The old peasant put up a spirited defence and defied the brigade leader. 'Do you know whose ducks these are?' Guo asked. 'These ducks are Chairman Mao's ducks. One is for Old Liang, to repay my debt to him. But I'm sending the other five to Peking for Chairman Mao to eat. And whoever is crazy enough to kill my ducks, well, he's the one opposing Chairman Mao.'

Not only in Old Guo's village but in the rural areas generally, the Great Proletarian Cultural Revolution exacerbated the problems it was supposed to solve. The attack on bureaucracy failed miserably. The authority of central planners remained intact. Despite changes in institutional forms, the idea that workers could gain control over their own lives proved illusory. Unsurprisingly, the Great Proletarian Cultural Revolution abruptly ended in 1969.

In the post-Cultural Revolution period, a crack soon appeared in the edifice of self-reliance. In 1972, Premier Zhou Enlai and President Nixon issued the Shanghai Communiqué, which pledged that China and the US would work toward the normalization of relations. Chinese planners knew that they had to relieve pressure on peasant production. They sought to purchase grain, technical inputs and even industrial plants from the US.

From the close of the Great Proletarian Cultural Revolution to 1975, agriculture and industry registered moderate growth. But the real wages of industrial workers in 1975 remained at the same level as in 1956, and the population continued to increase by about 2 per cent per year. The effort to build an accumulation fund still hinged on the appropriation of surplus from workers who lived at a near-subsistence level. Notwithstanding the reorganization of production and the development of productive forces, the mass of Chinese experienced little material improvement in their lives during the period from 1957 to 1976.

MAO'S LEGACY

Inasmuch as underdevelopment means the blockage that restrains the rational transformation of a social structure, the CCP did make some swift strides by eliminating China's old alignment of Nationalist power and feudal privilage. From the end of the Civil War in 1949 to Mao's passing in 1976, China underwent a metamorphosis in relations of production as well as in industry and, to a lesser extent, in agriculture. Inflation remained low. The party achieved structural change through land reform, collectivization and industrial control. At the same time, Mao avoided incurring a sizeable external debt and minimized dependence on foreign technology and raw material inputs. Faced with the cancellation of Soviet aid and a Western boycott, China formulated an inward-oriented strategy. By no means a blanket withdrawal from the world political economy, this strategy significantly reduced reliance on external market forces.

On the other side of the ledger, a large number of economic policies were introduced only to be reversed later. The reversal of policies took a toll, for any citizenry's tolerance for experimentation is not without limits. Mao's policies entailed extensive coercion and bloodshed. The rights of direct producers in a society under the weight of an elephantine bureaucracy were not protected. Top-heavy governmental structures and ritualized participation forestalled political competitiveness. All in all, China in 1976 was, and still is, a one-party state dominated by a bureaucratic class. In the final analysis, China under Mao was unable to solve the problem of underdevelopment through policies designed to generate internal accumulation and (though not entirely by choice) to constrict external sources of capital accumulation.

7 The Alternative Path, Weaving through Global Capitalism: Mozambique

Shortly after independence in 1975, a Marxist government in Mozambique sought to loosen its ties to South Africa's apartheid system. Mozambique approached multinational corporations in the US and Western Europe to do business. Their reply was: sorry, chum, you must deal with our regional affiliate (which is in Johannesburg). Even today, if a parent company does agree to fill an order, say, for urgently needed spare parts, delivery time from Europe is at least four or five months. It can take weeks to get a technician out to Mozambique from Europe to repair one of the country's few printing presses, but only a couple of days from Johannesburg, an eight-hour drive from Maputo.

In Mozambique, the practicalities of what is required to break out of the web of underdevelopment cannot be understood without reference to the country's past. It is not enough to recount the activities and practices that exist today, because to gain an appreciation of the current situation one must explain how present patterns took shape in the colonial era, and then examine the independent government's programme for reconstructing the national political economy.

THE COLONIAL LEGACY

Only two aspects of the historical context need concern us here: the peculiarities of Portugal's position in Europe and the all-important shift in colonial policy in the 1960s locking Mozambique into the southern African orbit. Traditionally, not only was Portugal the weakest country in Europe, but also the metropolitan economy itself

129

was subordinate to that of England. Dating from 1373, the Anglo–Portuguese pact is one of the most durable alliances on record. The 1703 Treaty of Methuen assigned to Portugal the role of providing primary products for British manufactured goods. With the deterioration of Lisbon's textile industry and the development of a chronic trade deficit, economic dependence became the pattern. In the twentieth century, under the longest lived fascist regime in history, Portugal neither promoted industrialization nor modernized the agricultural sector, as did other European countries.

At the 1884–5 Berlin Conference, at the behest of England, Portugal agreed to take state control in Africa to ward off French and Belgian claims to hegemony. In Mozambique, Portugal skimmed surplus from traditional colonial activities without engaging substantially in the modern sectors, which were largely the province of the non-national concerns. Big business in Lisbon did not invest heavily in the colonies, preferring instead safer markets elsewhere in Europe and Brazil. Seeking to guard against the 'denationalization' of Portuguese interests in the empire, Prime Minister Antônio Salazar introduced protectionism in the 1930s; however, when the colonial wars erupted in 1961, he was forced to reverse this policy, for the government desperately needed funds from foreign sources to fight a military campaign in three territories in Africa: Angola, Guinea-Bissau and Mozambique.

With Portugal faltering in its efforts to bear the burden of empire in the 1960s, the hinterland territories of South Africa and Rhodesia took a commanding position in the economy of Mozambique. They oriented it not to the needs of the mother country, but to their own burgeoning economies, and investment concentrated on developing infrastructure. Indeed the basis for transforming Mozambique into a service economy linked to the interior had been established early in this century in a series of agreements between Lisbon and Pretoria. Lisbon was to supply a vast amount of cheap labour to fuel capital accumulation on the Transvaal. More precisely, Portugal would export at least 100 000 African workers per year to the mines provided that South Africa routed at least 47.5 per cent of its Transvaal transit trade via Mozambique's traffic facilities. After the first six months of their 12–18 month contracts, the workers received deferred payments for 60 per cent of their wages. With the introduction of the two-tier gold price in 1968, the mines remitted this premium to Lisbon in gold valued at the official rate of $42 per ounce, which the metropolitan treasury then sold at the free market price of

$162 per ounce, retaining a windfall profit of perhaps $150 million per year. Largely as a result of this transaction, South Africa provided, before 1975, between 50 and 60 per cent of Mozambique's foreign exchange earnings. In addition, from 1965 to 1976, Maputo and Beira were the principal sanctions-breaking routes for Rhodesia, handling 85 per cent of Salisbury's imports and exports. From this traffic, Mozambique derived about 13 per cent of its total annual exchange earnings.

Portugal built and improved railways for use by the neighbouring countries without linking up domestic transportation routes. Today the rail line between Maputo and Beira, Mozambique's two major cities and ports, runs through Zimbabwe, and that between Beira and Nacala, the country's third largest harbour, is in Malawi. The railways all stretch east–west, from the coast to the interior; there is no all-weather road from north to south in this long, narrow country. Around this transportation network emerged an elaborate service sector to administer port traffic as well as major tourist centres for South Africans and Rhodesians.

The foremost monument to the combination of Portuguese political will and South African capital is Cabora Bassa, the largest dam in Africa and the fourth in size in the world. Portugal launched the project in 1969 with the intention that it would develop the whole Zambezi Valley, attract a large influx of white settlers and thereby serve as a bulwark against FRELIMO. The massive dam was built by Consórcio Hidroelétrico do Zambeze, a multinational consortium led by the Anglo-American Company of South Africa. South Africa was not only a major sponsor of Cabora Bassa but is also the chief beneficiary of its hydroelectric power; all current on the DC high voltage line from the dam's giant generators, even for Mozambique, must be relayed via the Apollo converting station in the Transvaal.

Colonialism thus implanted a mega-infrastructure without laying the foundations upon which Mozambicans themselves could build a nationally integrated economy. We can now turn our attention to how independent Mozambique has sought to extricate itself from the colonial heritage.

MOZAMBIQUE'S STRATEGY OF ACCUMULATION

Following one decade of armed struggle, Mozambique promptly formulated a post-colonial development strategy. Its principal features are creating new party and state organs, hastening a rural transformation, promoting heavy industry and redefining links with the international economy. After calling attention to Mozambique's professed goals, I will turn to the strengths and weaknesses of this strategy.

The Party and the State

At the core of the political programme is an effort to form a tightly knit organization between the leadership and the masses. Whereas the front had been a broad coalition of anti-colonial elements, the party was launched at the Third Congress of FRELIMO in February 1977 as a vanguard of workers and peasants. It retains the name FRELIMO, and is open exclusively to those politically engaged citizens who did not collaborate with the colonial government. In order to enlarge the working-class component of the party, preference among applicants is given to the proletariat, which numbers only about 200 000. While embracing the familiar Marxist tenet that the working class is the 'leading force' in society, the Third Congress took issue with the classical Marxist position which views the peasantry as a residue of an antiquated mode of production, and accorded a central role to Mozambican peasants. Not only does the peasantry constitute the most numerous stratum in Mozambique, but it also 'had already great proof of its engagements in the revolutionary transformation of our society'.

Following the completion of a campaign known as 'structuring the party' in 1978, FRELIMO has primary responsibility for dismantling the colonial state, and is assigned a leading role in relation to the new state. In practice, FRELIMO has proceeded gingerly in winnowing the colonial legacy. Without going into detail, it is clear that remnants of the old state machinery – in particular, complicated administrative departments such as customs – remain intact. However, Mozambique, like other countries aiming at a socialist transition, promptly introduced measures to place the economy under state control. The government nationalized the main branches of the economy, including private banking in 1978, and invited foreign concerns to submit claims for compensation. The assets and liabilities of the private banks – Casa Bancaria de Mozambique, Banco de Credito Comercial e Industrial and Banco de Angola – were transferred to the Bank of Mozambique. A newly created People's Development Bank replaced the Portuguese quasi-state banks – Banco de Fomento and Banco

Pinto e Sotto Mayor – which were given one year to conclude their business in Mozambique without incurring new assets and liabilities.

Added to this, the state took over all private property in land, apartment buildings and rental properties. It nationalized funeral parlours and all activities in the fields of medicine, law and education. But apart from such basic necessities in sectors related to social services, the state has nationalized relatively few holdings (in most cases abandoned enterprises).

There are numerous other innovations in the state apparatus. Among them, the army is a new entity; the Ministry of Foreign Affairs was created from scratch without typical, crash-training in diplomacy by the departing colonial power; the Ministry of Agriculture provides extension services that the metropolitan authorities would not furnish; and the legal system is being remoulded along the lines of the juridical principles established in the liberated zones. (The commission charged with the task of revamping the legal system studied the practices of various other countries, including the socialist ones. While this was an instructive exercise, it was immediately obvious that the law as it evolved in other countries had limited applicability in Mozambique. In capitalist countries courts sanction principles which Mozambicans do not wish to uphold. In socialist countries such as Cuba, courts have no experience settling disputes over, say, polygamous marriages or initiation rites, which are major sources of civil conflict in Mozambique.)

When Mozambicans began to abuse their positions of authority, FRELIMO inaugurated the 'Political and Organizational Offensive'. In 1980 the then President Samora Machel made a dramatic round of surprise visits to state enterprises, exposing incompetence and corruption. The president's initiative was symbolic, signalling FRELIMO's intention to revitalize inefficient structures and to call upon the people to take state institutions to task. In the wake of the president's announcements, some leading members of FRELIMO were relieved of their ministerial duties. Their new responsibility was to reinvigorate the party and, in a subsequent move toward decentralization, top officials were assigned to the provinces. Today, many key figures in FRELIMO are no longer based in Maputo.

Special mention should be made of the social sector, an area where there was nearly a void under Portuguese rule. In health care, the situation was appalling. Of the 440 doctors in Mozambique on the eve of independence, only 87 remained in the country. An expensive private medical system catered to white settlers in the towns. Apart from traditional medicine, health services were practically unknown in the countryside. Thus not only did FRELIMO ban private medicine, but it also organized a rural health service and emphasized preventive rather than curative medicine. Most importantly, FRELIMO introduced free medical treatment, including a massive vaccination campaign that reached 90 per cent of the population by 1979. Within five years of independence, infant mortality declined by 20 per cent. And against a background of a 5 per cent literacy rate at independence, 27 per cent of the population could read and write within eight years.

To give substance to this programme at the grass-roots level, locally elected mobilizing committees known as dynamizing groups organized political education projects, instilling FRELIMO's ideology into the rank and file. The dynamizing groups, envisaged as transitional entities, have gradually been supplanted by party cells, which are regarded as a more mature form of political institution. To stimulate greater political participation by the workers and peasants, the party draws on the 'mass democratic organizations': the Mozambique Women's Movement, the Mozambique Youth Movement and production councils.

The party's major step was to hold elections throughout the country for people's assemblies. In 1977, for the first time, all adult Mozambicans (except for those who had served the colonial state) were entitled to vote for candidates for political office within the single-party framework. The composition of these assemblies is a telling measure of the state's social base. Tabulations by a Mozambican weekly publication show that at the district level 20 per cent of the deputies elected were workers and 40 per cent peasants; at the Popular Assembly, the country's national parliament, 32 per cent of those elected were workers and 29 per cent peasants. An indicator of changing social relations, too, is the representation of women in Mozambique's legislative bodies. Proportionally there are more women in Mozambique's Popular Assembly than in the US House of Representatives. Of the 219 deputies in the Assembly, 28 are women. Their presence is more pronounced in the local and district assemblies, where 28 and 24 per cent respectively of the deputies are women.

The party attempts to stimulate political consciousness by organizing a weekly meeting in ministries on Saturday mornings to discuss texts, party documents and speeches. At these sessions, which are essentially political science seminars, men and women are encouraged to voice their opinions and criticize the implementation of socialism in Mozambique. Some Saturday morning meetings are lively and constructive, while others are boring and ineffectual.

The decisions taken at the Third Congress marked a new stage in the growth and evolution of FRELIMO's ideology. The guiding principle in FRELIMO's thinking is the notion that the lessons of the liberated zones can be generalized to provide the basis for developing the entire country along socialist lines. For FRELIMO the liberated areas are the key, the embryo of the future Mozambique. Unfortunately there is no easy explanation for understanding what constitutes a liberated area. Its essence lies in how problems are solved, how the people are organized and how social relationships have changed. Integral to this process are debate, discussion, criticism and self-criticism. In principle, Mozambicans talk out trying issues until mutually satisfactory solutions are reached. This procedure derives from the practices of self-rule established before independence day, when peasants engaged in armed struggle to oppose Portugal's attempt to move them into protected villages. These strategic hamlets, as they are also called, were modelled on those used by the US in Vietnam. Given that Mozambicans were scattered throughout the countryside, they had to concentrate their forces and join together, forming new communities to counter the Portuguese offensive. These dramatic changes in the life-styles of peasants generated the impetus for dispensing with antiquated agricultural practices, adopting improved technologies and forging cooperative work habits.

Lessons from the popular struggle – the need for continual self-criticism and innovation – played an important role in the debates at the Fourth Congress, held in 1983. Jarred by military raids from South Africa, widespread drought and its own management errors, especially overcentralization, FRELIMO ran the risk of losing peasant support. The economy had pushed the peasantry into subsistence, for there was little to buy. Neglect of family farming contributed to a material crisis which mushroomed into political and ideological crises. Planners, meanwhile, believed that there were no fundamental problems because the class base of the state was in order. The Fourth Congress thus developed a sharp critique of the Marxism practised by FRELIMO. It was viewed as too abstract and outside the popular experience. Questions of policy and options, it was said, must be kept open. In the political realm, the primary problem was heavily economic: how to generate a socialist accumulation fund. According to the congress, the solution is to develop new linkages between agriculture and industry, between rural and urban areas, in order to revive the economy.

A Rural Transformation

Central to the deliberation at the Fourth Congress was the plight of the countryside, where FRELIMO had sought to reorganize production units in order to take advantage of Mozambique's fertile soil. (Mozambique is also endowed with sizeable mineral deposits – including coal, bauxite, iron ore, copper and precious metals – reserves of natural gas, and a large fisheries potential.) Approximately 12 million Mozambicans, out of a population of 15 million, are involved in agriculture and, FRELIMO believes, only this sector can raise a surplus to rouse other sectors. Increasing agricultural production is deemed an urgent matter because the exodus of Portuguese settlers in 1975 and 1976 caused a sharp decline in yields on commercial farms, and Mozambique faces critical shortages of food.

At independence, FRELIMO established twin vehicles of rural development: state farms and communal villages. Formed from large plantations abandoned by the Portuguese, the 2000 state farms were meant to be the major source of the country's food supply. They were seen as the key to reducing food imports and to generating surpluses that could be invested in peasant production. While allocating considerable funding to the state farms, the government made a political decision not to transfer appreciable resources to the communal villages. The purpose of the village scheme, which in 1982 encompassed almost two million people (nearly 15 per cent of the population), was to regroup peasants in order to provide them with social services and to increase production. FRELIMO has called on residents to work together to build temporary housing, which is subsequently upgraded through self-help projects and small loans tendered by the state. In theory, the villages will achieve self-sufficiency and serve as the poles of socio-economic development throughout the countryside.

The resettlement strategy has been most successful in the Limpopo Basin and the Zambezi Valley, the areas devastated in February 1977 and March 1978 by the worst floods of this century in Mozambique, impelling thousands of peasants to seek a new life. The pace has not been as fast elsewhere, and some peasants have returned to their former homelands. Let us see why and how FRELIMO has responded.

Peasants in Mozambique are in a different position from their counterparts in neighbouring Tanzania or other African countries. Flying over rural Mozambique, one is struck by the diffuse distribution of the population. Peasants are generally grouped in clusters of two or three homesteads. They do not form medium-sized communities as in the adjacent countries, and neither do they live in large villages as do peasants in parts of West Africa. This pattern reflects a combination of historical factors: ancient wars among ethnic groups and the slave trade depopulated certain provinces; the Portuguese dispersed Mozambicans to prevent resistance to colonial rule; and many Mozambicans fled to avoid serving as contract labourers, often preferring to work in South Africa and Rhodesia. Today distinct difficulties are encountered in the formation of communal villages, owing partially to the isolation and narrowness of rural existence which is quite pronounced even in comparison to other African countries.

Inspired by its success with the techniques of education and persuasion, FRELIMO encourages peasants to attend meetings whose task is to examine Portuguese colonialism and the objectives of FRELIMO. Organizers explain that the current form of settlement obstructs economic advancement and the provision of social services. Organizers review the fundamental principles of agricultural economics, showing concretely the prospect of improvement. Then when a village is formed, peasants from nearby areas are invited to visit, to see for themselves the material and social benefits of living and working together, including increased productivity, schools, clinics and bore holes for water.

In some cases, peasants are simply tired of authorities and of moving. In the former war zones in Tete Province, for example, the Portuguese army had shifted a large number of peasants into strategic hamlets and given them free food. Not only are these peasants unaccustomed to hard work, but they expect the post-colonial state to feed them too, and otherwise just want to be left alone. FRELIMO is not attempting to transfer them, and will continue to sponsor discussions until such time as the peasants take the initiative to move.

Whereas FRELIMO has emphasized voluntarism and persuasion, the structural problem of accumulation must still be solved. With few consumer goods to buy, peasants lack incentive to produce. Without consumer goods to stimulate surplus production, increased foreign exchange earnings are not forthcoming. Such features of the world economy as declining terms of trade for primary products and stiffening conditions for loans exacerbate the accumulation problem in independent Mozambique.

Meanwhile performance in the agricultural sector falls short of FRELIMO's expectations. Total production has clearly plummeted since 1975. Key cashew and sugar exports are down. At the beginning of the 1980s, Mozambique grew only about one-third of the food it consumed. Not only have food imports risen, but also the government has squandered precious foreign exchange. Heavy equipment for state farms has consumed the bulk of the funds budgeted for agricultural development.

FRELIMO made a mistake investing in the large state farms without supporting millions of family farmers. The peasants now produce little beyond subsistence. What explains the lack of goods on the market is a blend of historical factors, bad luck and FRELIMO's errors. More specifically, the crisis is directly related to capital flight, military raids by South Africa and the rebels it has sponsored, adverse weather and a misguided policy of high technology in an impoverished country.

Although FRELIMO has acknowledged such mistakes and has engaged in thoroughgoing self-criticism, it still must determine where a surplus is to be produced and how Mozambique will generate internal capital accumulation to finance industrial development.

Industrialization

Whereas FRELIMO views a viable agricultural sector as an essential element in its quest for socialism, it initially regarded heavy industry as the driving force of an advanced economy. In other words, Mozambique is officially committed to a completely different path from that plotted by Tanzania or the other countries in Africa. In the initial years after independence, industrial activities centred on recovery from acts of sabotage perpetrated by vindictive settlers and from the exodus of skilled labour. The goal, defined by the Third Congress of FRELIMO, was to restore 1973 levels of production by 1980. This was achieved in some sectors but not others.

A noteworthy development in industry was the formation of production councils in each enterprise. Their avowed purpose is to bridge the separation between immediate producers and control of the means of production. To this end, workers in the councils are encouraged to set production targets and play an active role in decision making. To take one example of this in practice, Belita

Clothes Factory in Beira, nationalized in 1975 when the owners fled, is now run by its workers. A production council comprising 43 elected members determines goals and procedures. Workers are further organized into teams of 10, each of which includes an elected leader and party stalwart. Employees grow their own rice and other food staples on the factory's farm, where they labour one day ($9\frac{1}{2}$ hours) per working week (which is $5\frac{1}{2}$ days long). They also participate in sports together, and attend literacy classes, which they requested, at Belita. Production levels and wages reportedly doubled within three years after independence. The extent to which the reorganization at this factory meets the broader goals of the country's development strategy is evident. Belita is more successful than most production units in Mozambique, and illustrates what FRELIMO is seeking to achieve.

To improve working conditions in factories and offices, FRELIMO established labour unions in 1983. The first union, the Organization of Mozambican Workers, draws upon the experiences of its fore-runner, the production councils. The objectives of the new structure are to increase worker participation and to improve the coordination of state power and workers' action both in the rural areas and urban factories. According to labour legislation, unions are responsible for protecting workers against health and safety hazards. Employers have a legal obligation to provide medical care and disability security. The law affirms that women have rights equal to those of men in the work-place. There is special provision for mothers, including 60 days of paid leave during or after pregnancy. While the legislation is laudable, one must investigate its implementation in ensuing years. At the time of writing, it is an open question whether Mozambique's unions will become bona fide organizations of civil society which defend the rights of workers or transmission belts of the state to secure domination over the working class.

One constraint in organizing the urban proletariat is the large wage differentials among industrial workers emanating from the colonial period and hiked in the wake of wildcat strikes in 1974. After independence, FRELIMO imposed wage ceilings in the public sector, but wages in the private sector remained higher and unrestricted. Building heavy industry is problematic, too, because even in compari-son to other parts of Africa the level of technology in Mozambique is very low. At the tea estates in Gúrùe, for instance, the Portuguese proprietor had not imported machinery directly from the UK, where it was manufactured, but purchased second-hand equipment from

Malawi and India. In any event, most operations at Gúrùe are manual, not automated. A tea factory in Mozambique staffed by 70–100 workers produces a yield equivalent to that of a factory in Kenya with a complement of 10.

In the short term, top priority is accorded to strengthening consumer industries and building agricultural-processing activities. The long-term goal is to develop transforming industries in order to reduce dependency on foreign imports and to expand exports. Thus the government is constructing textile plants, aluminium smelting facilities, a paper and pulp complex and an iron and steel mill. Planners envisage that many of the industrial projects will be placed in northern Mozambique, close to most of the country's raw materials and away from the axis in the south designed by colonialism and overshadowed by Johannesburg. But before Mozambique can forge ahead with new industrial units, more detailed information is needed about the country's resource base and about industrialization in neighbouring countries. Duplication must be avoided, and it is crucial for Mozambique to coordinate its industrialization strategy with those of Tanzania and Zambia.

Ties with the International Economy

In international economic relations, FRELIMO has charted a middle course between acquiescing to the situation it inherited from colonialism and rejecting established ties. Having professed a desire to expand economic dealings with countries of diverse orientations, Mozambique first had to decide how to deal with Rhodesia and South Africa. Maputo distinguished between them in principle in that the former was a colony and the latter is a sovereign country. Unwilling to tackle both minority regimes simultaneously, for to do so would have been economic suicide, FRELIMO initially challenged the more vulnerable of the two. Thus FRELIMO complied with UN sanctions, closing its border with Rhodesia in March 1976, forfeiting its lucrative transit-trade earnings and causing large-scale unemployment in the transport sector. According to UN figures, the direct financial cost to Mozambique of imposing sanctions was $550 million.

FRELIMO has repeatedly expressed its determination to end its dependence on South Africa, but it understands that it would be self-defeating to attempt an overnight divorce. In the short run Maputo and Pretoria still need each other. The long-run strategy for disengagement from South Africa is to build an independent home economy and to diversify international economic relationships. Thus the number of Mozambican mineworkers in the white redoubt tumbled from a peak of 115 000 in 1975 to less than 40 000 in 1983. FRELIMO wanted to cut back the supply of migrant labourers in the future. However, this decline is directly attributable to the decision of the mining industry to vary the countries of origin of foreign labour and to increase the size of the domestic contingent as well as to the South African government's desire to punish Mozambique. The effective abolition of the gold bonus, resulting from South Africa's revaluation of its gold reserves in 1978 in conjunction with an amendment to the Articles of Agreement of the IMF, deprived Mozambique of its major source of foreign-exchange earnings. To compensate for a portion of this drop in revenue, post-colonial Mozambique has raised the price of Cabora Bassa energy above the amount agreed to by Lisbon and Pretoria, and jacked up the harbour dues charged to South African shippers.

FRELIMO views international assistance as a stop-gap measure to unshackle itself from the colonial heritage. Burdens arising from the application of sanctions and numerous costly attacks on Mozambique by South Africa and rebel forces have compounded Mozambique's need for aid. Special UN and Commonwealth funds, though substantially less than the amount requested, have met a portion of the country's stated requirements.

Maputo carefully considered the question of membership in international institutions. After enlisting in the African Development Bank, Mozambique joined the Lomé Convention of the European Economic Community and applied to COMECON, but was rejected. Whether Mozambique would benefit by entering the World Bank group has been more controversial. Mozambique is eager to receive the concessionary terms that the International Development Association, the soft-loan arm of the World Bank, offers to the least developed countries, but initially balked at the idea of joining its Bretton Woods partner, the IMF, as a precondition. Having noted the influential role which the fund plays in such countries as Portugal and Zaire, FRELIMO is wary of its enormous power. The IMF aroused suspicions in Mozambique when it urged Zambia to reopen its border with Rhodesia, and FRELIMO knows that the fund typically insists on conditions – reductions in government spending, especially in the social sector – that are inconsistent with the goals which FRELIMO seeks to achieve. Nonetheless in 1984 Mozambique, beset by widespread drought, direct South African military raids and attacks by insurgents, joined the IMF in a move calculated to draw multiple sources of external capital.

On balance, Mozambique's strategy for overcoming under-development is bold, yet tentative and perilous; by its very nature it injects profound tensions into the social fabric and engenders a distinctive set of problems.

ACHIEVEMENTS AND DIFFICULTIES

Emerging from the experience in the liberated areas, there is a deeply ingrained tradition of collective leadership in Mozambique (and this is what sets Mozambique apart from many other Third World countries). The nucleus of FRELIMO is compact and united. It is a highly cautious group with a penchant for protocol and painstaking analysis. A visitor may be surprised to find revolutionary *élan* and old-world formality bound up together in socialist Mozambique. FRELIMO's orderly style, too, distinguishes it from revolutionary groups whose political gatherings are, by comparison, impassioned and undisciplined.

The strength of FRELIMO is a theoretically sophisticated leadership combined with solid grass-roots support. The only challenges to its rule were an abortive military uprising in December 1975, which did not receive civilian backing, and protracted attacks by the MNR (also known by its Portuguese acronym, RENAMO), a contra movement that has operated in every province in Mozambique. Those at the top combine intellectual acumen with practical skills. They take a long view of politics, approaching it historically in the light of broad social forces and movements, not as an arena of personalities and episodes.

FRELIMO's leaders came to theory through diverse routes. President Machel, an intellectual driving force in his own right, was a former medical orderly and military commander. He explained that his first political education came 'not from the writing in books. Not from reading Marx and Lenin. But seeing my father forced to grow cotton for the Portuguese and going with him to the market where he was forced to sell it at a low price – much lower than the white Portuguese cotton grower.' It was practical experience in Mozambique as a wage earner, Machel added, which impelled him to seek theoretical understanding. Following Machel's death in a plane crash in 1986, FRELIMO's Central Committee elected Mozambique's next president, Joaquim Chissano, the foreign minister since 1975 and prime minister in the nine-month transitional period leading to independence in 1975. In colonial Mozambique, he was one of the first black students enrolled at Maputo's principal secondary school and received a scholarship to study medicine in Lisbon. He later went to Paris, where he met Marcelino dos Santos and helped to unite rival Mozambican liberation movements. Dos Santos, now a high-ranking official in FRELIMO, is an accomplished poet who spent many years in the circle around Jean-Paul Sartre in France. Dos Santos is widely regarded as a profound thinker and an eloquent speaker.

How deep in FRELIMO does this sophistication run? A major weakness in Mozambique is an acute shortage of middle cadres. There are simply too few qualified lieutenants to maintain links between top and bottom. This gap developed because Portugal denied Africans access to higher education and because FRELIMO expected the anti-colonial war to last longer than it did. The upshot is that not enough intermediaries were trained. It may be hypothesized – though conjecture cannot change history – that if the war had continued for a longer period, the liberated areas would have been extended to other provinces (but at the cost of much greater loss of life) and FRELIMO could have had a stronger foundation for building socialism.

To provide scientific and technical personnel capable of organizing a modern society, Mozambique is upgrading its educational system. At the time of independence, fewer than 30 Mozambican Africans were represented in an enrolment of over 2000 at Lourenço Marques University. Even today there are too few secondary school graduates to fill the places for full-time students at Eduardo Mondlane University, as it is now called. Some of the students at the university, particularly the sons and daughters of settlers, are products of the old elitist system, and still embrace the values transmitted by their former teachers.

Mozambique, like many underdeveloped countries, requires foreign technicians to meet its immediate manpower needs. At least half of the 240 000 Portuguese in Mozambique quit the country by independence day, and perhaps 90 per cent of them departed within the next year. The government has recruited *cooperantes*, contractees from Eastern and Western countries who are technically skilled and politically committed, to fill the void. In addition, in March 1980 the government invited former residents to return to Mozambique and invest in the private sector. Small businesses, shops, garages and so on, which had come under state control when their owners had gone into exile, were placed in private hands. For some commentators abroad, this policy signified a retreat from socialism. Other observers held that at independence, the state, faced with sabotage, abandonment and the lack of know-how by Mozambicans, had no choice except to fill the vacuum in commerce and transportation; it was not surprising that, in the first five years of independence, the state had failed at these tasks. In the light of this admitted failure, Machel counselled that the state should concentrate on the priority sectors (production and social activities such as education, health and housing), rather than on selling matches, eggs or a dress.

Another question worth considering is whether FRELIMO is confining resolution of major issues within too narrow a circle. Practical matters, especially social programmes, are aired in public, but little is known about divergent views among the leaders. Axiomatic to democratic centralism is the tenet that various oppositions engage each other until a decision is reached. The case for competition among different tendencies is predicated on the belief that a broad exchange of perspectives is essential to party life and that a battle between rival positions is the surest way to rectify mistakes.

While FRELIMO is free of schisms, it is not a monolith. FRELIMO is by no means a homogeneous whole. It is inconceivable that Mozambique's senior officials would be of one voice: by definition a front is a broad coalition of elements. Further, since a transition to socialism subsumes two or more modes of production and spurs conflict between them, divergent interests necessarily clash and the contention is reflected in a political party.

FRELIMO has tempered internal criticism because attempts by external forces – the minority regime in Rhodesia, former Portuguese settlers, ex-PIDE (secret police) agents and MNR forces – to discredit and divide independent Mozambique have been relentless. Also, endless discussion of practical matters within the broad FRELIMO framework deflects fragmentation, and distinct currents simply have not formed. It is important to note in this regard that a pitched battle between two factions was fought out at the Second Congress in 1968, when the socialists who are now in power defeated a moderate nationalist group. Thus a centrist FRELIMO position and collective leadership exist today since sharp differences were resolved in the turbulent pre-independence years.

A third area of concern is the proliferation of state bureaucracies caused by socialist development. This problem is inherent in the transition period owing to the rapid expansion of the state sector and the simultaneous contraction of the private sector. The question, however, at bottom is one of social relations rather than scale. Bureaucratism is a qualitative condition, in this case the awkward combination of archaic Lusitanian practices and modern revolutionary zeal, in part old ideological habits and the persistence of state structures from the colonial era, and in part a manifest inability to match political cohesion with administrative cohesion. More concretely, coordination among ministries is inadequate and liaison between Maputo and the provincial capitals is weak. While top officials in the bureaucracy are competent, the standard drops perceptibly as one moves down the ladder. At the middle and lower levels youthful exuberance is admirable, but executive experience and pronounced capacity are lacking. Only a small coterie of extremely hard-working officials is willing or able to make decisions, and those people are saddled with countless minor issues. Thus the Council of Ministers handles routine matters which are managed by an intermediate echelon in other countries. Candidly expressing his concern for this problem President Machel, in a key speech, spoke out against corruption in the State Housing Corporation. He also made a series of unannounced visits to ports, warehouses, factories and clinics, exposing red tape and black marketeering.

The formation of a National Planning Commission in July 1977 was a step in the right direction, provided that it ultimately helps to streamline the bureaucracy. In 1979 the commission formulated a detailed ten-year economic plan for the 1980s. Implementation has been delayed by the combined effect of natural calamities, the dire situation created by the insurgency, a shortage of trained personnel and lack of statistical data. At present fashioning the planning mechanism is an urgent matter; investment choices must be clearly defined; and finely honed techniques and specific timetables need to be worked out. Even though converting a market economy into a planned economy is a protracted and complex process, if planners in Mozambique do not act with dispatch to simplify and refine administrative procedures, it is an open question whether, to use Antonio Gramsci's felicitous phrase, democratic centralism will degenerate into bureaucratic centralism.

A closely related danger is repression. Remember that in a transitional period, fragments of both capitalism and socialism coexist. The attempt to achieve socialism is punctuated by a constant struggle between the sector of the economy subject to the law of value and the planned state sector. The capitalist classes typically favour restoration, and seek succour in foreign countries for the *ancien régime* or another form of reaction. They do not stand idly by as their interests are thwarted, but instigate capital flight and perhaps sabotage. Under these conditions it is exceedingly difficult for the fledgeling economy to meet the weight of economic ills. Then coercion may be used again, this time against disgruntled labourers as well as against the bourgeoisie, to ensure the survival of the new order. Coercion is not aberrant but endemic to the transition to socialism. In the long run, there remains the problem of how to disembowel the repressive apparatus so that democratic socialism can flourish.

The question of repression has been raised by top government officials in Mozambique. In a 1981 address to the nation, President Machel reported on official corruption and abuses of power by the police, members of security forces, the army and people's militia. The president called for popular control so that the perpetrators could be punished. The director of Machava Prison was dismissed over complaints of mistreatment of prisoners. In the face of alleged police brutality, several police and security officers were similarly dismissed. FRELIMO made clear its intention to continue to invite popular redress to stem repression.

This pledge is evidently discounted by the US government, particularly in the Department of State's human rights reports. For example, the 1983 report on Mozambique, required by Congress, concluded that FRELIMO has made important advances in health care and education. Despite the Marxist regime's differences with the Catholic Church, FRELIMO has loosened control of organized religion. However, the State Department did express reservations about restrictions on political participation imposed by a 'small cadre of senior officials' which dominates all political activity in the country. Acknowledging that there are no indications of government-sponsored disappearances, the State Department noted the practice of detention without trial in 'reeducation centers' where political prisoners and other 'anti-social elements' are interned.

FRELIMO's case is that the colonial power was not blacklisted for violations of human rights; meanwhile, the liberation movement led the campaign to attain the main right to political independence. After the ravages of colonialism, FRELIMO contends, it is no wonder that Mozambique's urban centres – like Saigon (today Ho Chi Minh City) – were replete with prostitutes, drug addicts and smugglers. Since the days of Portuguese rule, the government has in fact closed prisons, not opened them, according to FRELIMO.

By most accounts, the major problems are that the length of time that one must spend in a centre is unspecified and that the administrative system for releasing those who have completed the re-education process is faulty, causing some inmates to serve for indeterminate periods. Medical personnel who have treated inmates reveal that conditions are grim, but then again peasant life in Mozambique is spartan, and facilities in the centres are no worse than those in rural areas generally. The crux of the matter is that Mozambique's re-education centres must be considered in the national context as well as in relation to universal standards of human rights. Quite clearly, Western standards are not a historical alternative for Mozambique. A balance must be struck between a cultural-relativist position and a position which would establish global norms. One yardstick is the situation that obtained before independence and the direction in which Mozambique is moving. That Mozambicans readily dissent and are encouraged to voice criticism in the single party, but not in public, is certainly a step forward from what they knew under colonialism. Limits on open and democratic participation are attributable both to Mozambique's internal dynamics and external pressure on the country.

THE GLOBAL CONTEXT

The Subcontinent

In foreign affairs, one of Mozambique's avowed goals is to strengthen relations with neighbouring countries and the liberation armies of southern Africa. As a front-line state, Mozambique has sought to coordinate its foreign policy with those of Angola, Botswana, Tanzania, Zambia and Zimbabwe. It is cordial to other African countries whose political systems differ from its own. The adjacent kingdom of Swaziland, for example, is landlocked and relies on port facilities at Maputo.

To build their economies and to reduce dependence on South Africa, Mozambique and eight other states (Angola, Botswana, Lesotho, Malawi, Swaziland, Tanzania, Zambia and Zimbabwe) formed the SADCC in 1979. Each member state was placed in charge of a functional aspect of cooperation. SADCC delegated responsibility for transportation and communications, perhaps the most important part of the plan, to Mozambique. Over 40 per cent of the SADCC budget has been earmarked for expenditure in Mozambique.

Meanwhile Mozambique has sacrificed dearly in giving material and political support to southern African refugees and liberation movements. It hosted training camps for guerrillas belonging to the Zimbabwe African National Union wing of the Patriotic Front but has not permitted military preparation within its borders against apartheid rule. In all likelihood, repeated bombing raids emanating from Rhodesia were meant to pressure Machel to embrace Cuba and the Soviet Union and thus draw in the US against the insurgents. But Mozambique refused to allow the Salisbury regime to internationalize the war in any way. Maputo's policy was to encourage the Patriotic Front to enter into negotiations while keeping up the armed struggle. FRELIMO understands, too, the differences between conditions in Mozambique which led to the demise of colonialism and those in other territories which impede a transfer of power. It believes that the impetus for change must be internal. The Mozambique Revolution is not for export.

For Maputo the critical policy issue is its relationship with Pretoria. After the collapse of settler domination in Rhodesia, South Africa targeted two military attacks on ANC residences in Matola, a suburb of Maputo, and nurtured the MNR. Created by the white authorities in Rhodesia, the MNR comprises a medley of former members of the Portuguese colonial army, secret police and defectors from the liberation struggle. The insurgents have terrorized the civilian population, destroyed numerous development projects and fundamentally disrupted transportation and communications facilities. The MNR offers no ideology or governmental alternative to FRELIMO. Its only goal is destruction.

The costs of the destabilization campaign are enormous. In January 1984, the government of Mozambique assessed its losses since 1975 at $556 million ($6 million above the UN estimate) for destruction and sanctions during the Rhodesian war; and since Zimbabwe's independence in 1980, $3463 million for South Africa's reduction in railway-port traffic and mine-worker recruitment, plus $333 million for direct military aggression by South Africa and the MNR. Against a GNP of $2.05 billion in 1982, a seven-year loss of $4.02 billion is a staggering sum.

Under heavy military and economic stress, in March 1984 Mozambique signed the Nkomati Accord, a non-aggression pact with South Africa. Pretoria and a beleaguered Maputo agreed to halt insurgents from attacking the other country and to pave the way for improved economic relations. Not only did South Africa want to seal the Mozambican border, but also the *modus vivendi* was an opportunity to split the coalition of front-line states and liberation movements.

Military ventures have cost South Africa dearly: over $1 billion per year for the occupation of Namibia alone. In 1983 and 1984, the overall financial pressure mounted appreciably: a sagging gold price, a severe drought, poor export performance and mushrooming government spending in several sectors. Yet another source of pressure was the Reagan administration's needs during an election year. President Reagan's aides advised him to achieve diplomatic victories in order to silence critics who accused the administration of militarizing foreign policy in such Third World areas as Lebanon, Grenada and Central America. Hence the US urged South Africa – described by Mr Reagan as 'a friendly country that has stood behind us in every war we've ever fought' – to tone down its response to the furies of guerrilla warfare. Since South Africa could not have a more supportive president in the White House, it was in Pretoria's interest to comply with Washington's overture.

For war-ravaged Mozambique, striking the Nkomati bargain was a matter of survival. Not only has the country been battered by the MNR, but also a prolonged drought caused widespread starvation. What Maputo hoped to gain by calling off the undeclared war is time. The diplomatic setback suffered by FRELIMO was supposed to be the means to give Mozambique its first chance to implement its development strategy in times of peace. However, Pretoria continued to train and support the MNR in violation of its pact with Maputo. In the post-Nkomati period, the conflict with rebel forces has worsened and is draining Mozambique's economy.

The Socialist Countries

Just as it did before independence, Mozambique is now steering clear of the Sino–Soviet dispute and keeping its foreign policy options open. That FRELIMO is cultivating relations with a variety of nations can be best understood by examining how its foreign policy has evolved.

In the colonial era, external support played a secondary role, and FRELIMO relied on its own resources because it had to do so. For one thing, unlike Algeria or Vietnam, Mozambique could not count on an anti-war movement in the metropole to constitute an effective force, for the fascist government in Lisbon would not permit dissent. To be sure, in the early 1960s some cadres, including Machel, received military training in Algeria. But confidence in its own ability led FRELIMO to reject an offer of Cuban aid in 1967. Mozambique turned down Cuba's overture after Che Guevara, who had been instructing guerrillas and leading them in battle in the Congo from April to December 1965, travelled to Dar es Salaam and met representatives of FRELIMO. Guevara and FRELIMO differed in their theories of guerrilla warfare. Whereas Guevara advocated that a military campaign carried directly to select localities would trigger a spontaneous peasant uprising, FRELIMO believed in the efficacy of long, patient spadework by political activists as a precondition for a mass-based, armed insurrection. In FRELIMO's view, Guevara was trying to impose theories emerging from Latin America without understanding the concrete conditions that obtained in Mozambique. FRELIMO's own theorists repudiated any attempt to generalize lessons from another context.

By independence, Mozambique and Cuba revived their friendship. The two countries share an Afro–Iberian heritage and speak similar languages; both have experienced foreign rule and fought to cast off the yoke of colonialism. In the late 1970s, there were between 650 and 750 Cubans in Mozambique, a presence far smaller than that in Angola and Ethiopia. At the same time, Maputo maintains cordial but strict relations with Moscow. Shortly after independence, in a now celebrated incident, Chissano, who was then foreign minister, publicly rebuked the Soviet ambassador by saying that Moscow should not attempt to pressure Maputo. Chissano was referring to an attempt by the Soviets to persuade FRELIMO to grant them military base facilities, which Mozambique has steadfastly refused to do. Nonetheless Mozambique, embracing the ideal of socialist cooperation, voted against the UN resolution deploring Soviet intervention in Afghanistan.

Compared to Soviet technical assistance in Mozambique, the level of Chinese activity is modest. Sino–Mozambican relations are grounded in the amity established before independence, when Beijing provided instructors and engineers for FRELIMO's training camps. The independence of Mozambique came at a time when China was sorting out its own problems, as well as supporting the FNLA and UNITA in Angola. Unlike Mozambique, which backed the Popular Movement for the Liberation of Angola exclusively, China promoted a united front. In fact their differing policies in Angola do not explain contemporary relations between the two countries, as is sometimes argued, for China and Tanzania also took opposing stands on Angola but their relations did not suffer. Nor did Mozambique's condemnation of China's invasion of Vietnam lead to a general deterioration of relations between Maputo and Beijing. In recent years, there has been a general congruence in policy changes. Both Mozambique and China have introduced market reforms and have moved towards an accommodation with the US.

In seeking technical assistance, FRELIMO believes that the experiences of socialist countries are closer to Mozambique's than are those of the capitalist world. But FRELIMO has found that problems arise in negotiations with all countries, the socialist nations included. Technical assistance is a contractual agreement, and skill and expertise are required to set the terms. FRELIMO is now acquiring that specialized, practical knowledge. Meanwhile, it has made mistakes and some aspects of the agreements that have been signed are not favourable to Mozambique. Particular difficulties are encountered in obtaining technical assistance from planned economies, since orders must be placed well in advance of the date of delivery; the exigencies of Mozambique's needs frequently do not permit proper anticipation and accurate timing.

The West

Friendship with the socialist world has not precluded cooperation with the West. FRELIMO recognizes that Western countries themselves have divergent policies, and distinguishes among distinct interests within each country. It deeply appreciates the generous assistance tendered by the Nordic states and the concessionary terms granted by the Netherlands and Britain. But until 1982, Mozambique spurned West Germany because Bonn insisted that an agreement include reference to West Berlin. FRELIMO wanted to maintain its ties with East Germany. Mozambique subsequently concluded a food aid agreement with West Germany, tacitly acknowledging Bonn's interpretation of the status of Berlin. Maputo also contracted with Lisbon to purchase small arms, an emblem of reapprochement with the former colonizer and member of the North Atlantic Treaty Organization.

In its relations with the US, FRELIMO believes that powerful groups – senators who supported the Byrd Amendment, which allowed chrome imports from Rhodesia, and American executives investing in South Africa – are opposed to Mozambique, and that there are also good friends, both in the government and among the public, who are working for ends which are consonant with those of Mozambique.

Strategically Washington tries to protect and promote US interests, mainly through South African channels. The aim is to avert confrontation with the Soviet Union and Cuba in southern Africa. Politically, Washington seeks to enlist FRELIMO's assistance in assuring an orderly transition to majority rule, anchored to moderate leadership in Namibia and South Africa. Economically, the US strives to secure a hospitable climate for American firms in the subcontinent. US bilateral interests in Mozambique are nonetheless minimal; private investment is nominal. Although trade with the US is important to Mozambique, this commerce does not figure seriously in the American global pattern.

The US is the leading customer for Mozambican sugar and cashews, two of the country's major exports. Mozambique maintains a favourable balance of trade with the US: $28.5 million in exports versus $20 million in imports in 1983, a marked decline in the surplus from the previous year and a modest overall level to be sure.

To woo US capital, Mozambique organized an investors' conference in New York. General Tire of Akron, Ohio, holds a small equity share in a Mozambican tyre factory, Mabor de Moçambique. And in 1983, the government negotiated contracts with Exxon and Shell for exploration of petroleum and natural gas. Other US firms, however, hesitated to operate in Mozambique. Potential investors have criticized Mozambique's Decree Law 18/77 of April 1977, the legislation governing foreign investment, for its lack of specificity. Equally problematic, they say, is the paucity of detailed information about the economy.

Of greater concern to Washington than the bilateral stakes in Mozambique is keeping the economies of its Western allies buoyant. Although US trade with and investment in South Africa are marginal to the vitality of the American economy, the sturdiness of the South African economy is directly related to the strength or weakness of Britain. It has not passed unnoticed in Washington that events in South Africa could seriously damage the British economy, which in turn would have major repercussions in the US.

To understand more fully US–Mozambican relations, recall that at independence, in 1975, the policy of President Gerald Ford and Secretary of State Henry Kissinger was to bring an FNLA–UNITA coalition to power in Angola. Mozambique rightly feared activity by the CIA within its own borders. It is not surprising in the light of this history that the US was not invited to independence-day celebrations. However, some individuals such as Senator Richard Clark and Congressman Charles Diggs attended in their private capacities and not as representatives of the government. On that day, after the US Consulate had closed down and was no longer accredited in Mozambique, the former US Consul-General flew the American flag. Added to what FRELIMO regarded as a clear affront was the consistently bad press given to Mozambique in 1975 and 1976 by American journalists, who often picked up their information in Johannesburg or Salisbury from embittered Portuguese *émigrés* and conveyed stereotyped images of 'rigid Marxism' in Mozambique.

In Lusaka on 27 April 1976, Kissinger unveiled what he touted as a completely new US policy in southern Africa based upon acceptance of the principle of majority rule for Rhodesia and Namibia and a commitment to end 'institutionalized inequality' in South Africa. The Lusaka speech conceded that the US had made mistakes in the subcontinent, a reference to American support for Portugal in the colonial war. The Secretary of State offered $12.5 million in assistance to Mozambique. He sought to engage Machel in settling the Rhodesia issue, but FRELIMO doubted Kissinger's sincerity and scotched his bid to visit Maputo.

The Senate balked at Kissinger's promise to give Mozambique a $10 million grant and $4.7 million in food aid – the figure was raised from the original one of $2.5 million – on the grounds that the country was communist, that assistance would contribute to terrorism and that three Americans were imprisoned in Mozambique. In addition to barring development assistance (though not food aid) to Mozambique, the US lobbied against loans to Maputo by the African Development Bank. The Ford administration sought to fulfil its prior commitment (of April 1976) to Mozambique, but failed to lift the Congressional ban.

After the Nixon–Ford years, FRELIMO was pleased by signs of change in Washington, such as Ambassador Andrew Young's statement that Cubans are a 'stabilizing influence' in Angola and the repeal of the Byrd Amendment in 1977. FRELIMO looked favourably on participation by the US in the UN Conference in Support of the Peoples of Zimbabwe and Namibia, held in Maputo in 1977, but disapproved of Young's performance there, especially his patronizing refrain about his own experience in the US civil rights movement. Mozambicans do not want an American solution to African problems. They do not regard the legislative techniques used to accomplish integration in the American South in the 1950s and 1960s as a model for ending colonialism and accelerating the liberation struggle in southern Africa in the 1980s.

In a sharp reversal of policy, in December 1980 Secretary of State Edmund Muskie certified that aid to Mozambique would be in the foreign policy interests of the US. While planning was under way for aid to Mozambique, FRELIMO exposed CIA activity and charged that the agency had relayed information which facilitated a South African raid on Maputo. As a result, the US suspended plans to provide development assistance.

Section 512 of the Foreign Assistance and Related Programs Appropriation Act, 1982, specifically bans development assistance to Mozambique, unless the president favours a waiver of the prohibition and reports to the Congress that furnishing assistance would further the interests of the US. In 1982–3 there was talk in the Congress of enacting new legislation to supersede Section 512 and to place Mozambique in the category sometimes facetiously referred to as 'the hit list'. Set forth in Section 513 of the Act, the hit list comprises the countries proscribed from development assistance under any conditions: Libya, Iraq, South Yemen, Angola, Cambodia, Cuba, Laos, Vietnam and Syria.

In the spring of 1984, however, President Reagan and the Congress waived the ban on development assistance to Mozambique and approved commencement of bilateral programmes. Technical assistance, commodity import programmes and the provision of small agricultural equipment are envisaged. In 1984 the Reagan administration allocated more emergency food aid to Mozambique than to any other African country. Weighing into the decision to reverse US aid policy were the emergency situation in Mozambique, FRELIMO's overtures to US investors, the easing of relations between Maputo and Pretoria and, perhaps, to some small extent the administration's desire to moderate its hard-line image during an election year.

PROBLEMS AND PROMISES

To sketch out the main points, Mozambique has encountered an awesome combination of natural and social disasters: the departure of most of the country's skilled personnel, a consequent decline in productivity and critical food shortages, the return of thousands of exiles and migrant workers, the loss of the major source of foreign exchange (South African gold paid for black labour), a drop in world prices for the nation's agricultural exports, costly border wars, an insurgency backed by a powerful neighbour and severe floods followed by drought and famine. Even if Mozambique is not converted into a Bantustan (a black ethnic reserve dependent on South Africa), it will still face objective conditions which allow an opposition movement to gain momentum. Perhaps the main problem is that in a climate of insecurity, when the survival of the state is at stake, security, not development, necessarily takes precedence. The diversion of resources from development to war drains the economy. Under such conditions accumulation for productive investment is not yet a reality. By all accounts the economy is in a state of acute distress.

Yet several vital factors which foster development may be found in Mozambique. Among them are substantial reserves of arable land, vast mineral wealth, abundant energy and determined leadership with popular support. To get out from under, the government must not only offer a vision, a conception of a better and an achievable future, but also unmistakably demonstrate the capacity to execute its plan. Mired in particularly abject conditions of underdevelopment, Mozambique, more than most countries, has produced a clear idea of how to move the country ahead. Mozambique's leaders are free of the fallacies enshrined in prevalent ideologies of accumulation, and have replaced them with a strategy of development which blends theoretical understanding and their own indigenous experience. In executing this strategy they have mobilized the masses and have by and large relied on voluntarism: coercion is the exception.

To be sure, Mozambique's strategy of accumulation is highly egalitarian, but attempting to implement it under inauspicious circumstances has undermined FRELIMO's legitimacy. Specifically, the state has had to intervene massively in the economy, even in sectors where its capacity is notably lacking. When intervention in the accumulation process does not work, the state loses legitimacy. The difficulty is that without other sources of accumulation, the state seeks to extract surplus from the peasant sector. At the same time, those who hold state power also rely on the peasants as their source of political support. How long the peasants will wilfully play this dual role is hard to say. Even if Mozambique's dilemmas overwhelm FRELIMO, elements of its strategy for escaping underdevelopment could suggest important lessons for the Third World.

Part IV
The Big Question

8 What Works in the Third World?

When an acquaintance in Dar es Salaam invited me to visit her family in an *ujamaa* (communal) village, I jumped at the opportunity. Hemmed in by the Indian Ocean on one side and groves of mango trees, coconut palms, jackfruit (which resemble large basketballs) and the infamous durian plant, with its succulent pulp of fine flavour but skunk-like smell, on the other, we careered southwards for 100 miles along a washboard road to the Rufiji River. There we navigated inland over a series of dirt paths until we reached our destination: numerous clumps of neat, thatched huts nestled astride the river bank.

Following a warm welcome, an exchange of gifts and a tour of the village, an elder recounted the origins of the community, whose inhabitants had been moved to this location by the government. Asked whether she preferred to live in this communal setting or her former domicile, this wizened old woman merely shrugged. My question was too iffy for her taste. Perhaps she thought that such hypothetical matters may interest naive Westerners, but given the practicalities of the struggle to scratch a jagged patch of earth for subsistence, why bother?

Later, after establishing some rapport, I asked whether force had been used to transfer rural dwellers to this site. 'No,' she said. 'Was the army present?' 'Yes.' 'Did the soldiers carry guns?' 'Yes,' she nodded knowingly. The implications were obvious, and so the conclusion drawn by various commentators was that, as in other resettlement schemes in Africa, the threat to use force was as effective as actual coercive practices.

The homegrown rice served for lunch was delicious, much better than the American and Chinese varieties in the supermarkets in Dar es Salaam, where Tanzanian rice, an export item, was not available. Malnutrition was quite apparent, for the children's bellies protruded markedly. But how could the sons and daughters of fishermen suffer from protein deficiency? The villagers explained that the government had decreed that the catch was for export only and that violators faced stiff penalties.

We were surrounded by another vital source of protein, an abundance of cashew trees. The villagers said that cashews, too, were an export product. I then inquired about the price paid to the producer of cashew nuts: 'One shilling and five cents per kilo'. Asked if they knew the retail price for the same grade of cashews in Dar es Salaam, the villagers replied unhesitatingly, '20 shillings per kilo'. Allowing for transportation costs and processing the crop, is a producer price pegged at about 5 per cent of retail justified? Or is a relatively large surplus being siphoned? If the latter is the case, are the peasants truly aware of the mechanisms of exploitation?

The matter was resolved when I inquired about the extent of communal farming versus family farming. I was told to look yonder at the communal plot. 'We till those fields only on the days when government officials make their rounds. Otherwise, we produce for our own families, just as we've always farmed.'

The conflict of interest between the direct producers and the state is unmistakable. Resistance is passive, not active. Although political consciousness is rudimentary, the peasants share a notion that they do not wish to feed the consumption habits of a voracious bureaucratic bourgeoisie. Such is the blockage that restrains productive forces in underdeveloped countries.

Whether this blockage can be cleared is controversial. The argument to be developed in this chapter is basically positive. Some things do, or can, work in the Third World. After all, there are glimmers of hope in a number of countries once viewed as sunk in despair. Twenty years ago who would have thought that India's teeming population could learn to feed itself? Bangladesh, widely touted as a basket case two decades ago, is approaching self-sufficiency in the production of food. China, which suffered a devastating famine in the late 1950s and early 1960s, is today an exporter of food. Not that these countries have found the master-key to escape underdevelopment, but guiding principles illuminate the way out from under. These principles do not offer an instantaneous solution. There are no magic remedies. However, the lack of a simple solution does not lessen the urgency of the problem. With wide variations within and among regions of the world, there is a continuing need to adapt these principles to changing realities, learning from experience as we proceed.

WHAT IS THE PROBLEM?

In the final analysis, underdevelopment is a historical process cul-minating in the stifling of human creativity, skill and self-confidence. It is maintained by the exterior squeeze of a changing world economy and the inner functioning of an exploitative social system. In the context of dependent capitalism, this process is reproduced and extended by such structures as international agencies, foreign aid, technology, multinational corporations and banks. This course of affairs is not inevitable, however. These same structures may play an entirely different role, contributing to a country's accumulation fund, if an alliance with broad support for a fundamental transformation of the political economy controls state power.

To head off any misunderstanding, it must be clear that for both liberals *and* Marxists, the principles that elucidate the way out from under cannot be abstracted from human agency. By human agency, I mean a general capacity for moral personality and individuality. Liberals and Marxists agree that the abolition of systematically oppressive conditions – slavery, serfdom and contemporary dis-criminatory practices – is a prerequisite for the realization of human good, including individuality. The main liberal claim is that a legiti-mate political regime must facilitate individual agency, and vice versa. Likewise, Marxists defend such broad judgments about human good, but locate the basis of inequality in a mode of production. Just as slavery is at odds with modern individuality, 'wage slavery' conflicts with self-respect. Marxism's moral claims stem from a notion of social agency. The central argument rests on an appreciation of a society which nurtures social individuality. It is structure that sets the limits and defines the range of individual choice. But beyond modern liberal and Marxist arguments, the deeper issue concerns the proper ratio between structural determination and human will, which permits intervention in social change. One should obviously avoid a one-sided analysis resting exclusively on structural determination or voluntar-ism. Very concretely, the question of agency is tied into such matters as the relationship between foreign technology and inventiveness in the Third World, moral and material incentives as spurs to productiv-ity, and what drives individuals to join liberation movements.

To take this one step further, the problem of underdevelopment is two-fold, having both subjective and objective dimensions. As far as the subjective aspect is concerned, fatalism and defeatism on the one

hand and a naive romanticism on the other obscure possible solutions
to the hard core of underdevelopment.

Fatalist attitudes precipitated by economic frustration can be illustrated briefly in Mauritania, a country whose external debt exceeds its
GNP, and home to an ancient desert culture that may already be
dead. Today the desert is void of what was one of the world's largest
nomadic populations and their tireless caravans. Before the drought
hit, Mauritanian farmers were growing enough sorghum, wheat and
other grains to feed the country. In 1984, however, they furnished
only 6 per cent of total food consumption. Two-thirds of what
Mauritanians ate represented donations, causing concern about
creating dependencies on foreign aid.

The recent drought in Mauritania intensified hunger, but the
problem has been several centuries in the making. Desertification
goes back at least 2500 years, and humans have increasingly compounded the impact of atmospheric pressure systems. When the
Sahara was mostly grass, and parts of North Africa were the bread-
basket of the Roman Empire, large caravans began to denude the
prairies of trees used for firewood. In the eighteenth and nineteenth
centuries, Europeans destroyed the gum forests along Mauritania's
coast (now part of the desert). Boundaries drawn by the colonizers
made it difficult for nomads to migrate to greener pastures in neighbouring lands, and overgrazing has quickened the pace of the spreading sand.

Efforts to stave off the desert, which is expanding at about four
miles per year, are not succeeding. The construction of dams is costly
for a country whose principal export, iron ore, fetches low prices on
the world market. Fishing has potential, but Mauritania lacks a
navy to patrol against foreign fleets exploiting its marine resources.
Officials have authorized oil exploration, without result.

For Mauritanians, disillusionment is an obstacle to surmounting
underdevelopment. Asked to foretell his future, a herdsman balked,
saying there is only one option: 'In sha Allah' ('Whatever God wills)'.
Reflecting the attitude with which these wanderers have coped with
the drought and desert, he added, 'We are ready for whatever comes
from God.'

Many Westerners share that man's pessimism, which is fed by a
coterie of artists and writers. Prominent among them is V. S. Naipaul,
himself a gifted spinner of tales about 'half-made societies', flawed
civilizations, places where 'the West is packing its boxes, waiting for
the helicopters'. The theme that ignites Naipaul's pages is the area of

darkness just outside town; in the trail of colonial empires, always the bush remains. By 'the bush', Naipaul means ignorance and obscurity: contempt for what he left behind in his native Trinidad, dubbed 'a place with no history', where his grandfather, a Brahmin from Uttar Pradesh, India, had immigrated as an indentured worker.

Naipaul, the winner of every major literary award in Britain, and often described as quite possibly the greatest author writing in the English language today, claims that he is not a spokesman for anything. He sees little hope for a Third World whose future and past travel along parallel paths in the present. In over 20 books of fiction and non-fiction, a psyche that has internalized colonial values reflects a pervading pessimism, a dark vision.

Naipaul's view of Third World politics is uncomplicated: a quick-sand of corruption, decadence and vice. Without liberal democracy, non-Western countries can have only barbarism. There is no middle ground, no alternative route. Naipaul's description of Argentina is a prototypical account of all Third World countries: 'Politics reflect a society and a land. Argentina is a land of plunder, a new land, virtually peopled in this century. It remains a land to be plundered, and its politics can be nothing but the politics of plunder.' Something must be wrong with all 23 million Argentines. Evidently the missing element is Western laws, achievements and aspirations. As with Africa, life in this Third World setting, clearly an unnecessary country, is but a graveyard. 'You were in a place where the future had come and gone.'

Whereas Naipaul's odysseys made by people who become aliens in other civilizations point to a basic political conservatism and forlorn acceptance of the status quo, Frantz Fanon, another West Indian writer, also an interpreter of the mind of the colonized, provided one of the most powerful inspirations to revolutionaries in our time. Born in Martinique in 1925, Fanon studied medicine in France, fought in the French army during the Second World War, and served as a psychiatrist in Algeria, where he experienced revolution as both observer and participant. He died young of leukaemia at the age of 36, before the independence of Algeria. One can only conjecture about the impact of the masterly books which this prolific author would have composed had he lived longer.

For Fanon Third World countries, not social classes, are the agents of change, and psychological factors are the main movers of history. Racism should be understood not as an independent phenomenon but rather as 'the most visible element of a given structure'; it is an ideological weapon accompanying domination. The underlying dynamic is decolonization, an inherently violent phenomenon; the nation is consecrated in blood, and the creative power of revolution is purified by the flame of violence. According to Fanon, it is repressive violence which breeds revolutionary violence. When the electrodes are put to the genitals, the native becomes a man and can no longer afford random or purely destructive outlets for repressed aggression. Thus violence often occurs as collective behaviour, allowing for the possibility of a social transformation. Far from celebrating violence as an end, Fanon looks to its transcendence by a new and higher social order.

When nationalist movements in Algeria, Angola and elsewhere were developing into social revolutions, Fanon, unlike many of his contemporaries, warned about emerging forms of dictatorship and about the pitfalls of the one-party state, potentially a shield for private ambition. The bourgeoisie in the Third World, he claimed, is not the inventive, productive, entrepreneurial class of the *Communist Manifesto* but a parasitical stratum profiting from a subordinate economy. Also, the proletariat in the Third World is not a suppressed class but a privileged element with much more to lose than its chains. In Fanon's view, the key sources of revolutionary change are the peasantry and the lumpenproletariat, both natural allies of urban intellectuals.

Fanon's writings contain more fresh ideas on the nature of colonialism than any piece of scholarly literature and have had an enormous impact on the thinking of revolutionaries, but his notion of spontaneous peasant revolution is an emblem of Third World romanticism, a harbinger of the misguided optimism of some of his followers. Fanon's idea of spontaneous peasant revolution is a myth. It does not account sufficiently for political organization, ideological work and discipline: who is to mobilize the peasantry? And how is political consciousness to be formed? Moreover, Fanon's emphasis on psychology and the individual give short shrift to history, especially in regard to the lumpenproletariat. He offers not a single example of revolutionary dynamism among the lumpenproletariat, and fails to distinguish between the hard-core lumpen and the urban proletariat. While many of Fanon's prophecies concerning decolonization and settler rule have come to pass, his programme was vague and incomplete.

Both aspects of the subjective barrier to identifying possible solutions to underdevelopment – a cornucopia of defeatism and romanticism – resonate among contemporary Western observers. In the pregnant controversies over whether the developed countries have a moral responsibility to share resources with the Third World, one option sometimes advocated, though under a different banner, is *triage*, a term first used in reference to the treatment of the most severely wounded during the First World War. Given scarce medical resources, those who could not be easily saved were allowed to die. Such hard-nosed politics is epitomized in the 'lifeboat ethics' of the biologist, Garrett Hardin. Those nations which cannot make it on their own should not be admitted to the lifeboat of the rich lest we lose our safety factor and threaten our own, as well as our progeny's, survival. The ethics of the lifeboat mean that sharing is impossible; the downtrodden should be permitted to go their own way even if innocent people die, harsh though that may be. As far as Hardin is concerned, there are no solutions for Third World countries. Let them wallow in the mire.

In contrast to this gloomy interpretation, contemporary romanticism offers a sanguine view, typically expressed in the form of triumphalism. The most recent revolution is regarded as a beacon for the Third World. Sympathetic observers sometimes celebrate the promise of liberation struggles without taking a hard look at the enormous structural problems endemic to post-revolutionary societies.

Leaving aside prevalent attitudes and cultural expressions, the objective nature of underdevelopment seems, at first sight, straightforward. Today almost 20 per cent of the global population resides in the advanced countries. But as population skyrockets in the rest of the world – while holding steady in the developed countries – the proportion cocooned in the advanced nations is expected to tumble to only 4 per cent by the middle of the twenty-first century. Unless the poor become richer, 24 out of every 25 people will then be living in poverty.

In fact the persistent and mounting problem in the global political economy cannot be solved by economic growth: a large portion of the world's population is unable to get a foothold in an expanding economy. In some cases, slow economic growth over past decades has worsened the ravages of underdevelopment, and rapid economic growth is not a cure.

On a world scale, there is a fundamental disproportion between accumulation, a profitable rate of return, and consumption. Burgeoning economies require increasing capital accumulation, but the current reality is insufficient profit and irrational disposal of surplus.

Capitalist accumulation is not only a ceaseless process, but also a necessary, albeit insufficient, condition for augmenting the value of labour. In another historical era in Western Europe, capitalist accumulation became the spearhead of social development. The process differs in the contemporary Third World because the internationalization of capital entails redirecting a large share of surplus, the margin between production and consumption, from one sphere to another sphere of the global economy. For a capitalist economy to become self-sustaining, the bulk of the surplus must be invested in domestic production, not transferred to other countries. Yet this transfer from underdeveloped countries to the advanced capitalist world is a hallmark of international economic relations. Although capital flows in both directions, a startling feature of the global economy, according to a World Bank announcement, was a $22 billion transfer from the Third World to the advanced countries in 1985. This figure reached a staggering level because interest payments and amortization of debts exceeded total new loans and investment.

Typically, capitalist economies in the underdeveloped world are extroverted organisms. Their outward orientation invites control by international capital. Foreign investors have the opportunity to shape domestic economies, including decisions over where equipment and inputs are purchased, what commodities are produced, how production is organized, where and to whom goods are sold and so forth. The net effect is usually to mould internal social relations to conform to the existing social structure of accumulation.

This process dovetails nicely with the use of foreign aid as an instrument of policy. Increasingly the aid policies of certain Western governments are biased against state intervention in Third World economies and favour the expansion of the private sector. Notwithstanding the emphasis upon strengthening dominant socio-economic structures, much aid is earmarked for the military in the Third World.

The build-up of arms in fact often contributes to political instability. Official development assistance is only a small fraction of world spending on armaments. Total aid comes to a mere $20 billion per year, while overall military expenditure is around $450 billion per year. As observers as far apart as the Brandt commissioners and Fidel Castro have argued, if only a small share of the money, effort and research devoted to military uses were ploughed into development, the availability of resources would make the prospects of the Third World look much brighter. Rather, at present, each dollar sunk into military procurement may be viewed as an opportunity lost in development expenditure. Military dollars lessen security, for the war economy makes the world poorer.

Long before it became fashionable for contemporary conservatives to argue that military spending is beneficial to the economy, conventional Keynesians claimed that the Second World War had remedied the problems of the depression of the 1930s. In 1940, John Maynard Keynes declared that it seemed 'politically impossible for a capitalist democracy to organize expenditure on the scale necessary to make the grand experiments which would prove my case – except in war conditions'. This was to reupholster the old Marxist argument that war is a capitalist means to realize surplus value through military production.

In fact, military expenditure yields fewer jobs per dollar than does most American business, according to the US Bureau of Labour Statistics. Military contracts bid up the cost of skilled labour and provide employment for expensive, technical people. Moreover, a large ratio of military to civilian capital formation saps the civilian economy. Extensive research by Seymour Melman shows that, in the US, capital is increasingly concentrated in a fund that renders no goods useful for consumption or further production. Hence by 1977, out of every $100 of new (producers') fixed capital formation, the US applied $46 to the military economy. In Japan, the figure was $3.70. Melman observes that the investment of Japan's capital in productive economic growth is no doubt a major feature of that resource-poor country's amazing industrial surge.

In recent years, the advanced countries have helped to pay for the huge cost of developing their new weapons systems through arms sales to the Third World. Export sales have offset the rising cost of weapons research and have enabled Western and Eastern countries to go on producing sophisticated equipment for their own forces. The spiral of arms sales to the Third World has been astounding: an increase in current dollars from $19.7 billion in 1975 to $45.6 billion in 1980 (US Library of Congress figures). Some Third World countries, most notably Brazil, have developed arms industries of their own and compete with the big suppliers – the US, the Soviet Union and France – in the export market.

The key problem for Brazil, like other underdeveloped countries, however, is not guns and bombs or population. By what grotesque priorities could this troubled nation give birth to a billion dollar a year arms industry? Fundamentally, the challenge of underdevelopment is how to both reduce structures of inequality and build an accumulation fund. Some state capitalist countries, such as Brazil, have achieved higher levels of capital formation and have broadened social inequalities. The structural changes made by countries aiming at socialism have lessened social inequalities but have not fuelled the accumulation process. Herein lies the dilemma.

WHAT HAS BEEN TRIED?

To say that all Third World countries are tottering is to overlook the differences. Some strategies have provided the material base to expand the domestic economy.

The 'miracle' of *unfettered capitalist accumulation* was built on a fundamental premise: a transfer of wealth from the needy to the well-to-do would power the engines of capital accumulation. The dominant strata would then take the economy in tow, expanding the stock of machinery and other productive equipment. Putting this strategy to work, with a nod toward regulating the worst abuses by foreign capital, Brazil became a paragon of rapid industrialization. The gains of dependent capitalist development were quite considerable during the 1970s. Pushing for growth at any cost, Brazil erected numerous factories, attained profit rates that were among the world's highest, and offered stable right-wing rule.

Brazil is one of a galaxy of Third World countries, called NICs, which are often touted as a viable model for the rest of the Third World. NICs are defined as a category of countries in which the per capita income exceeds, and the share of the manufacturing sector in the gross domestic product surpasses, a given statistical threshold. It is also the particular position that a country has reached in the international division of labour which denotes its status as a NIC. Usually, a NIC specializes in the production of intermediate, manufactured goods.

The main features of the NIC model are maximum integration in the world economy, especially through multinational corporations, direct *state-led* industrialization, low wages and a predisposition for authoritarian rule. What has facilitated industrialization in these countries is a substantial domestic market or access to one, heavy investment in economic infrastructure and large-scale external aid.

To what extent is the NIC model an exemplar for the rest of the Third World? Since the category itself glosses over the diversity among countries, it can only be employed with great caution. First, there are at least two groups of NICs. The so-called modern Japans, or 'Asian Gang of Four' (Hong Kong, Taiwan, Singapore and South Korea) maintain fairly open economies. They differ in essential respects from the large Latin American NICs, namely Brazil, Mexico and Argentina. One major difference is that extensive land reforms in South Korea and Taiwan contributed importantly to relative income equality. No significant land reforms have been undertaken in Brazil and Argentina, countries with a highly skewed pattern of income distribution. Following reforms in Mexico during the 1930s, there has been a reconcentration of landholdings and worsening inequality. Additionally, unlike the comparatively open economies of Asia, the Latin American NICs have at times applied extremely high tariffs. To safeguard infant industries, powerful local entrepreneurs have sought to maintain a high level of protection.

Within each group, the divergence is striking. Most especially, as city states and entrepôts without a substantial agricultural sector, Hong Kong and Singapore are unlike the other NICs. Also, the resource endowments and historical trajectories marking the various national experiences are quite dissimilar. For example, Taiwan's success in the export of manufactures was accompanied by such factors as the proximity of the Japanese market, massive aid, the presence of a formidable entrepreneurial class and favourable trade conditions arising from the Vietnam War. In comparison, Brazil has drawn on its huge domestic market, large population and vast resources. In the case of South Korea, it is clear that a broad range of import-substitution industries was developed and that various non-price measures were used to promote export industries.

The chances of these experiences being repeated in most parts of the Third World – in, say, sub-Saharan Africa – are slim. As global capitalism continues to expand, some national economies, much like competing firms, will emerge as winners and others as losers. The international division of labour will change: what is to prevent Brazil and England from switching places? But at least for the duration of the twentieth century, the underlying system will remain in place. There is no reason to think that the NIC model illuminates the way to wipe out underdevelopment. Even for the handful of NICs whose economies grow rapidly, questions can be raised about repressive state structures and the social cost of export-oriented industrialization, which is not inconsiderable. The Latin American NICs suffer severely from the debt burden and have adopted austerity measures that ride on the back of the poor, whereas the other economic parvenus, the modern Japans, are still stalked by the broad social and political problems characteristic of the Third World.

The term 'modern Japans', increasingly in currency, is a misnomer. The Japanese pattern of independent capitalism is not an option for contemporary Third World countries. For one thing, Japan was never a colony. In 1638 the Tokugawa Shogunate adopted a policy of strict seclusion, and the imperialist powers became ensnarled in rivalries in more lucrative areas, especially the Middle East, India and China. The heyday of imperialism was punctuated by such explosions as the Crimean War beginning in 1854 and the US Civil War, tying down the Western powers. Lacking raw materials of its own, Japan sought to keep foreign capital at arm's length until the state could control it. Unequal treaties were imposed, however. Gradually poking out from isolation, Japan proscribed the importation of luxury items and cheap consumer goods, purchasing instead raw materials and capital goods for industry. Subsequently, Japan launched a sustained drive to become the world's third leading economy, engaging in military adventurism and colonial conquest, rapidly expanding its munitions and export industries. Japan itself emerged as an imperialist power: a course that obviously is not the way for Third World countries to surmount underdevelopment.

Is there evidence to commend the policy of seclusion as a prelude to a high rate of capital accumulation? Not in the few instances when _go-it-alone strategies_ have been tried in the context of underdevelopment.

A telling case is Burma where, following the 1962 *coup d'état*, a technocratic–bureaucratic regime backed by the military proclaimed autonomy as its goal, but ever since it has run into a tangle of political and economic troubles, especially maintaining minimal living standards, with the parallel or subterranean economy posing an intractable problem. The attempt of Pol Pot's Kampuchea to withdraw from the world economy was more extreme. Rusticating the urban population and striving for an agriculturally self-sufficient rural order, the regime relied on repression and provoked the ire of many other countries, as the Vietnamese invasion showed.

As we have seen, China under Mao also inaugurated an inward-looking policy. Faced with US intransigence and Soviet pressure to toe the line, Beijing cut itself off from Moscow, its major source of foreign investment and aid, largely excluding itself from the world economy. The burden of accumulation weighed heavily on the agricultural sector. Peasants were required to hold consumption near subsistence, and the state soaked up the rest of what they produced as surplus for investment. Yet a labyrinthine bureaucracy hindered productive investment, ritualized participation and discouraged peasant initiative. With a new class in the making, China's inward-looking strategy could not attain requisite levels of accumulation for mounting an industrial base. Clearly a country cannot forge an autonomous path to development merely by breaking its external ties and initiating central planning. The way out from under lies not in seclusion, but in the maelstrom of international relations.

More concretely, if it is agreed that autarchy is not the solution, the task becomes one of participating in the global political economy while simultaneously undercutting a contradictory world order. More purposefully than most countries, Mozambique has tried this route. Drawing on substantial support from the popular classes, FRELIMO adopted a strategy of *managing the ties of dependency* inherited from colonialism.

Before waging a frontal assault on the colonial state, the liberation movement wrought multidimensional changes in civil society. FRELIMO accorded priority to establishing alternative norms and laying new social foundations in zones wrested from Portuguese colonialism. The goal was to assign socio-economic content to political independence. Rejecting various formulas for decolonization handed down by Lisbon, FRELIMO accelerated the moral–intellectual phase of revolutionary development and fostered a different cultural–ideological milieu. This entailed a 'war of position', a concept developed by Gramsci to refer to the erosion of the ideological bonds which cement the ruling class and popular classes, a process that paves the way for winning control of the state apparatus. The essential element in challenging the dominant hegemony is the moulding of a new culture and innovative institutions within the old order.

From independence in 1975 to the Third Congress in 1977, FRELIMO opened a debate on how to conquer underdevelopment. FRELIMO envisaged state farms and communal villages, along with heavy industry, as the locomotives which would pull the economy out of the rut that it was left in by almost 500 years of Portuguese colonialism. In the international sphere, Maputo sought to diversify its economic relationships, reducing some forms of dependence on South Africa, developing ties with the socialist world and selectively engaging in trade and securing assistance from the West.

The period between the Third Congress in 1977 and the Fourth Congress in 1983 was one of trial and error. The experimentation entailed both a refinement of the development strategy and serious mistakes. FRELIMO invested substantially in large state enterprises without supporting millions of family farmers. Heavy industry remained but an intention. In foreign economic relations, FRELIMO sought more actively to engage foreign capital, yet until 1984 withstood pressure to conform to the policies of international monetary institutions. FRELIMO paid a heavy price for its blunders during this period: a substantial demobilization of the peasantry. After the Fourth Congress, FRELIMO attempted to correct its errors by ploughing capital into family farms, the source of livelihood for 80 per cent of the population. Top priority was assigned to building agricultural processing industries and to producing more consumer goods. The long-term goal is to develop transforming industries in order to reduce dependence on foreign imports and also to expand selected export sectors. FRELIMO is trying to create an independent home economy while encouraging private investors to help meet the country's immediate objectives.

Thus in terms of social relations, though not economic accomplishments, the significance of the Mozambique Revolution is that it is a prototype of building counter-hegemony in the Third World. Vast modifications in society have taken place under the surface of formal institutions. In the wake of the ideological erosion of the old order, Mozambicans developed an acute understanding of their predicament and conceptualized the requirements for transforming an underdeveloped economy in utter shambles at the time of independence. Unlike most countries in the Third World, Mozambique has relied primarily on local initiative. But all of this political and theoretical activity failed to produce the economic bonanza FRELIMO had hoped for. The debilitating effects of Mozambique's security situation and the drought in the 1980s, along with ill-advised attempts to implement the development strategy, are a stoppage that FRELIMO has been unable to clear out.

The South African-based insurgency is not primarily the result of FRELIMO's inept policies. It stems from Pretoria's fear of a democratic socialist alternative on its border. But as long as Mozambique is pummelled by its powerful neighbour, it can offer no definitive evidence that a tightrope approach to the global political economy is the path to success. This strategy is more promise than positive performance. Like other underdeveloped countries, Mozambique is still saddled with the problem of how to gather an investable surplus for productive investment.

Having noted the merits and shortcomings of strategies that embrace, repudiate and balance ties with global capitalism, let me underscore the principal trade-offs in terms of who benefits and who loses. Evidently, the way to achieve the highest rate of economic growth is to embrace global capitalism. But maximum integration in world capitalism heightens a national economy's vulnerability to external forces. Moreover, economic gains for the few do not demonstrably help to overcome underdevelopment, understood as removal of the blockage that warps a social structure and prevents the interests of the majority from becoming increasingly dominant. Whereas disengagement from global capitalism does not generate substantial economic growth, this strategy permits the redistribution of wealth and an egalitarian ethic. This is not to overlook the ascendancy of a new bureaucratic class, anchoring another set of rigidities in the social system. The strategy of selectively managing the ties of dependency also has a poor record for economic growth, yet there is much to commend this programme. It entails subordinating external capital to the requirements of the local economy and providing channels, both internal and external, for the creation of an accumulation fund. It also involves submerging the blockage in the social structure and repeatedly adopting measures to stop abuses of power. Without being laudatory or blind to the costly mistakes of policy makers, it is evident that a strategy of balancing the ties of dependency offers a clear chance for productive economic growth on terms consistent with the needs and aspirations of ordinary people.

Objections to this strategy arise from critics who believe that it invites foreign intervention. It is true that a country which adopts a balancing strategy becomes a tempting target for foreign intervention, but surely the sceptics' argument is a classic case of blaming the victim. Another challenge, one with much substance, is the call for evidence of successful economic performance. Setting aside debates over the yardsticks for measuring economic performance, I have already shown that in at least one instance where this balancing act has been tried, the economy is almost prostrate. Nonetheless, flawed execution of a strategy does not invalidate its underlying concept. If we were living in the late fifteenth century in Western Europe, how could one 'prove' the potential of capitalism, whose stirrings did not match the achievements of feudal units of production? Evidence would have been altogether lacking.

Looking to the future, some writers flatly assert that independent national development is impossible within the world capitalist system, thus making development strategies a delusion, at least within that system. Those who advance this position hold that, to be meaningful, anti-systemic change must come at the world level. Others argue that practical development strategies can be enhanced through a Third World partnership based on self-help. It is claimed that in these hazardous times, collective self-reliance is the key to Third World power.

Emblematic of the potential for concerted action by Third World producers was the hike in the price of oil from $1 per barrel in 1970 to over $30 per barrel in 1980. The drama of how Colonel Muammar el-Qaddafi of Libya successfully spearheaded a rebellion against big oil, while too convoluted to rehearse fully here, is instructive in its implications for a collective response to the problems of under-development. Setting the stage for OPEC's price explosion, the inter-national oil companies exercised a near monopoly and disciplined any producer who tried to evade their price controls. The major oil companies, or Seven Sisters (Exxon, Gulf, Texaco, Mobil, Socal, British Petroleum and Shell), derived enormous profit from their power to determine where and how much to prospect, set levels of production, command refinery technology, dominate world markets, and share pipelines and tankers among themselves.

Playing the independent oil companies against the majors, Qaddafi employed a divide-and-rule strategy against those who had practised it so successfully in the past. The Libyan leader singled out Occidental as his first target, abruptly cutting the amount of oil the company could produce. There was no love lost been Occidental and the Seven Sisters. Not only did the other oil companies refuse to defend Occidental, but the US government chose this inopportune moment to abandon its long-standing support for the companies. Relative to Western Europe and Japan, the US stood to gain from the boost in oil prices because it is only partially dependent on imported oil. Moreover, financial reinforcement for the Shah and the Saudis would strengthen two regional powerhouses allied to the US. As the syndi-cated columnist Jack Anderson and his colleague James Boyd point out in their book, *Fiasco*, President Nixon and his National Security Adviser, later Secretary of State, Henry Kissinger, maintained that the oil companies should accede to Qaddafi's demands, Nixon because of his reluctance to expand domestic production and Kis-singer because he was wrapped up in his grand strategy of high politics. The Nixon administration's oil expert, Jim Akins, advised that the oil companies had no reason to fear that a leapfrog effect would take place among the oil-producing countries. With this avenue of opposition to Qaddafi closed, the oil companies acquiesced in the negotiations. The oil companies lost what they had fought for decades to win: control over production. The die was cast for a group of underdeveloped countries, organized since 1960 into OPEC, to initiate the era of high-cost oil and to raise the spectre of producer power.

Indeed, the short period of OPEC power was a genuine challenge to the international order. In the 1980s, however, the price of oil cascaded into a depressed market. Although OPEC succeeded for a time in jacking up oil prices, it never effectively regulated production. The organization set production quotas, but it had no means of enforcing them. Conflicting interests among its 13 members have hobbled common action. A territorial dispute between Iraq and Kuwait and the protracted war between Iraq and Iran are but two of the rivalries that have bedevilled the organization. Other measures of OPEC's diversity include geography, population and average per capita income. Algeria is more than 30 times the size of the UAE. Indonesians number about 150 million, over 700 times the population of Qatar. And the average per capita income in the UAE is $26 850, in excess of 60 times that of Indonesia.

OPEC's problem has not only been how to share a dwindling market among its members, but how to organize itself to share demand with non-OPEC exporters. Mexico and the North Sea producers have the option of offering cheaper oil. To adjust to a reduced market, some OPEC members have moved increasingly from pumping oil to processing and marketing it.

Indeed, as control of oil reserves shifted, the companies became service outfits, specializing in high technology activities, buying smaller energy concerns and purchasing big businesses outside the energy field. And as oil prices rose in the period from 1973 to 1980, energy company profits soared. Critics accused American oil companies and OPEC nations of being allies in profiteering, placing the heaviest burden on ordinary people in both the advanced countries and the non-oil-exporting countries in the Third World. Notwithstanding the phenomenal run-up in oil prices, the gains for producer countries were primarily at the state level; there is little evidence to suggest that the mass of people in the OPEC countries benefited from the boom.

Underdeveloped countries cannot, through their producers' associations, capture the bulk of the surplus from the sale of their resources because they lack a common identity of interests and a monopoly of key minerals. OPEC, with less than half of the world's oil output, is an assembly of producers, not a cartel whose members are bound to act in unison.

A cartel implies massive concentrated power. In the second half of the twentieth century, its activities are tightly coordinated and backed by government and other concerns. Failure to comply with the cartel's policy means that enforcement action will be taken. By this definition, the underdeveloped countries are faced with what amounts to a creditors' cartel.

Not only do private lending institutions command vast resources, but the banks concert their policies and protect each other through cross-default clauses: a declaration of default against one bank in effect trips an automatic pronouncement against others, ensuring joint action by creditors in many countries. Private banks are bolstered by their governments, the IMF and the World Bank. A break with these lending institutions would be likely to cause the cessation of all international credit, thus cutting off trade with foreign countries.

Can a debtors' cartel exercise reverse leverage over the creditors' cartel? In Cuba, Fidel Castro has called for a suspension of all debt by Latin American countries. In Peru, President Alan García Peréz unilaterally set a limit – 10 per cent of annual export earnings – on the debt service his nation will pay foreigners.

Threatened by the debt bomb, Western bankers are moving swiftly to prevent the superdebtors from ganging up on them. The Westerners seek to separate Mexico and Brazil from the rest of the pack. These two countries owe over two-thirds of the total Latin debt and more than one-third of the debt of all underdeveloped countries. Hence Jacques de Larosière, managing director of the IMF, reportedly informed Mexico that it would receive easier terms than other debtors for putting its economic house in order. Similarly, Walter B. Wriston, a confidant of President Reagan, told Brazil that it, too, would receive favoured treatment for complying with prescribed policy. Guarding their options, the big banks are buying up Brazilian debt notes from the smaller banks, which are more likely to knuckle under.

Additionally, lending countries can always play their trump card: the food weapon as a means to enforce financial discipline. After all, most countries are borrowing in order to eat. Debt repudiation is unlikely as long as creditors can impose famine as a penalty for violating the rules of the international financial system.

Many borrowing countries are in fact in arrears on their debt payments, but all parties tiptoe around the term 'default', preferring instead euphemisms like 'rescheduled agreements' and 'stretchouts'. Insolvent borrowers obviously do not have the economic wherewithal to pay, and their governments would find it politically suicidal to try to do so. Therefore, as Celso Furtado has argued, the only way to avoid a showdown between debtors and lenders is for the private international banks to strike a deal with their central banks. If Western governments do alleviate the burden of the debt, they will defuse the worst aspects of the present crisis. But the system that produced the debt crisis in the first place will remain intact, with the majority of the world's population still ravaged by ingrown structures of underdevelopment.

WHAT HAS BEEN LEARNT?

If it is by no means self-evident that tried national strategies of development and tested forms of international action point the way out from under, what general lessons can be derived from a sometimes diffuse and contradictory experience in the Third World? Although there are no ready-made formulas for overcoming underdevelopment, it would be wrong to muddle through with improvised solutions. The task is to identify principles which can be adapted to varied conditions.

The first step is to recognize that *Third World countries cannot break the structures of underdevelopment by relying on the impulses generated in the heartlands of world capitalism.* The stimulus cannot come from the advanced capitalist countries, although elements within those countries may play an important role in the struggle. Closely related, one impulse that reinforces underdevelopment and strengthens world capitalism is an export-promotion strategy in the Third World.

The establishment of export platforms for Third World industrialization is but one aspect of a historical process rooted in the economic crisis of the 1930s and accelerated after the Second World War. In that wrenching realignment of the international division of labour, underdeveloped countries began to assemble and manufacture industrial goods. The advanced countries have increasingly focused on the service sector, particularly banking and insurance, and high-technology, speciality products such as seamless pipe for the oil industry and alloys for the aerospace industry. Meanwhile, underdeveloped countries continue to supply commodites for the West, but now the Third World provides low-technology products that it can make cheaply. In this two-tier system of world production, large ratios of underdeveloped countries' manufacturing activities are within the province of foreign affiliates of multinational corporations. Since this contemporary version of an export-oriented industrialization strategy accentuates reliance on external market forces, and thus widens the gulf between domestic production and local consumption, it is not the answer to the problem of underdevelopment.

The second lesson is that *it is possible to set limits to exploitation*. Underdeveloped countries are not suspended in a state of torpor, and by learning from experience along the way, they can embark on a purposeful course to reduce the outflow of surplus and to redirect it for social needs. Although specific policy proposals would take us too far afield, it may be useful to offer some guidelines for practical action.

With the redeployment of industrial activities from the advanced to the underdeveloped countries, the old international division of labour is a dead letter. Underdeveloped countries now compete with the advanced countries in some sectors. For example, six producers – Brazil, Argentina, Venezuela, Mexico, Taiwan and South Korea – became exporters of basic steel when their new-found capacity outstripped domestic demand. South Korea's state-of-the-art steel mill, designed and built by Japan, has stirred resentment in Tokyo, where steel makers plead that the world market is already overclogged and that the government should adopt a policy of import protection. Their counterparts in the West have switched to increasingly sophisticated products, conceding basic steel making to cheaper producers. Some analysts thus see a growing symbiosis between enterprises in the advanced and underdeveloped countries.

The emerging international division of labour does not, however, include thoroughgoing redeployment of scientific and technological activities. Most Third World countries are passive users, relay agents and imitators in international production. Creative capacity in the accumulation process continues to be concentrated in the advanced countries. At issue are not only resources but also resourcefulness. Inventions are less important than inventiveness. Indigenous, innovative capacity goes to the heart of releasing human energies, which is the essence of development.

In the drive to develop an innovative capacity, Third World producers can take effective measures to curb multinational corporations – entities with no inherent interest in advancing indigenous scientific potential in host countries – and to assert greater control over the home economy. Health care is one sector in which such action is essential. The vast majority of the population in the Third World urgently needs drugs for disease control and primary medical care; the lack of these drugs is an important constraint on development. Research carried out by multinational pharmaceuticals is not geared to the development of tropical drugs for diseases predominant in the Third World. Their resources are directed instead to the production of 'me-too drugs', goods similar to existing ones. These goods are produced not primarily to improve health care but to boost a firm's market share and profit margins.

In the face of the drug companies' enormous market power, most Third World countries have appeared helpless; however, Cuba's challenge to the pharmaceuticals suggests the type of limits that may be placed on exploitation. Before the revolution, the Cuban drug market was unregulated, with little coordination among government agencies. In 1958, imports represented 80 per cent of Cuba's drug supply. However, by 1980, domestic drug production met 81 per cent of local needs.

The government vested responsibility for the procurement and distribution of drugs in one agency, the Ministry of Public Health. The ministry established a national formulary guide, which identifies the drugs deemed essential and their active ingredients. Only drugs listed in this guide may enter the country, reducing the inflow from 20 000 registered medicinal products in 1962 to 689 products in 1979. Next, the ministry launched facilities to manufacture, test and carry out research on pharmaceuticals. The research and development effort is centred on the health problems of Cuba, and allows for quality control and inspection of drugs purchased abroad. Special attention is given to the veracity of advertising claims and safety hazards.

The government also created MediCuba, a foreign commerce enterprise that imports and exports all items in the medical–pharmaceutical sector. The sole link between the international and the local drug market, MediCuba is able to offer multinational corporations exclusive access. Rather than relying on the public tender system, MediCuba invites bids from select companies: those with proven performance as well as some new bidders. In discharging this responsibility, MediCuba gathers systematic data on previous purchases, including volume, delivery time, terms of payment and price fluctuations. MediCuba also collects information on the economic profile of suppliers, their production capacities, the latest technical and scientific advances and so on. In short, the Cuban strategy in the health care sector is not to try to get rid of multinational corporations but to harness them by changing the environment in which they operate.

By playing on the competition for foreign markets among enterprises which, according to capitalism's own inner logic, require expansion, underdeveloped countries can turn adversity to advantage. The first measure is to empanel a centralized agency to regulate the procurement and distribution of goods. This should not be a bureaucratic jungle where the economically fit thrive; safeguards are required to prevent undemocratic control, a profusion of state organs and corruption. An equally important measure is limiting access to the internal market. To perform both of these tasks in a shrewd and enlightened manner, policy makers must be apprised by a market intelligence system equipped to provide information on the latest developments in the advanced countries.

Building an innovative capacity and limiting the excesses of multinational corporations would, however, be an incomplete programme if the problem of foreign exchange flows were left to fester. The question that arises, therefore, is what are the alternatives for underdeveloped countries trying to cope with the awesome financial challenges confronting them while avoiding the pitfalls of IMF structural adjustments? Since the fund has few powers of enforcement apart from the withdrawal of its seal (and hence international credit), what is the touchstone of formulating a strategy which forges macro-balance and growth, equity in income distribution and national economic integration?

To answer this question, it is not necessary to start from scratch. A great deal can be learnt from the structural adjustment programme Tanzania negotiated with the IMF and the World Bank, some elements of which have been implemented and others abandoned. According to economist John Loxley, the alternative to the IMF model of accumulation centres on shifting purchasing power to rural areas after the provision of incentive goods up-country. In other words, goods would first be made available in the stores and then producer prices would rise. Subsequently, adjustment policies would be phased in after emergency balance of payments support became available. This would mean a postponement of most investment projects, with concentration instead on rehabilitation and the utilization of existing capacity. Equally important is increased efficiency in state agencies, allowing cooperatives and small traders to fill gaps, as well as a reduction in recurrent budget expenditure in the areas of administration and defence. The monies thereby released would be used to protect minimum wage earners through wage adjustment and basic needs expenditure.

Foreign exchange would be targeted on directly productive activities, especially essential goods, export earnings and recurrent budget revenue. This strategy entails lessening dependence on project aid and heightening state action to ensure coordination among aid donors. The task is to enhance both production and efficiency, while shunning shock treatment, all-out export promotion and an unbearable burden on poor urban workers.

Obviously one should not be utopian about this scheme's chances of success. Its feasibility hinges on the presence of a resolute political will within the state apparatus, the depth of support or opposition among local classes, the options for outside financing, and the danger of destabilization, whether the political riposte is threatened or real.

WHAT SHOULD BE DONE?

Since the structures of underdevelopment are varied and durable, it is not easy to identify concrete measures which can be adopted across the board. But analysis can eliminate snares and delusions as well as provide principles for escaping underdevelopment.

In a pioneering analysis, *Dependence and Transformation*, Clive Thomas (an economist from Guyana) broke new ground by showing that the situation in the Third World is far from hopeless and by outlining an alternative to orthodox doctrines of development. He argues that for underdeveloped countries the way out is to design a programme of 'dynamic convergence'. The core idea is to converge resource use, local demand and basic needs. There follow two 'iron laws of transformation: one is realigning resources and demand, and the other is realigning needs with demand. The overall objective is to harmonize the sectors of an economy so that indigenous peoples produce what they consume and consume what they produce. This principle would govern investment choices, encourage the growth of local technologies, suggest new possibilities for resource-based industries and point the way towards an integrated, self-sustaining economy.

Up to a point, Thomas is right about the need for a basic economic realignment. Yet in the absence of a strong political will among the masses, domestic resources would be used to meet local demand which, in turn, would be luxury goods coveted by the well-to-do. A country that adopted this strategy could wind up in the position of Brazil, with basic industries ringed by squalor and poverty. In other words, a strategy of dynamic convergence could lend support to technocratic, nationalist interests.

Thomas assumes that, if this strategy is to be implemented, a peasant-worker alliance must first control the state. This presupposition wishes away such vexing political questions as how do classes acquire political consciousness, organize themselves, manage the coalition, and grab state power? Clearly it is not sufficient to focus on productive forces and to evade the issue of social relations.

Restructuring is a continuous process both in the physical aspects of production and the social organization of production. In this context, restructuring means that the majority of direct producers comes to dominate the use of resources and state power. Although the forms will vary from country to country, thoroughgoing political participation is essential to continually orient the state to meet mass needs and to correct abuses of state power. The whole population must be involved in politics and the economy more equitably; without sustained mobilization, the development effort is bound to falter.

Countries where the peasant producers are dispersed, poor and unorganized face formidable obstacles to changing their historical trajectories. Since social structures constantly reproduce underdevelopment, a radical realignment means that we must rearrange human relationships. This is true both in our bonds with nature and in relations between the sexes. Official policy making is dominated by men, but most food in the Third World is produced by women, and yet the state allocates the lion's share of agricultural training, development assistance and rural credit to the male population.

Rehabilitation of a feeble agricultural sector is of major importance for development. So long as the advanced countries can wield the food weapon, the underdeveloped countries will be in a disadvantaged position. Within Third World economies, balance between the agricultural and industrial sectors is a prime necessity. Although there is no pat formula for striking an appropriate balance in each and every case, it is clear that pumping capital into economic infrastructure and neglecting productive activities is the wrong way to go.

In principle, building economic infrastructure can contribute enormously to development efforts by involving peasant producers more fully in the national economy. Nonetheless, in the context of a dependent capitalist economy, sinking investment into this sector may only eliminate impediments to the further penetration of foreign capital, facilitate the exploitation of cheap labour, and reduce the time of turnover of capital, which helps to enlarge the profits reaped by the few. If a key to escaping underdevelopment is to create value from nature's bounty, injecting capital into infrastructure is a means to enable men and women to extract more value; however, first the level of productivity must be raised.

Are the penetration of foreign capital and a policy that emphasizes the mobilization of domestic resources inherently contradictory? Inviting in external capital is risky, but a rupture with the global economy is not the way out of underdevelopment. In theory, it can be argued that foreign capital may help to build the state economy in a transitional period. Credit obtained from abroad increases the accumulation fund: it can provide technical equipment for the sectors of the economy governed by the planning principle, thereby augmenting the forces of production, and allows the state to employ workers who previously had no opportunity to take part in social production. This contribution, however, is contingent upon the conditions of capital. The interest paid must be less than the value created for accumulation. It is a question, too, of what obligations are made to international creditors and how credit is allocated within the domestic economy. Frequently, investment choices are compromises; the state's political resolve is typically weakened by the needs to placate or pay off local groups, play for time and even mortgage development projects to capitalist investors.

Within the confines of global capitalism, the Third World should do more than set limits to exploitation. *Underdeveloped countries must learn to exploit international market forces and to hitch them to the domestic economy*. If they are incapable of doing so, and even if they attain real economic growth, these countries would be in the position of runners on a track who can at best maintain their distance from the front of the pack by accelerating at about the same rate as the leaders. This analogy, I believe, correctly captures the reality at the state-to-state level but not at the people-to-people level, each of which requires a fundamental realignment.

The only way to get out from under is for the underdeveloped countries to *grasp the contradictions driving the global political economy*. An analytic capacity is essential to this task, but it is important to avoid being overly abstract or metaphysical about the contradictions in world capitalism. Structural analysis has its contextual limits.

At the risk of repeating a few points, let us again consider, from another perspective here, the action taken by Libya in the 1970s. Qaddafi cleverly manipulated inter-imperialist rivalries, the contradictions between Western states and multinational corporations and the conflicts among the enterprises themselves.

The conditions under which Qaddafi acted are essential to understanding the outcome: the continued closing of the Suez Canal forced oil tankers to take the long route from the Middle East's main energy reserves to Western Europe. Then, too, Syria's decision to shut down the Trans-Arabian pipeline denied half-a-million barrels of oil per day to Europe, previously supplied from Middle Eastern fields, thus heightening the West's reliance on Libyan oil. Western consumers were unable to use nearby oil fields because the legacy of imperialism ensnarled countries such as Nigeria and later Iran in internal turmoil.

The Libyan oil offensive followed a severe winter that had depleted most of Europe's reserve stock and had elevated demand. Compounding the problem of Western vulnerability was the shortage of tankers to carry oil from Saudi Arabia and other exporting countries to Europe and the US. Despite concern about consumer demand, Western governments were reluctant to rescue the oil companies, which had been widely regarded in the US as greedy profiteers, culminating in an anti-trust suit filed by the Justice Department and a civil suit during the Eisenhower years. As noted, host governments put pressure on the firms to comply with Libyan demands, and Qaddafi played the contradictions between the state and the multinational corporations to the hilt.

The oil companies were by no means a united group. Qaddafi adroitly managed the schism between the independent and major oil companies by choosing a small fry as his first target. He recognized that the independents were more dependent on Libyan oil than were their heavyweight counterparts, and calculated that their plight would not arouse much sympathy or support from the Seven Sisters. For their part, the Sisters viewed the independents as upstarts who were making foolish mistakes in business negotiations, jeopardizing the control over production and pricing long maintained by the seven majors, and threatening to upset the lucrative, vertically and horizontally integrated oil industry. Noting the ill will between these concerns, Qaddafi cut the amount of oil Occidental could produce, giving birth to the worldwide oil crisis of the 1970s.

Is this experience singular because of oil's uniqueness as a commodity? Whereas each case has its special features, Libya's action against the oil industry does highlight structural contradictions within global capitalism as well as the latitude for political manoeuvre. Libya's encounter with multinational enterprises illustrates both the possibilities and bounds of what can be accomplished under present historical conditions. Although a large increment of oil revenue flowed into OPEC coffers, these countries were unable to release human creativity and energies because of the rigidities clogging their social systems. From the point of view of democratic values, Qaddafi's dictatorship is repugnant; Libya's type of social system hinders meaningful international action and, perforce, blocks development. Western capitalists benefited handsomely from OPEC power because inflation reduces real wages, effectively redistributing income to the privileged segments of society. Far-reaching changes were wrought in state-to-state relations without basic transformations in the domestic divisions of labour.

What should Western-based movements do to help bring about basic transformations in the Third World? There are several important measures. One is opposition to military build-ups. Another is lobbying for the conversion of armaments' expenditure to investment in genuine agricultural reform. Similarly, pressure on Western governments to adopt a non-interventionist policy in countries undergoing fundamental structural change is essential. But policy makers do not usually act against the interests of the groups that put them in power. To ask capitalists to refrain from expansionism is to ask them to cease being capitalists. This is not to suggest that tactical decisions are predetermined. Surely the anti-war movement influenced the US decision to withdraw from Vietnam. Nonetheless, it is not enough to stop Western states from interfering in the Third World.

Basic change must come about within underdeveloped countries themselves. In this process, Western support for realigning the domestic divisions of labour in the Third World should be linked more closely to the internal situations within the advanced countries. Just as production is increasingly international, struggles in various parts of the global political economy must be intertwined. As the ideological struggles intensify, moralizing about the evils of exploitation should not replace sober analysis of the crisis.

Equally important for Westerners to contemplate is the question of what has not been done adequately or at all. Although state actions must be continually challenged, it is wrong to allow those who hold the reins of power to set the agenda. Unfortunately, many Westerners who oppose their governments' policies in the Third World have largely been reactive, their strategies crisis-oriented. Typically, critics have formed single-issue movements. Until recently, many US citizens regarded the liberation struggle in southern Africa as a 'minority issue', a foreign policy matter for blacks to contest; Latin Americanists pursue their causes; and so on. What is required is an interlinking of movements that mobilize constituencies around such diverse issues as militarism, feminism and intervention in different parts of the world. It is essential to bring home to workers, community groups and intellectuals precisely how individuals are personally involved in Third World struggles. Are bank deposits, pension funds and taxes supporting repressive structures in the Third World? How can these levers be used to gain control and change policy?

Surely there is a long road to travel before underdevelopment is overcome. Setting aside the exaggerated optimism of the early postcolonial period and the profound pessimism about the Third World which ensued, it is a truism to say that massive struggles in earlier historical epochs, such as the passage from feudalism to capitalism, a transition which engulfed the entire globe, have spawned fundamentally new world orders. It is out of the crucible of crises and from hard-fought struggles that new social forces emerge and invent creative solutions to deeply embedded problems. The praxis of struggle cannot be defined in advance. Improvements do not come steadily; there are traps and confusions, followed by sudden breakthroughs. And even then it can be hard to measure progress. Although the escape from underdevelopment calls for a monumental feat, we can devise novel ways to abolish the grim conditions in which the majority of humankind has been condemned to live and chart strategies for the course ahead.

Notes and References

1. Public Platitudes and Unfounded Attitudes

The interview with Fidel Castro by Barbara Walters was aired on 9 June 1977. I have corrected some stylistic errors in the ABC transcript, pp. 8–12, which the television network generously shared with me. Moynihan's statement is noted by Michael Harrington, *The Vast Majority: A Journey to the World's Poor* (New York: Simon & Shuster, 1977) p. 18 (emphasis in original). Brzezinski was interviewed by George Urban. The interview appeared under the title 'The Perils of Foreign Policy: A Conversation in Washington', *Encounter* 56(5) May 1981, especially p. 13; and in condensed form, 'A Talk with Brzezinski', *New York Times*, 22 April 1981 (emphasis in original). Mr Gromyko's quip is taken from 'Russians Come and Russians Go, but Not Gromyko', *New York Times*, 4 October, 1982. Xan Smiley's 'Misunderstanding Africa' can be found in *The Atlantic Monthly*, 250(3) September 1982, pp. 72; 74. See Ngugi Wa Thiong'o, *Petals of Blood* (New York: Dutton, 1978) p. 326.

Data on the gap between rich and poor countries are drawn from the Independent Commission on International Development Issues, *North–South: A Program for Survival* (Cambridge, Mass.: MIT Press, 1980) p. 32. Indicators of the gap can be found in World Bank, *World Development Report 1981* (New York: Oxford University Press, 1981) p. 3, and International Monetary Fund, *World Economic Outlook* (Washington, DC: IMF, 1985) pp. 148–9 and 162–3.

On the meaning of political economy, see W. Ladd Hollist and James A. Caporaso, 'International Political Economy Research: What Is It and Where Do We Turn for Concepts and Theory?', in W. Ladd Hollist and F. LaMond Tullis (eds), *An International Political Economy*, International Political Economy Yearbook (Boulder, Col.: Westview Press, 1985) vol. 1, pp. 27–49. The classical tradition is surveyed by Robert L. Heilbroner, *The Worldly Philosophers: The Lives, Times, and Ideas of the Great Economic Thinkers* (New York: Time Incorporated, 1961). Another valuable study is Ernest Mandel, *Marxist Economic Theory*, trans. Brian Pearce (London: Merlin, 1968). For an overview of various schools of thought, consult Robert W. Cox, 'In Search of Political Economy', *New Political Science*, 5/6, Winter/Spring 1981, pp. 59–78, and Michael Barratt Brown, *Models in Political Economy: A Guide to the Arguments* (Boulder, Col.: Lynne Rienner, 1985).

Diverse perspectives on the Third World are represented in People's Daily, *The Theory of Three Worlds* (New York: Books New China, 1977); Kwame

187

Nkrumah, 'The Myth of the "Third World", *Labour Monthly*, 50(10) October 1968, p. 465; 'Mrs. Gandhi Welcomes Dawn of Era of Detente', *India News*, 4 September 1973, cited by Allen H. Merriam, 'Semantic Implications of the Term "Third World"', *International Studies Notes*, 6(3) Fall 1979, p. 14; and Immanuel Wallerstein, *The Capitalist World-Economy* (Cambridge, Mass.: Cambridge University Press, 1979) p. 348.

2. Sources of Received Ideas About the Third World

The quotations from Okot p'Bitek's *Song of Lawino* (Nairobi: East African Publishing House, 1966) are taken from pp. 140, 141, 142, 155, 156, 207 and 208. The backdrop to *Song of Lawino* is the subject of James H. Mittelman, *Ideology and Politics in Uganda: From Obote to Amin* (Ithaca, NY: Cornell University Press, 1975). The comments by Hugh Trevor-Roper, 'The Rise of Christian Europe', *Listener* (London), 28 November 1963, p. 871, are reported by Ali A. Mazrui, *Cultural Engineering and Nation-Building in East Africa* (Evanston, Ill.: Northwestern University Press, 1972) p. 7. Severeid's remarks were on CBS Evening News, 15 July 1975. The quote from Option 2 can be found in NSSM-39, edited and introduced by Mohamed A. El-Khawas and Barry Cohen, *The Kissinger Study of Southern Africa* (Westport, Conn.: Lawrence Hill, 1976) p. 105. Seymour M. Hersh, *The Price of Power: Kissinger in the Nixon White House* (New York: Summit Books, 1983) p. 263, describes the Nixon–Valdés meeting. Hersh cites material in Armando Urbie's memoir, *The Black Book of American Intervention in Chile* (Boston: Beacon Press, 1975) pp. 30–3.

Cecil Rhodes is quoted in *Imperialism, the Highest Stage of Capitalism* (Beijing: Foreign Language Press, 1973) p. 94, by V. I. Lenin. The same theme appears in Sir Sidney James, 'Personal Recollections of Cecil Rhodes; 1, Some Conversations in London', *The Nineteenth Century*, 51, May 1902, pp. 832; 835.

The five phases on the road to modernization are outlined by W. W. Rostow, *The Stages of Economic Growth: A Non-Communist Manifesto* (London: Cambridge University Press, 1960). The anecdote about peasant farmers is borrowed from Philip Raikes, 'Rural Differentiation and Class Formation in Tanzania', *Journal of Peasant Studies*, 5(3) April 1978, pp. 315–17. On the failure of modernization theory to come to grips with causality, see Geoffrey Kay, *Development and Underdevelopment: A Marxist Analysis* (New York: St Martin's Press, 1975) pp. x; 2. The legacy of the modernization school is examined by Richard Higgott, 'From Modernization Theory to Public Policy: Continuity and Change in the Political Science of Political Development', *Studies in Comparative International Development*, 15(4) Winter 1980, pp. 26–58.

Perhaps the best book in the dependency framework is Fernando Henrique Cardoso and Enzo Faletto, *Dependency and Development in Latin America*, trans Marjory Mattingly Urquidi (Berkeley: University of California Press, 1975). In responding to criticism levelled by Marxists, Cardoso and Faletto conflate the dependency concept and class analysis. They surrender the distinctive features of this concept – the notion that the mainspring of Third World political economies is the exploitation of the periphery by the centre –

substituting dialectical reasoning rooted in history and based on the identification of contradictions. The thrust of their analysis is therefore dependency in name only. On the origins of underdevelopment, a seminal work which informs my analysis is Walter Rodney, *How Europe Underdeveloped Africa* (London: Bogle-L'Ouverture Publications, 1972). The economic legacy of imperialism and a suggested antidote are presented by Clive Thomas, *Dependence and Transformation: The Economics of the Transition to Socialism* (New York: Monthly Review Press, 1974). This vast literature is reviewed by Ronald H. Chilcote, *Theories of Development and Underdevelopment* (Boulder, Col.: Westview Press, 1984).

3. Received Ideas and International Institutions

The quip by an African diplomat is drawn from 'Invasion Debate: U.N. Weakness Displayed', *New York Times*, 5 March 1979. Commentary on the UN by various US delegates can be found in John E. Stoessinger, *The Might of Nations: World Politics in Our Time* (New York: Random House, 1975) p. 301; William F. Buckley, Jr, *United Nations Journal: A Delegate's Odyssey* (Garden City, NY: Anchor Books, 1977) p. 237; and Daniel Patrick Moynihan, *A Dangerous Place* (Boston: Little, Brown, 1978) p. 188. In criticizing these views, I am summarizing arguments that I have made elsewhere: 'American Double Standards on African Issues at the UN', *New York Times*, 22 January 1977. The relationship between international organization and capital accumulation is explored by Robert W. Cox, 'Production and Hegemony: Toward a Political Economy of World Order', in Harold K. Jacobson and Dusan Sidjanski (eds), *The Emerging International Economic Order: Dynamic Processes, Constraints and Opportunities* (Beverly Hills: Sage, 1982) pp. 37–58.

The passage from the Independent Commission on International Development Issues (also known as the Brandt Commission) appears in *North–South: A Program for Survival* (Cambridge, Mass.: MIT Press, 1980) p. 264. A sequel to this report is the Brandt Commission, *Common Crisis, North–South: Cooperation for World Recovery* (Cambridge, Mass.: MIT Press, 1983).

On the pitfalls of foreign aid, see Yashpal Tandon (ed.), *Technical Assistance Administration in East Africa* (Stockholm: Dag Hammarskjöld Foundation, 1973). Apart from the information drawn from personal experience, my sources on Tanzania are 'Third World Saga: Tanzania's Case Shows the Pluses and the Many Minuses of Big Foreign-Aid Programs', *Wall Street Journal*, 27 August 1982, and Andrew Coulson, 'The Automated Bread Factory', in Coulson (ed.), *African Socialism in Practice: The Tanzanian Experience* (Nottingham: Spokesman, 1979) pp. 179–83.

The conventional view on the role of modern technology in a developing economy is exemplified by Rostow, *The Stages of Economic Growth: A Non-Communist Manifesto* (London: Cambridge University Press, 1960) pp. 4; 32–3. The need to understand the context for technology transfer is stressed by Harvard professors Robert H. Hayes and Modesto A. Maidique, 'The Technology Gap', *New York Times*, 2 June 1981. Two historical treatises explore this theme in depth: Perry Anderson, *Passages from Antiq-*

uity to Feudalism (London: New Left Books, 1974), especially pp. 203–4, and Maurice Dobb, *Studies in the Development of Capitalism* (New York: International Publishers, 1963) pp. 22–3. Excellent studies of technology and the changing international division of labour are Folker Fröbel, Jürgen Heinrichs and Otto Kreye, 'The New International Division of Labour', *Social Science Information*, 17(1) 1978, pp. 123–42; Charles Bergquist (ed.), *Labor in the Capitalist World Economy* (Beverly Hills: Sage, 1984); and Joseph Grunwald and Kenneth Flamm, *The Global Factory: Foreign Assembly in International Trade* (Washington, DC: Brookings Institute, 1985). Multinational-driven research and development efforts in the Third World and India's technology policy are discussed by Helge Hveem, 'Selective Dissociation in the Technology Sector', especially pp. 280; 298–303, in John Gerard Ruggie (ed.), *The Antinomies of Interdependence: National Welfare and the International Division of Labor* (New York: Columbia University Press, 1983). The argument that technology transfer is leakage from multinational corporations is advanced by Charles-Albert Michalet, 'From Unequal Industrial Development to Unequal Scientific and Technological Development: Toward the New International Economic Order?' (paper presented to the annual meeting of the International Studies Association, St Louis, 1977).

On why multinational corporations forestall the emergence of centres of innovation and technology in the Third World, see Stephen Hymer, 'The Multinational Corporation and the Law of Uneven Development', in Jagdish N. Bhagwati (ed.), *Economics and World Order: From the 1970s to the 1990s* (New York: Macmillan, 1972) pp. 113–40. Much of the data cited here on multinational corporations is derived from John Cavanagh and Frederick F. Clairmonte, 'From Corporation to Conglomerates: A Review of Multinationals over the Last Twenty Years', *Multinational Monitor*, January 1983, pp. 16–19. The quotation by Kissinger appears in Hersh, *The Price of Power: Kissinger in the Nixon White House* (New York: Summit, 1983) p. 265. A compelling account of efforts by the ITT and the CIA to get rid of Allende can be found on pages 258–96 of Hersh's book. Dr Yudkin's report is summarized in 'Western Drugs and Third World Markets', *Guardian* (London), 21 August 1977. The lessons of the Bhopal tragedy are discussed in 'Disaster in India Sharpens Debate on Doing Business in Third World', *New York Times*, 16 December 1984.

The figures on the ratio of loans to unpaid debt were compiled by Mark Hulbert, 'Will the US Bail Out the Bankers?' *The Nation*, 235(12) October 16, 1982, p. 365. Dimensions of the debt crisis are examined in Lester B. Thurow, 'America's Banks in Crisis', *New York Times Magazine*, 23 September 1984; 'Records Show Citicorp Acted to Skirt Foreign Bank Rules', *New York Times*, 13 September 1982; and Anthony Sampson, *The Money Lenders* (Harmondsworth: Penguin Books, 1981). The emergence of a secondary market which trades international loans at discount is reported in 'The Market for Latin Debt', *New York Times*, 17 July 1985, and Richard S. Weinert, 'Swapping Third World Debt', *Foreign Policy*, 65, Winter 1986–7, pp. 85–97. An appraisal of the IMF's record is provided by John Loxley, *The IMF and the Poorest Countries: The Performance of the Least Developed Countries under IMF Stand-by Arrangements* (Ottawa: North–South Institute, 1984). The increasing frequency of debt rescheduling is documented by the Department of State, Bureau of Public Affairs, 'Foreign Indebtedness to US Government' (October 1983), n.p. The quotation by the former Brazilian president appears in Jeff Freiden, 'On Borrowed Time,' NACLA *Report on the Americas* 19(2) March–April 1985, p. 2. The political economy of debt is the subject of a special issue of *International Organization*, 39(3) Summer 1985.

4. Back to the Nineteenth Century for New Ideas

A lucid explanation of why capitalism must expand may be found in Robert L. Heilbroner, *The Nature and Logic of Capitalism* (New York: W. W. Norton, 1985). See especially Chapter 2, 'The Drive to Amass Capital'. Important background readings on the nexus between the state and the market are Charles Lindblom, *Politics and Markets: The World's Political Economic Systems* (New York: Basic Books, 1977); Theda Skocpol, *States and Social Revolutions: A Comparative Analysis of France, Russia, and China* (New York: Cambridge University Press, 1979); and Peter B. Evans, Dietrich Rueschemeyer, and Theda Skocpol (eds), *Bringing the State Back in* (New York: Cambridge University Press, 1985).

Walter Wriston's comment appears in 'Wriston: A Summing Up', *New York Times*, 21 June 1984. The parable about the interconnection between production and circulation is taken from Arghiri Emmanuel, *Unequal Exchange: A Study of the Imperialism of Trade* (New York: Monthly Review Press, 1972) p. 152. For the vignette about Zimbabwe, I am indebted to David Martin and Phyllis Johnson, *The Struggle for Zimbabwe: The Chimurenga War* (New York: Monthly Review Press, 1981) pp. 54–5. On land hunger, see also Terence Ranger, *Peasant Consciousness and Guerrilla War in Zimbabwe* (Berkeley: University of California Press, 1985). Marx's comment on his own life is drawn from Martin Nicolaus' Foreword to Karl Marx, *Grundrisse: Foundations of the Critique of Political Economy*, trans Martin Nicolaus (Harmondsworth: Penguin Books, 1973) p. 11. The illustration about the English manufacturer is provided by Marx, *Capital*, 3rd edn (New York: International Publishers, 1975), vol. 1, p. 766. On Marx's mistaken notion about underdevelopment, see *Capital*, 3rd edn (London: George Allen & Unwin, n.d.), vol. 1, p. xvii, quoted and discussed by Geoffrey Kay, *Development and Underdevelopment: A Marxist Analysis* (New York: St Martin's Press, 1975) p. 11. The literary works cited here are Henrik Ibsen, *Arthur Miller's Adaptation of An Enemy of the People* (Harmondsworth: Penguin Books, 1980) and Chinua Achebe, *Man of the People* (Garden City, NY: Anchor Books, 1967).

5. The Conventional Route, Joining Global Capitalism: Brazil

The acquisition of Hills Brothers by Corpersucar is discussed in 'Brazil's Coffee (with Sugar) Billionaire', *Fortune*, 46(1) July 1977, pp. 82–8. The scale of Brazil's economy is surveyed by Marsha Miliman, 'Brazil: Let Them Eat Minerals!' *NACLA's Latin America and Empire Report* 3(4) April 1973, pp. 5–7. Information on the historical backdrop may be found in Alfred

Stepan, *The Military in Politics* (Princeton: Princeton University Press, 1971) and Alfred Stepan (ed.), *Authoritarian Brazil: Origins, Policies, and Future* (New Haven: Yale University Press, 1972). Specifically, I am drawing on Sylvia Ann Hewlett, *The Cruel Dilemmas of Development: Twentieth Century Brazil* (New York: Basic Books, 1980) p. 34, and Peter Evans, *Dependent Development: The Alliance of Multinational, State, and Local Capital in Brazil* (Princeton: Princeton University Press, 1979) pp. 110–11. An excellent discussion of import substitution is provided by José Serra, 'Three Mistaken Theses Regarding the Connection between Industrialization and Authoritarian Regimes', in David Collier (ed.), *The New Authoritarianism in Latin America* (Princeton: Princeton University Press, 1979) pp. 99–163.

The Johnson administration's view of the Goulart government is quoted by Hewlett, *The Cruel Dilemmas of Development*, p. 72. On repression and labour organization, see Kenneth S. Mericle, 'Corporatist Control of the Working Class: Authoritarian Brazil Since 1964', in James M. Malloy (ed.), *Authoritarianism and Corporatism in Latin America* (Pittsburgh: University of Pittsburgh Press, 1977) pp. 303–38; Kenneth Paul Erickson and Kevin J. Middlebrook, 'The State and Organized Labor in Brazil and Mexico', in Sylvia Ann Hewlett and Richard S. Weinert (eds), *Brazil and Mexico: Patterns in Late Development* (Philadelphia: Institute for the Study of Human Issues, 1984) pp. 213–63; and Maria Helena Moreira Alves, *State and Opposition in Military Brazil* (Austin: University of Texas Press, 1985).

Mr Delfim's remarks appear in Cheryl Payer, *The Debt Trap: The International Monetary Fund and the Third World* (Harmondsworth: Penguin Books, 1974) p. 161. For information on Brazil's state-run corporations, see Douglas H. Graham, 'Mexican and Brazilian Economic Development: Legacies, Patterns and Performance', in Hewlett and Weinert (eds), *Brazil and Mexico*, especially p. 32; 'Brazil's Economy after the Miracle', *New York Times*, 17 July 1983; and Eul-Soo-Pang, 'Brazil's New Democracy', *Current History*, 82(481) February 1983, p. 56. Attitudes on state intervention in the economy are reported by Evans, *Dependent Development*, p. 238. On the involvement of multinational corporations in the local economy, see Hewlett, *The Cruel Dilemmas of Development*, p. 135, and 'Brazil', *Encyclopedia of the Third World: Afghanistan to Guinea-Bissau*, rev. edn, ed. George Thomas Kurian (New York: Facts on File, 1982) vol. 1, p. 234. The figures on the repatriation of profit can be found on p. 144 of Hewlett, *The Cruel Dilemmas of Development*. Data on income distribution are provided by Hewlett, 'Poverty and Inequality in Brazil', in Hewlett and Weinert (eds), *Brazil and Mexico*, pp. 317–38.

The remark by the former cabinet minister appears in Janet Shenk, 'Don't Believe in Miracles', *NACLA Report on the Americas* 12(3) May–June 1979, p. 10, citing 'After Fifteen Years, Military Rule Dies Hard in Brazil', *Washington Post*, 31 March 1979. Mr Reagan's gaffe is reported in 'President Promises to Give Brazilians a \$1.2 Billion Loan', *New York Times*, 2 December 1982. The declining confidence of international banks in investment in Brazil is noted in 'IMF Plans Pressures on Banks to Help Brazil', *New York Times*, 15 December 1982. The plight of the Pereiras is described in 'Poorer Brazilians Are Going Hungry, While the Rich Worry about the Future', *Wall Street Journal*, 6 May 1983. The changing political climate is assessed in 'A Country That Is on the Verge of Exploding', *Business Week*, 2 May 1983. President Figueiredo's reaction to the wave of civil unrest is reported in 'Blowup: Jobless Workers on a Rampage', *Time*, 18 April 1983. The European ambassador's statement appears in 'Brazilians Condemn Liberalization Foes', *New York Times*, 11 April 1983; the lawyer's observation is in Penny Lernoux, 'The "Model" Shattered: Brazil, the Banks, the Third World', *The Nation*, 237(14) 5 November 1983, p. 435. On the debtors' cartel and the huge profits reaped by international banks in Brazil, see Pang, 'Brazil's New Democracy', p. 55, and Lernoux, 'The "Model" Shattered', p. 435, respectively. Mr Delfim's reaction to the pileup of debt is quoted by Payer, *The Debt Trap*, p. 161.

On dependent state capitalism, see James Petras, *Critical Perspectives on Imperialism and Social Class in the Third World* (New York: Monthly Review Press, 1978) pp. 47; 89; 92. The 1985 economic recovery is reported in 'The Ash Wednesday Awaiting Brazil's Revelling Politicians', *Economist* (London), 8 February 1986. A statistical profile of trade with Brazil is provided by the US Bureau of the Census, *Statistical Abstract of the United States, 1982–83*, (Washington, DC: Government Printing Office, 1983) p. 880. On p. 435 of 'The "Model" Shattered,' Lernoux examines the options facing Brazil.

6. The Exit Option, Withdrawing from Global Capitalism: China Under Mao

The major sources for this chapter are Vivienne Shue, *Peasant China in Transition: The Dynamics of Development toward Socialism, 1949–1956* (Berkeley: University of California Press, 1983) and Andrew Walder's dissertation, 'Work and Authority in Chinese Industry: State Socialism and the Institutional Culture of Dependency' (University of Michigan, 1981). Essential background reading is Lucien Bianco, *Origins of the Chinese Revolution, 1915–1949*, trans Muriel Bell (Stanford: Stanford University Press, 1971) and William Hinton, *Fanshen: A Documentary of Revolution in a Chinese Village* (New York: Random House, 1966).

The land reform is assessed by C. K. Yang, *Chinese Communist Society: The Family and the Village* (Cambridge, Mass.: MIT Press, 1959). Another important work on the rural sector is Nicholas R. Lardy, *Agriculture in China's Modern Development* (Cambridge: Cambridge University Press, 1983). The comparison of economic performance in 1952 and the pre-revolutionary period appears in Xue Muqiao, *China's Socialist Economy* (Beijing: Foreign Languages Press, 1981) p. 22. The data on income in the agricultural sector are drawn from Shue, *Peasant China in Transition*, p. 283; her explanations quoted here appear on p. 332. An excellent discussion of relations between the central authorities and local cadres may be found in Ezra Vogel, *Canton under Communism: Programs and Politics in a Provincial Capital, 1949–1968* (Cambridge, Mass.: Harvard University Press, 1969). The incentive system is reviewed in Walder's seminal study, 'Work and Authority in Chinese Industry', *passim*. The tale of Old Guo is told by Liang Heng and Judith Shapiro, *Son of the Revolution* (New York: Alfred A.

Knopf, 1983) p. 184. On the shortcomings of the Cultural Revolution, see Victor Lippitt, 'Socialist Development in China', in Mark Selden and Victor Lippitt (eds), *The Transition to Socialism in China* (Armonk, NY: M. E. Sharpe, 1982), especially pp. 131–2. A provocative account is provided by Samir Amin, *The Future of Maoism*, trans Norman Finkelstein (New York: Monthly Review Press, 1983). Debates about the sequel to Maoism appear in Stephan Feuchtwang and Atar Hussain (eds), *The Chinese Economic Reforms* (New York: St Martin's Press, 1983).

7. The Alternative Path, Weaving Through Global Capitalism: Mozambique

Some of the information in this chapter is drawn from James H. Mittelman, *Underdevelopment and the Transition to Socialism: Mozambique and Tanzania* (New York: Academic Press, 1981). The statement on the role of the peasantry appears in Mozambique Information Agency, *Information Bulletin*, 9–10, 1977, p. 6. The composition of the people's assemblies is described in 'Assembleia Popular', *Tempo* (Maputo), 378, 1 January 1978, pp. 53–4; Allen and Barbara Isaacman, 'A Rare Glimpse of How Mozambique Governs Itself', *Christian Science Monitor*, 27 December 1979; and Stephanie Urdang, 'The Last Transition? Women and Development in Mozambique', *Review of African Political Economy*, 27–28, 1984, pp. 13–14.

An interpretation of the changing rural economy in Africa that differs from my own is offered by Goran Hyden, *No Shortcuts to Progress: African Development Management in Perspective* (Berkeley: University of California Press, 1983). Hyden hypothesizes that an 'uncaptured peasantry' exits the formal economy. According to him, Africa's pre-capitalist societies are without states that can be used for economic expansion and development. Undoubtedly, Hyden identifies an important phenomenon – the informal market or parallel economy – but his explanation is open to challenge on the ground that the mode of production in contemporary Africa is predominantly a capitalist, not pre-capitalist, structure. Moreover, rather than choosing the exit option, peasants are being pushed out of the system.

Samora Machel was interviewed by Herb Shore in Dar es Salaam, Tanzania, in 1970. The interview is quoted by George Houser and Herb Shore, *Mozambique: Dream the Size of Freedom* (New York: The Africa Fund, 1975) p. 11. The US State Department's assessment of Mozambique's human rights performance can be found in *Country Reports on Human Rights Practices* (Report to the Committee on Foreign Affairs, US House of Representatives, and the Committee on Foreign Relations, US Senate, Washington, DC, 1984). The costs of South Africa's destabilization campaign have been computed by the Government of Mozambique in its *Economic Report* (Maputo: National Planning Commission, 1984) p. 41. Data on the economy are taken from 'Mozambique', *Foreign Economic Trends and Their Implications for the United States* (FET-66) (US Department of Commerce, Washington DC, 1984) pp. 2; 4–5. The ban on development assistance was contained in *Legislation on Foreign Relations through 1982*, Current Legislation and Related Executive Orders, vol. 1

(Committee on Foreign Relations, US Senate, and Committee on Foreign Affairs, US House of Representatives, Washington, DC, 1983) p. 361.

For readers interested in post-colonial Mozambique, the most authoritative studies are Allen Isaacman and Barbara Isaacman, *Mozambique: From Colonialism to Revolution, 1900–1982* (Boulder, Col.: Westview Press, 1983); Joseph Hanlon, *Mozambique: The Revolution under Fire* (London: Zed Press, 1984); Barry Munslow, *Mozambique: The Revolution and Its Origins* (London: Longman, 1983); and John S. Saul (ed.), *A Difficult Road: The Transition to Socialism* (New York: Monthly Review Press, 1985).

8. What Works in the Third World?

A penetrating essay on human agency, on which I have drawn, is Alan Gilbert, 'Democracy and Individuality,' *Social Philosophy and Policy*, 3(2) Spring 1986, pp. 19–58. Some of the material on Mauritania is borrowed from 'Drought Turns Nomads' World Upside Down', *New York Times*, 3 March 1985, and 'Poorer Nations Get Poorer as Recession Eases', *Africa News*, 21(13) 26 September 1983, p. 6. The sentences quoted from V. S. Naipaul can be found in *The Return of Eva Peron* (New York: Alfred A. Knopf, 1980) p. 141, and *A Bend in the River* (New York: Vintage Books, 1979) p. 27. Frantz Fanon's remark on the ideology of racism is taken from 'Racism and Culture', in Fanon, *Toward the African Revolution* (Harmondsworth: Penguin Books, 1964) p. 43. See the commentary by Aristide Zolberg, 'Frantz Fanon – A Gospel for the Damned', *Encounter*, 27(5) November 1966, pp. 56–63. Garrett Hardin's views are set forth in his 'Lifeboat Ethics: The Case Against Helping the Poor', *Psychology Today*, 8(4) 8 September 1974, pp. 38ff.

Seminal work on the 'objective problem' is Celso Furtado, *Accumulation and Development: The Logic of Industrial Civilization*, trans Suzette Macedo (New York: St Martin's Press, 1983); Celso Furtado, *No to Recession and Unemployment: An Examination of the Brazilian Economic Crisis* (London: Third World Foundation, 1984); and Peter Evans, *Dependent Development: The Alliance of Multinational, State, and Local Capital in Brazil* (Princeton: Princeton University Press, 1979), especially pp. 80–1. Data on arms sales are derived from the Independent Commission on International Development Issues, *North–South: A Program for Survival* (Cambridge, Mass.: MIT Press, 1980) p. 117; and 'Cost-Effective Job Creation', and 'The Third World Limits Its Arsenals', articles in the *New York Times* on 22 September 1982, and 18 March 1984, respectively. Keynes's comment appears in *The Collected Writings of John Maynard Keynes: Activities 1939–1945; Internal War Finance*, ed. Donald Moggridge (Cambridge: Cambridge University Press, 1978) vol. 22, p. 149. Seymour Melman summarizes his research findings in 'Looting the Means of Production', *New York Times*, 7 October 1980.

I have borrowed information on the NICs from Stephan Haggard and Chung-in Moon, 'The South Korean State in the International Economy: Liberal, Dependent, or Mercantile?', in Ruggie (ed.), *The Antinomies of Interdependence: National Welfare and the International Development of*

Labor (New York: Columbia University Press, 1983), especially, pp. 132–41 and 185–9. Extensive research on capitalist development in Japan has been carried out by Jon Halliday, *A Political History of Japanese Capitalism* (New York: Monthly Review Press, 1978).

On restructuring ties with the world order, see Furtado, *Accumulation and Development*, pp. 115; 118, and Immanuel Wallerstein, *The Politics of the World-Economy: The States, the Movements, and the Civilizations* (Cambridge: Cambridge University Press, 1984) p. 10. The strategy of managing the ties of dependency is assessed by Robert W. Cox, 'Production and Hegemony: Toward a Political Economy of World Order', in Harold K. Jacobson and Dusan Sidjanski (eds), *The Emerging International Order: Dynamic Processes, Constraints and Opportunities* (Beverly Hills: Sage, 1982) pp. 54–6, and André Tiano, *La dialectique de la dépendance: Analyse des relations économiques et financières internationales* (Paris: Presses Universitaires de France, 1977) pp. 402–6. The concept 'war of position' is developed by Antonio Gramsci, *Selections from the Prison Notebooks of Antonio Gramsci*, trans and ed. Quintin Hoare and Geoffrey Nowell Smith (London: Lawrence and Wishart, 1971), *passim*.

Much of my information on oil is derived from Anthony Sampson, *The Seven Sisters: The Great Oil Companies and the World They Shaped* (New York: Bantam Books, 1976); Jack Anderson, with James Boyd, *Fiasco* (New York: Times Books, 1983); and 'Energy Upheaval: Questions about OPEC, Past and Future', *New York Times*, 3 October 1983. On the leverage of Western banks, see 'Acting to Avert Debtor Cartel', *New York Times*, 20 June 1984, and Joan Robinson, *Aspects of Development and Underdevelopment* (Cambridge: Cambridge University Press, 1979) p. 132. Cuba's policy toward the pharmaceuticals is described by Mike Muller, *The Health of Nations: An Investigation of the Pharmaceutical Industry's Exploitation of the Third World for Profit* (London: Faber & Faber, 1982), especially p. 65, and Luis R. Capo, 'International Drug Procurement and Market Intelligence: Cuba', *World Development*, 11(3) November 1983, pp. 217–22. My discussion of an alternative to the IMF model of accumulation relies very heavily on John Loxley, 'IMF and World Bank Conditionality and Sub-Saharan Africa' (mimeo, n.d.). A compelling critique of Clive Thomas, *Dependence and Transformation: The Economics of the Transition to Socialism* (New York: Monthly Review Press, 1974) has been developed by Andrew Coulson (mimeo, Department of Economics, University of Dar es Salaam, n.d.). The argument about the division of labour in agriculture is presented in Kevin Danaher, *Myths of African Hunger* (San Francisco: Institute for Food and Development Policy, 1985) p. 2.

Index